Communications in Computer and Information Science

2365

Series Editors

Gang Li, *School of Information Technology, Deakin University, Burwood, VIC, Australia*

Joaquim Filipe, *Polytechnic Institute of Setúbal, Setúbal, Portugal*

Zhiwei Xu, *Chinese Academy of Sciences, Beijing, China*

Rationale
The CCIS series is devoted to the publication of proceedings of computer science conferences. Its aim is to efficiently disseminate original research results in informatics in printed and electronic form. While the focus is on publication of peer-reviewed full papers presenting mature work, inclusion of reviewed short papers reporting on work in progress is welcome, too. Besides globally relevant meetings with internationally representative program committees guaranteeing a strict peer-reviewing and paper selection process, conferences run by societies or of high regional or national relevance are also considered for publication.

Topics
The topical scope of CCIS spans the entire spectrum of informatics ranging from foundational topics in the theory of computing to information and communications science and technology and a broad variety of interdisciplinary application fields.

Information for Volume Editors and Authors
Publication in CCIS is free of charge. No royalties are paid, however, we offer registered conference participants temporary free access to the online version of the conference proceedings on SpringerLink (http://link.springer.com) by means of an http referrer from the conference website and/or a number of complimentary printed copies, as specified in the official acceptance email of the event.

CCIS proceedings can be published in time for distribution at conferences or as post-proceedings, and delivered in the form of printed books and/or electronically as USBs and/or e-content licenses for accessing proceedings at SpringerLink. Furthermore, CCIS proceedings are included in the CCIS electronic book series hosted in the SpringerLink digital library at http://link.springer.com/bookseries/7899. Conferences publishing in CCIS are allowed to use Online Conference Service (OCS) for managing the whole proceedings lifecycle (from submission and reviewing to preparing for publication) free of charge.

Publication process
The language of publication is exclusively English. Authors publishing in CCIS have to sign the Springer CCIS copyright transfer form, however, they are free to use their material published in CCIS for substantially changed, more elaborate subsequent publications elsewhere. For the preparation of the camera-ready papers/files, authors have to strictly adhere to the Springer CCIS Authors' Instructions and are strongly encouraged to use the CCIS LaTeX style files or templates.

Abstracting/Indexing
CCIS is abstracted/indexed in DBLP, Google Scholar, EI-Compendex, Mathematical Reviews, SCImago, Scopus. CCIS volumes are also submitted for the inclusion in ISI Proceedings.

How to start
To start the evaluation of your proposal for inclusion in the CCIS series, please send an e-mail to ccis@springer.com.

Zhongjun He · Yidong Chen
Editors

Machine Translation

20th China Conference, CCMT 2024
Xiamen, China, November 8–10, 2024
Proceedings

 Springer

Editors
Zhongjun He
Baidu
Beijing, China

Yidong Chen
Xiamen University
Xiamen, China

ISSN 1865-0929　　　　　　　ISSN 1865-0937　(electronic)
Communications in Computer and Information Science
ISBN 978-981-96-2291-7　　　ISBN 978-981-96-2292-4　(eBook)
https://doi.org/10.1007/978-981-96-2292-4

© The Editor(s) (if applicable) and The Author(s), under exclusive license to Springer Nature Singapore Pte Ltd. 2025, corrected publication 2025

This work is subject to copyright. All rights are solely and exclusively licensed by the Publisher, whether the whole or part of the material is concerned, specifically the rights of translation, reprinting, reuse of illustrations, recitation, broadcasting, reproduction on microfilms or in any other physical way, and transmission or information storage and retrieval, electronic adaptation, computer software, or by similar or dissimilar methodology now known or hereafter developed.
The use of general descriptive names, registered names, trademarks, service marks, etc. in this publication does not imply, even in the absence of a specific statement, that such names are exempt from the relevant protective laws and regulations and therefore free for general use.
The publisher, the authors and the editors are safe to assume that the advice and information in this book are believed to be true and accurate at the date of publication. Neither the publisher nor the authors or the editors give a warranty, expressed or implied, with respect to the material contained herein or for any errors or omissions that may have been made. The publisher remains neutral with regard to jurisdictional claims in published maps and institutional affiliations.

This Springer imprint is published by the registered company Springer Nature Singapore Pte Ltd.
The registered company address is: 152 Beach Road, #21-01/04 Gateway East, Singapore 189721, Singapore

If disposing of this product, please recycle the paper.

Preface

The China Conference on Machine Translation (CCMT) is a national annual academic conference held by the Machine Translation Committee of the Chinese Information Processing Society of China (CIPS) which brings together researchers and practitioners in the area of machine translation, providing a forum for those in academia and industry to exchange and promote the latest developments in methodologies, resources, projects, and products, with a special emphasis on the languages in China. Since the first session of CCMT in 2005, 19 sessions have been successfully organized (the first 14 sessions were called CWMT), and a total of 13 machine translation evaluations (2007, 2008, 2009, 2011, 2013, 2015, 2017, 2018, 2019, 2020, 2021, 2022, 2023) have been organized, as well as one open-source system module development (2006) and two strategic seminars (2010, 2012). These activities have made a substantial impact on advancing research and development of machine translation in China. The conference has been a highly productive forum for progress in this area and is considered a leading and important academic event in the natural language processing field in China.

This year, the 20th CCMT took place in Xiamen, Fujian. This conference continued the tradition of being the most important academic event dedicated to advancing machine translation research in China. It hosted the 14th Machine Translation Evaluation Campaign, featured two keynote speeches, and included four tutorials. The conference also organized four panel discussions, bringing attention to the frontier of machine translation, the industry of machine translation, a forum for students, and a special panel for the 20th anniversary of CCMT. A total of 52 submissions (including 17 English papers and 35 Chinese papers) were received for the conference. All papers were carefully reviewed in a double-blind manner and each paper was evaluated by at least three members of an international Program Committee. From the submissions, 13 English papers and 18 Chinese papers were accepted. These papers address all aspects of machine translation, including the robustness and efficiency of machine translation models, translation evaluation, large language models for machine translation, multi-modal machine translation, low-resource machine translation, shared tasks, etc. We would like to express our thanks to every person and institution involved in the organization of this conference, especially the Program Committee, the machine translation evaluation campaign, the invited speakers, the local organization team, the generous sponsors, and the organizations that supported and promoted the event. Last but not least, we greatly appreciate Springer for publishing the proceedings.

November 2024

Zhongjun He
Yidong Chen

Organization

General Chair

Hushur Islam — Xinjiang University, China

Program Committee Co-chairs

Zhongjun He — Baidu, China
Yidong Chen — Xiamen University, China

Organizing Co-chairs

Jiajun Zhang — Institute of Automation, Chinese Academy of Sciences, China
Jinsong Su — Xiamen University, China

Tutorial Co-chairs

Shujian Huang — Nanjing University, China
Kehai Chen — Harbin Institute of Technology at Shenzhen, China

Frontier- Trends Forum Co-chairs

Peng Li — Tsinghua University, China
Yang Zhao — Institute of Automation, Chinese Academy of Sciences, China

Co-chairs of Industrial Applications Forum

Tong Xiao — Northeastern University, China
Hao Yang — Huawei Translation Service Center, China

Students Forum Co-chairs

Xuebo Liu Harbin Institute of Technology at Shenzhen, China
Guanhua Chen Southern University of Science and Technology, China

Evaluation Chair

Rui Wang Shanghai Jiao Tong University, China

Sponsorship Co-chairs

Chong Feng Beijing Institute of Technology, China
Mieradilijiang Maimaiti Xinjiang Technical Institute of Physics and Chemistry, Chinese Academy of Sciences, China

Publicity Co-chairs

Jinan Xu Beijing Jiaotong University, China
Junhui Xu Soochow University, China

Publication Chair

Gongbo Tang Beijing Language and Culture University, China

Program Committee

Baosong Yang Alibaba Group, China
Biao Zhang Google, USA
Bojie Hu Tencent, China
Changxing Wu East China Jiaotong University, China
Chong Feng Beijing Institute of Technology, China
Chunliang Zhang Northeastern University, China
Cunli Mao Kunming University of Science and Technology, China

Dakun Zhang	Systran, France
Derek F. Wong	University of Macau, China
Fandong Meng	Tencent, China
Guoping Huang	Tencent AI Lab, China
Hailong Cao	Harbin Institute of Technology, China
Haitao Mi	Tencent America, USA
Heng Yu	Shopee, China
Hongfei Xu	Zhengzhou University, China
Jiajun Zhang	Institute of Automation, Chinese Academy of Sciences, China
Jinan Xu	Beijing Jiaotong University, China
Jinhua Du	Huawei UK Research & Development Ltd., UK
Jinsong Su	Xiamen University, China
Jun Xie	Alibaba DAMO Academy, China
Junhui Li	Soochow University, China
Junliang Guo	Microsoft Research Asia, China
Kehai Chen	Harbin Institute of Technology (Shenzhen), China
Lemao Liu	Tencent AI Lab, China
Liangyou Li	Huawei Noah's Ark Lab, China
Longyue Wang	Alibaba Group, China
Maoxi Li	Jiangxi Normal University, China
Mingxuan Wang	Bytedance AI Lab, China
Muhua Zhu	Meituan Group, China
Muyun Yang	Harbin Institute of Technology, China
Qiang Wang	Hithink RoyalFlush AI Research Institute, China
Quan Du	NiuTrans, China
Qun Liu	Huawei Noah's Ark Lab, China
Shengxiang Gao	Kunming University of Science and Technology, China
Shuangzhi Wu	Bytedance, China
Shujian Huang	Nanjing University, China
Tong Xiao	Northeastern University, China
Toshiaki Nakazawa	University of Tokyo, Japan
Wen Zhang	Xiaomi AI Lab, China
Xiang Li	Li Auto Inc., China
Xiangyu Duan	Soochow University, China
Xiaocheng Feng	Harbin Institute of Technology, China
Xing Wang	Tencent AI Lab, China
Xu Tan	Microsoft Research Asia, China
Yachao Li	Northwest Minzu University, China
Yang Feng	ICT, Chinese Academy of Sciences, China
Yang Liu	Tsinghua University, China

Yating Yang   XTIPC, Chinese Academy of Sciences, China
Yidong Chen   Xiamen University, China
Yufeng Chen   Beijing Jiaotong University, China
Yves Lepage   Waseda University, Japan
Zhaopeng Tu   Tencent AI Lab, China
Zhengxian Gong   Soochow University, China
Zhongjun He   Baidu, China

Organizers

Chinese Information Processing Society of China, China

Xiamen University, China

Sponsors

Platinum Sponsors

Alibaba Cloud

Organization   xi

HUAWEI Translate

VolcTrans

Youdao

Global Tone Communication Technology Co., Ltd.

Gold Sponsors

Baidu

OPPO Corporation

CloudTranslation

Silver Sponsors

NiuTrans Research

VirtAI Cloud

Contents

Robustness and Efficiency of Translation Models

A Data-Efficient Nearest-Neighbor Language Model via Lightweight Nets 3
   Qinhao Zhou, Xiang Xiang, Ke Wang, Yuqi Zhang, Yuchuan Wu, and Yongbin Li

Extend Adversarial Policy Against Neural Machine Translation via Unknown Token 11
   Wei Zou, Shujian Huang, and Jiajun Chen

Low-resource Machine Translation

Evaluating the Translation Performance of Multilingual Large Language Models: A Case Study on Southeast Asian Languages 27
   Hua Lai, Silei Han, Ying Li, Zhengtao Yu, and Zirui Guo

Quality Estimation

Critical Error Detection Based on Anchors Test 51
   Kaiyuan Huang and Junguo Zhu

Large Language Modes for Machine Translation

Enhancing Machine Translation Across Multiple Domains and Languages with Large Language Models 69
   Hao Lu, Rui Zhang, Hui Huang, Fuhai Song, Junkai Liu, Yican Ye, Lang Lang, Ziqing Zhao, Muyun Yang, and Rui Cong

Incorporating Terminology Knowledge into Large Language Model for Domain-Specific Machine Translation 82
   Xuan Zhao, Chong Feng, Shuanghong Huang, Jiangyu Wang, and Haojie Xu

Multi-modal Translation

Joint Multi-modal Modeling for Speech-to-Text Translation as Multilingual Neural Machine Translation 99
   Jiale Ou, Hongfei Xu, and Hongying Zan

Machine Translation Evaluation

CCMT2024 Tibetan-Chinese Machine Translation Evaluation Technical
Report 119
   Wenhao Zhuang, Dawa Cairen, Pengmao Cairang, and Yuan Sun

HW-TSC's Submission to the CCMT 2024 Machine Translation Tasks 128
   Zhanglin Wu, Yuanchang Luo, Daimeng Wei, Jiawei Zheng, Bin Wei,
   Zongyao Li, Hengchao Shang, Jiaxin Guo, Shaojun Li, Weidong Zhang,
   Ning Xie, and Hao Yang

ISTIC's Neural Machine Translation Systems for CCMT' 2024 141
   Zhuofan Hu, Ningyuan Deng, and Yanqing He

Lan-Bridge's Submission to CCMT 2024 Translation Evaluation Task 148
   Min Luo, Gang Hu, and Jie Wei

Technical Report of OPPO's Machine Translation Systems for CCMT 2024 155
   Yunbei Zhang, Tingxun Shi, Xiaolei Zhang, and Zhengshan Xue

Xihong's Submission to CCMT 2024: Human-in-the-Loop Data
Augmentation for Low-Resource Tibetan-Chinese NMT 162
   Jiawei Hu, Yincun Chen, and Hanyu Zhang

Correction to: A Data-Efficient Nearest-Neighbor Language Model
via Lightweight Nets C1
   Qinhao Zhou, Xiang Xiang, Ke Wang, Yuqi Zhang, Yuchuan Wu,
   and Yongbin Li

Author Index 175

Robustness and Efficiency of Translation Models

A Data-Efficient Nearest-Neighbor Language Model via Lightweight Nets

Qinhao Zhou[1], Xiang Xiang[1(✉)], Ke Wang[2], Yuqi Zhang[3], Yuchuan Wu[2], and Yongbin Li[2]

[1] Nat'l Key Lab of Multi-Spectral Info Intelligent Processing Tech, School of Artificial Intelligence and Automation, Huazhong University of Science and Tech, Wuhan, China
[2] Alibaba Group, Beijing, China
[3] Nat'l Practice Base for Outstanding Engineers (Digital Tech), Hangzhou, China

Abstract. Nearest-Neighbor Language Models (kNN-MT) leverage the contextual representations and next-word predictions of tokens to construct a vector-based database. During the inference stage, this database is utilized to assist the model in predicting the next word, resulting in impressive performance improvements. However, as the volume of data grows, the storage requirements for the vector-based database in kNN-MT continue to increase. Furthermore, the kNN retrieval performed for each predicted token introduces additional latency during the inference stage. To address these limitations, we propose training a lightweight neural network as a substitute for the vector datastore and kNN search. Our approach significantly reduces the storage overhead while maintaining fast inference speed, as demonstrated by our experiments on various translation datasets.

Keywords: Machine Translation · kNN · lightweight network

1 Introduction

The integration of retrieval-based approaches and language models has garnered substantial interest for enhancing specific NLP tasks [3,5,9]. This combination enables language models to leverage external knowledge, leading to improved performance in diverse NLP applications. kNN-MT [6] is a retrieval-based method that can improve the performance of the model on a specific translation dataset without training. Unlike other methods based on fine-tuning [2] or data augmentation [1,4,10,11], kNN-MT does not suffer from catastrophic forgetting, which is a limitation present in most existing methods.

However, kNN-MT requires storing the entire training data and comparing the contextual information from the NMT output with each entry in the training

---

The original version of the chapter has been revised. Author's affiliation was displayed incorrectly. A correction to this chapter can be found at
https://doi.org/10.1007/978-981-96-2292-4_14

data for every translation step. This results in significant storage requirements and slows down the inference speed of the entire system. To address the storage overhead problem, various works have proposed filtering algorithms to eliminate redundant training data entries. These methods reduce the storage burden through compression and filtering techniques. In contrast, we propose replacing the search process in kNN-MT with a lightweight network. Specifically, for each domain, we utilize the output of the decoder hidden state as input and use the nearest neighbors obtained from kNN search, along with the target token, as supervision to train a lightweight neural network. At test time, this network will serve as a replacement for the kNN search module. This approach significantly improves inference speed and greatly reduces storage burden in practical applications. Besides, our experimental results demonstrate that our method recovers between 92% and 99% of the translation performance of kNN-MT across different domains.

2 Background: kNN-MT

In this section, we first elaborate on the background and principles of kNN-MT, describe its inference process, and then introduce recent works based on it.

kNN-MT works as an auxiliary component to a base NMT model, using the training dataset to construct a datastore for translation without requiring additional training. The datastore consists of a large number of key-value pairs. For a given bilingual sentence pair (X, Y) in the training set, the NMT model translates every token y_t in t step with text information $(X, y_{<t})$. Then, the key is $f(X, y_{<t})$ and the value is y_t and the datastore is constructed by

$$(\mathcal{K}, \mathcal{V}) = \bigcup_{(x,y) \in (\mathcal{X}, \mathcal{Y})} \{(f(x, y_{<t}), y_t), y_t \in y\}. \tag{1}$$

kNN-MT requires traversing and storing the entire training data for every domain. During inference, for each decoding step t, kNN-MT predicts token $\hat{y}_t$ with the combination of the output distribution of NMT and the kNN search results in datastore based on $f(x, y_{<t})$. Assuming $N_k = \{(h_i, v_i), i \in \{1, 2, ..., k\}\}$ represents the nearest neighbors obtained from kNN search, the associated predictive distribution can be represented as

$$p(y_t|x, \hat{y}_{<t}) = \sum_{(h_i, v_i)} 1_{y_t=v_i} exp(\frac{-d(h_i, f(x, \hat{y}_{<t}))}{T}). \tag{2}$$

The expression involves the temperature coefficient denoted by T and the Euclidean distance or l_2 distance denoted by $d(,)$. The calculation of the distribution is essentially based on the distances between the nearest neighbors obtained from the search and the query hidden state. Based on the above calculation process, the final predicted probability distribution $\hat{y}$ can be expressed as

$$p(y_t|x, \hat{y}_{<t}) = \lambda p_{kNN}(y_t|x, \hat{y}_{<t}) + \\ (1 - \lambda) p_{NMT}(y_t|x, \hat{y}_{<t}), \tag{3}$$

where λ denotes the interpolated superparameter of the two distributions.

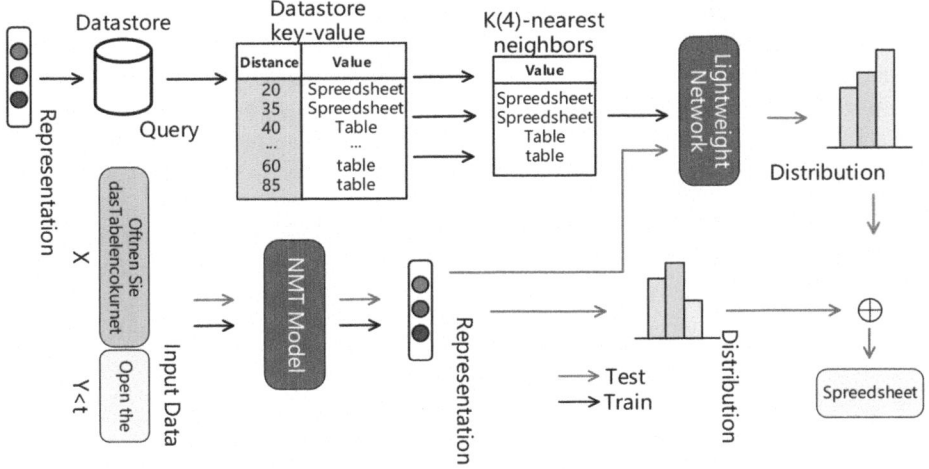

Fig. 1. The main framework of our proposed method.

kNN-MT significantly enhances the translation performance of NMT models on specific datasets. However, the substantial storage overhead and slower inference speed limit its practicality. In recent years, extensive research has been conducted to optimize kNN-MT by reducing storage overhead [12,15,16] and improve the search speed [7,13,14]. These efforts eliminate redundant key-value pairs in the datastore and to some extent enhance the translation performance of kNN-MT.

3 Methodology

Due to the necessity of computing distances between each query point and all points in the datastore, the computational complexity of kNN-MT is quite high. As illustrated in Fig. 1, we train a lightweight network as a replacement for the kNN datastore, while keeping the parameters of the NMT model frozen to ensure the retention of its existing knowledge. Specifically, we utilize the hidden state from the last layer of the NMT model as input. The nearest neighbors obtained through kNN search, along with the target token, are used as the ground truth for training. The corresponding loss function is formulated as

$$\begin{aligned}\mathcal{L}_{KL} &= \sum_i^N p_i^{KNN} \log \frac{p_i^{KNN}}{q_i^{nn}}, \\ \mathcal{L}_{CE} &= -\sum_i^N (y_i^{gt} \log q_i^{nn}),\end{aligned} \quad (4)$$

where p and q represent the probability distributions obtained from kNN search and the NMT output, respectively. We optimize the KL divergence loss of both.

y_i^{gt} is the target token for the current context, which we use to optimize a CE loss. The variable N represents the current batch size. We utilize the aforementioned loss to train the lightweight network as a replacement for the kNN search module. Compared to original kNN-MT, our method eliminates the need for extensive nearest neighbor search during the testing phase. Furthermore, the storage cost of retaining a lightweight network with only a few layers is much lower than storing all the training data.

Our lightweight network can be seen as an additional transformation of the feature space generated by the NMT, with the expectation of aligning the resulting feature space with the outcomes of the kNN search. However, even for the same token, it can have vastly different meanings in different contextual contexts, leading to highly complex decision boundaries in feature spaces. Therefore, it is challenging for the feature space transformed by lightweight networks to align perfectly with the results obtained from kNN search.

To address this issue, the feature space needs to be further optimized. Specifically, we propose further incorporating a sublinear layer between the lightweight network and the NMT. We train this layer to optimize a Mean Square Error (MSE) loss, aiming to reduce the distance between word vectors and improve the decision boundaries. We minimize the distance between the context representation, $f(x, y_{<t})$, generated by the NMT model, and the keys corresponding to y in the datastore. The corresponding loss function can be formulated as follows:

$$\mathcal{L}_{dis} = \frac{1}{N}\sum_i^N (h_i - \frac{1}{M}\sum_j^M h_j)^2. \quad (5)$$

In the formula, h_i denotes the hidden state produced by the decoder of the NMT model, h_j represents the contextual information stored in the datastore, and M represents the number of nearest neighbors retrieved through kNN search for the target token. The final training loss for training lightweight network can be obtained by combining these three losses and the corresponding formula can be expressed as follows:

$$\mathcal{L}_{total} = \mathcal{L}_{CE} + \alpha_1 \mathcal{L}_{dis} + \alpha_2 \mathcal{L}_{KL}, \quad (6)$$

where α_1 and α_2 are hyperparameters for each extra loss.

4 Experiments

4.1 Experimental Setup

Datasets. We use the WMT19 data for German-English [8] as the general domain corpus and we follow adaptive kNN-MT [15] which consider domains including IT, Medical, Koran, and Law as specific domain corpus. The statistics of the above datasets are illustrated in 2. Before training, we use Moses toolkit to tokenize the sentences and we split words into subwords with bpe-codes. We utilize ScareBLEU to evaluate the translation performance of different methods.

Table 1. The BLEU scores and additional storage overhead of different Methods. The baseline method does not involve additional storage, but fine-tuning disrupts the existing knowledge of NMT. "-" means no additional storage overhead.

	Method	IT		Koran		Law		Medical	
		BLEU	Params	BLEU	Params	BLEU	Params	BLEU	Params
	Ours	42.02	**2.09M**	19.87	**2.09M**	50.88	**2.09M**	47.56	**2.09M**
	PLAC kNN-MT	47.00	221M	19.9	34M	62.8	10B	56.2	3B
	Adaptive kNN-MT	**47.39**	369M	**20.30**	53M	**62.90**	19B	**56.10**	7B
	kNN-MT	45.23	369M	19.65	53M	54.98	19B	49.00	7B
Baseline	Mix domain Train	31.68	-	15.95	-	46.50	-	40.66	-
	Finetune	43.19	-	22.85	-	56.47	-	51.98	-
	General Train	36.81	-	16.96	-	45.50	-	39.51	-

Table 2. Statistics of dataset in different domains.

Dataset	IT	Medical	Koran	Laws
Train	222, 927	248, 009	17, 982	467, 309
Dev	2000	2000	2000	2000
Test	2000	2000	2000	2000

Implementation Details. We use the *fairseq* framework and accelerate the kNN search process using the *faiss* acceleration library, which is also used in most kNN-MT based work. We use the same training hyperparameters as in Adaptive-kNN-MT [15]. Specifically, we set the distribution interpolation parameter λ to 0.7, the initial learning rate to $3e-4$, the batch size to 8, and the update frequency to 16. We optimize the network parameters using the Adam optimizer.

4.2 Main Results

The main experimental results are presented in Table 1. We compare our method with other kNN-MT based approaches in various domains. For instance, Adaptive kNN-MT achieves 5.37 BLEU improvement in the IT domain. In comparison, our method achieves a significant optimization in storage overhead while sacrificing a small amount of translation performance. Similar effects can be observed on datasets of other domains. Moreover, it can be seen that fine-tuning in specific domain dataset can improve the translation performance to some extent. For instance, in the Medical domain, fine-tuning achieves a BLEU score of 51.98, surpassing the 49.00 BLEU score of kNN-MT. However, these approaches can disrupt the exisiting knowledge of the base model, leading to a decline in its performance in general domain.

4.3 Ablation Study

The kNN algorithm is highly sensitive to the choice of parameter K, which often needs to be manually set. A larger value of K may introduce irrelevant samples into the search, thereby causing interference in the training process. Conversely, a smaller value of K may result in the retrieval of a limited number of relevant samples, affecting the generalization ability of the trained lightweight network. We conduct experiments to investigate the impact of different K values on translation performance, as shown in Fig. 2 left. Based on experimental results, we uniformly set the K value to 4 in our experiments.

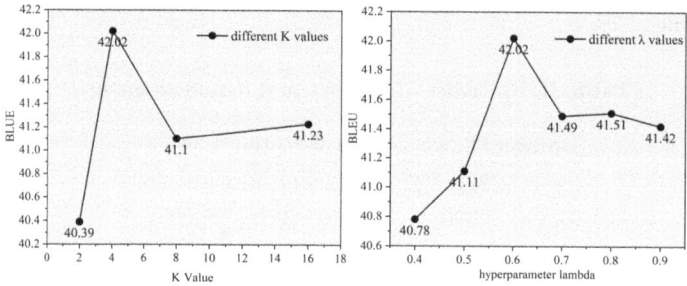

Fig. 2. Performance of lightweight network with different hyperparameters

Figure 2 right illustrates the translation performance of the lightweight network on IT domain data for different values of the distribution interpolation parameter λ. It can be observed that the translation performance is highest when the value of λ is set to 0.6. Moreover, when λ is greater than 0.5, the performance generally surpasses that when λ is less than 0.5, which indicates that when the distribution of the output from the lightweight network has a higher proportion, the performance improvement is more significant.

Table 3. The experiments of different α values in loss function on IT domain.

KL Loss	BLEU	MSE Loss	BLEU
0.1	40.05	0.1	40.93
0.3	41.15	0.3	41.03
0.5	41.35	0.5	41.45
1.0	**42.02**	1.0	**42.02**

We conduct experiments of different α in final loss function as shown in Fig. 3. We observe that as the α increases, the translation performance gradually improves and it can be seen that when the α_1 and α_2 are 1.0, the translation performance is best. We also explore the structure of lightweight networks and find that a single layer of nonlinear units yield best performance. Increasing the depth of the network make it difficult to train and fit kNN results.

5 Conclusion

In this paper, we propose a approach which replaces the search and matching process of kNN-MT with a lightweight network. Compared to using a datastore, the lightweight network significantly reduces storage overhead and ensure fast inference speed while sacrificing only a small amount of performance. We conduct cross-domain machine translation experiments on four datasets from different domains. Compared with the original kNN-MT, the performance loss of our method is acceptable while greatly reducing storage overhead.

Acknowledgement. The funding for this research was generously provided by the Natural Science Fund of Hubei Province (Grant 2022CFB823), the Alibaba Innovation Research program (Grant CRAQ7WHZ11220001-20978282), and grants from the National Key Lab of MSIIPT (Grant 6142113220309) as well as the MoE Key Lab of Image Processing and Intelligent Control, among others.

References

1. Chan, D.M., Ghosh, S., Rastrow, A., Hoffmeister, B.: Domain adaptation with external off-policy acoustic catalogs for scalable contextual end-to-end automated speech recognition. In: ICASSP 2023-2023 IEEE International Conference on Acoustics, Speech and Signal Processing (ICASSP), pp. 1–5. IEEE (2023)
2. Wilkinghoff, K.: Design choices for learning embeddings from auxiliary tasks for domain generalization in anomalous sound detection. In: ICASSP 2023-2023 IEEE International Conference on Acoustics, Speech and Signal Processing (ICASSP), pp. 1–5. IEEE (2023)
3. Chen, D., Fisch, A., Weston, J., Bordes, A.: Reading Wikipedia to answer open-domain questions. In: Proceedings of the 55th Annual Meeting of the Association for Computational Linguistics (Volume 1: Long Papers), pp. 1870–1879 (2017)
4. Chu, C., Dabre, R., Kurohashi, S.: An empirical comparison of simple domain adaptation methods for neural machine translation. arXiv preprint arXiv:1701.03214 (2017)
5. Gu, J., Wang, Y., Cho, K., Li, V.O.K.: Search engine guided neural machine translation. In: Proceedings of the AAAI Conference on Artificial Intelligence, vol. 32 (2018)
6. Khandelwal, U., Fan, A., Jurafsky, D., Zettlemoyer, L., Lewis, M.: Nearest neighbor machine translation. Distances **4**(3), 100 (2020)
7. Meng, Y., et al.: Fast nearest neighbor machine translation. In: Findings of the Association for Computational Linguistics: ACL, vol. 2022, pp. 555–565 (2022)
8. Ng, N., Yee, K., Baevski, A., Ott, M., Auli, M., Edunov, S.: Facebook FAIR's WMT19 news translation task submission. arXiv preprint arXiv:1907.06616 (2019)
9. Robertson, S., Zaragoza, H., et al.: The probabilistic relevance framework: BM25 and beyond. Found. Trends Inf. Retrieval **3**(4), 333–389 (2009)

10. Stergiadis, E., Kumar, S., Kovalev, F, Levin, P.: Multi-domain adaptation in neural machine translation through multidimensional tagging
11. Tars, S., Fishel, M.: Multi-domain neural machine translation. arXiv preprint arXiv:1805.02282 (2018)
12. Wang, D., Fan, K., Chen, B., Xiong, D.: Efficient cluster-based k-nearest-neighbor machine translation-nearest-neighbor machine translation. In: Proceedings of the 60th Annual Meeting of the Association for Computational Linguistics (Volume 1: Long Papers), pp. 2175–2187 (2022)
13. Wang, S., et al.: Faster nearest neighbor machine translation. arXiv preprint arXiv:2112.08152 (2021)
14. Xu, F.F., Alon, U., Neubig, G.: Why do nearest neighbor language models work? arXiv preprint arXiv:2301.02828 (2023)
15. Zheng, X., et al.: Adaptive nearest neighbor machine translation. In: Proceedings of the 59th Annual Meeting of the Association for Computational Linguistics and the 11th International Joint Conference on Natural Language Processing (Volume 2: Short Papers), pp. 368–374 (2021)
16. Zhu, W., Huang, S., Lv, Y., Zheng, X., Chen, J.: What knowledge is needed? Towards explainable memory for kNN-MT domain adaptation. arXiv preprint arXiv:2211.04052 (2022)

Extend Adversarial Policy Against Neural Machine Translation via Unknown Token

Wei Zou, Shujian Huang(✉), and Jiajun Chen

National Key Laboratory for Novel Software Technology, Nanjing University,
Jiangsu 210046, China
zouw@smail.nju.edu.com, {huangsj,chenjj}@nju.edu.cn

Abstract. Generating adversarial examples contributes to mainstream neural machine translation (NMT) robustness. However, popular adversarial policies are apt for fixed tokenization, hindering its efficacy for common character perturbations involving versatile tokenization. Based on existing adversarial generation via reinforcement learning (RL), we propose the 'DexChar policy' that introduces character perturbations for the existing mainstream adversarial policy based on token substitution. Furthermore, we improve the self-supervised matching that provides feedback in RL to cater to the semantic constraints required during training adversaries. Experiments show that our method is compatible with the scenario where baseline adversaries fail, and can generate high-efficiency adversarial examples for analysis and optimization of the system.

Keywords: Neural machine translation · Adversarial example · Reinforcement learning

1 Introduction

Neural machine translation [1,25, NMT] based on the encoder-decoder framework has proved its efficacy in modern industries. However, it's susceptible to textual noise that does not fit the training data distribution without affecting readers (Table 1). Saboteurs also craft adversarial inputs to achieve similar deterioration [2,14,29]. Due to the black-box nature of neural networks, it is difficult to safeguard such errors, posing threats to NMT systems. Some [3,8,11] handcraft adversarial tests against the NMT for system defects. However, the extravagant expert rules can hardly cover versatile scenarios and rely heavily on expertise in the target system.

Others turned to adversarial example generation against the target NMT. Adversarial example generation [9] is an annotation-preserving perturbation on input that triggers system degradation, leading to off-the-shelf cases for maintenance. The mainstream adversaries against NMT aim to search for optimal input perturbations, modeled by substitutions given corresponding tokenization. Some policies [4,5,15,19,26] focus on subwords in embedding vicinity against

Table 1. The Chinese input means "This work received an unprecedented number of complaints.", which is well-translated. However, textual perturbations (highlighted in bold) trigger significant errors without affecting readers.

in	本工作 收到 了 许多 投诉，数量 前所未有 。
out	We have received an unprecedented number of complaints.
in	本工作 **们** 收到 了 **许许多多** 投诉， **数** 数量 前所未有 。
out	he said, we have received a lot of complaints, the number of unprecedented.

Table 2. Character-level perturbations significantly modified the tokenization, invalidating substitution-based policy. '@@' indicates partition within words.

input	I love eating pineapple and kiwifruit.
tokenized	I love eating pine@@ apple and kiwi@@ fruit.
perturbed input	I love eating pi*en*apple and k*wi*ifuit.
tokenized perturbation	I love eating pi@@ en@@ apple and k@@ wi@@ i@@ f@@ uit.

mainstream NMT while others [6,7] focus on character substitutions against character-based NMT. The adversaries refer to corresponding search loss defined upon tokenization to guide the search. Though these methods achieve text adversary, the challenges remain as follows:

Firstly, the text adversaries are apt for the tokenization granularity of the target system, leaving out perturbations in different editorial granularity. Mainstream methods [14,15,19,26] must assume static tokenization during perturbations since the similarity-based substitution with corresponding search loss is defined upon the given tokenization granularity. Such modeling narrows the accessible adversaries since perturbations in smaller granularity risk invalidating the optimum search once it changes the overall tokenization (Table 2). Therefore, they can hardly reconcile perturbations across versatile granularity. That is, adversaries against mainstream NMT modeled by tokenized subwords [22] lack compatibility for common character perturbations such as homonyms [28] and synonyms [2,12]. A practical adversarial example generation requires expanding policies for perturbations in different granularity.

Secondly, it's hard to model the semantic constraints involving perturbations across different granularity to maintain output annotations. Unlike minor perturbations against the image classification, minor perturbations on characters do not correspond to similarity features based on embedding of off-the-shelf subwords when they significantly modify overall tokenization (Table 2). Though humans neglect their impact on semantics, mainstream deep learning modules tend to trigger *false-negative* classifications given significantly modified tokenization.

This paper extends the adversary [29, RL-attacker] based on reinforcement learning [24, RL]. Specifically, RL-attacker is trained by RL, where the NMT is an environment for rewards to constrain annotation-reserving semantics and promote adversary. The value estimation during RL circumvents handcrafted search loss given static tokenization in the mainstream adversaries. In this work, we propose the 'DexChar' policy to introduce dexterous character perturbations to the mainstream substitution-based adversarial policy. we additionally incorporate noisy data augmentation for the corresponding discriminator in environments, thus catering to false-negative classification, and providing compatible rewards for character perturbations during the RL.

The main contributions of this work can be summarized as follows:

- We propose the 'DexChar' policy which extends mainstream substitution-based adversaries with dexterous character perturbations across different granularity;
- Meanwhile, we implement noisy data augmentation to improve semantic constraints for adversary training to circumvent *false-negative* discrimination triggered by character perturbations;
- We conduct adversaries on mainstream NMT with different input module settings. The results show that our improved policy is compatible with the scenarios where the mainstream adversarial policy fails, and can intuitively analyze and maintain the model without losing much efficiency.

2 Preliminary

2.1 Annotation-Preserving Adversaries for Text

Mainstream text adversaries are modeled by constrained perturbations. Though some policies [23] adopt the perturbations in the latent vicinity, they will fail constraints within more delicate semantics. Therefore, major text adversaries [4,5,15,19,26] focus on token substitution in embedding vicinity. Given the tokenization with the corresponding word embedding representation, the adversary collects all the k-nearest neighbors by cosine-similarity for each token in the vocabulary as candidates, then keeps the candidates within a vicinity radius ϵ for perturbation. Others [6,7,10] focus on character substitutions against character-based NMT, e.g., transposition, insertion, substitution, and deletion. They rely on the morphology and phonetics of characters to ensure the reader's perception of the semantics under noise [10], thus apt for maintaining annotations without embedding similarity.

Theoretically, arbitrary text perturbations can correspond to a specific substitution. However, an applicable adversary must enumerate accessible perturbations for search loss defined upon a given tokenization as guidance. Since it's impossible to enumerate underlying perturbations beforehand, it fails to grasp defects by various perturbation granularity.

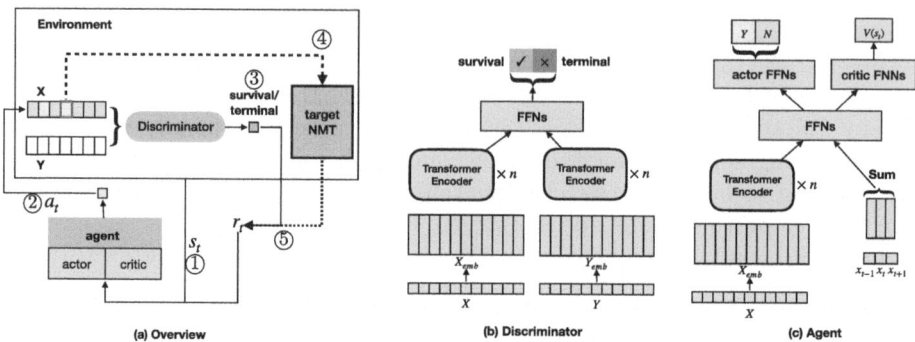

Fig. 1. The overview of RL-attacker [29]. (a) The overall algorithm loops the following steps: ① agent uses the current text as state input (s_t) to determine whether the current position t (framed in red) needs perturbation. ② The agent perturbs text if needed (highlight in yellow) by a candidate token substitution; ③ D determines whether perturbation is within semantic constraint: negative (red), the remaining perturbation is terminated with a punishment of -1; Otherwise, the 'survive' perturbation (green) is rewarded by the positive probability of D, and continuing follow-up perturbations; Loop ① to ③ until the policy survives to complete the sequential perturbations. ④ The perturbed sequence is re-segmented and tested by the target NMT for episodic reward; ⑤ Accumulate rewards r and update the agent. (b) The architecture of discriminator D, with n layers of Transformer encoder for input feature extraction. (c) The architecture of actor-critic agent with shared input feature extraction.

2.2 Adversarial Policy Against NMT via Reinforcement Learning

Adversarial example generation via RL [29, RL-attacker] trains the adversary by interacting with the target NMT to maximize the metric degradation. It inherits the mainstream adversarial substitution while circumventing the handcrafted search loss via value estimation for arbitrary guidance. RL-attacker involves consecutive GAN-style [9] updates of an *environment* and an *agent* (Fig. 1), where the environment contains a discriminator D for semantic constraints. For n_a rounds of policy updates, the environment's D is updated up to n_e rounds until its validation performance ρ reaches $\bar{\rho}$. Since the learned value estimation by critics provides policy guidance for training instead of a handcrafted search loss on a given tokenization, the corresponding policy is theoretically no longer limited to a given static tokenization and expert priors.

However, the RL-attacker only adopts the similarity-based substitution for the policy without covering character-level adversaries. Meanwhile, the discriminator D for semantic constraints is a neural net upon direct text embedding, thus prone to yield false-negative discrimination if the character-level perturbation significantly modifies the tokenization. D tends to negate character perturbations even within semantic constraints due to tokenization issues, thus hindering underlying character adversarial policy training.

3 Methodology

In this section, we detail our methods with the corresponding motivations. First, we propose the 'DexChar' policy, which introduces dexterous character perturbations of different granularity by harnessing the 'unknown' token (noted as 'UNK') for the existing substitution-based adversarial policy. Then, we implement noisy data augmentation for the corresponding self-supervised discriminator in the environment to alleviate the false-negative semantic discrimination for the extended policy.

3.1 'DexChar' Policy

The major issue in introducing arbitrary perturbations for policy is to present an entry for innumerable underlying substitutions. Note that perturbations of different granularity impact systems by introducing **low-frequency** character combinations as shown in Table 2 which disturb the language model upon trained tokenization, we propose to add candidate 'UNK' to all substitutions as the entry for various underlying perturbations. Once a token adopts the 'UNK' for perturbation, generating its **valid low-frequency substitution** introduces perturbations of different granularity. Note that 'UNK' indicates low-frequency rather than unrecognized text, since low-frequency character combinations are ubiquitous although the SOTA tokenization algorithms present arbitrary character strings. Therefore, the DexChar policy is still viable against systems with the SOTA tokenization algorithms.

Algorithm 1. 'DexChar' Perturbation $\Delta(w, ACT, kwargs)$

Require: $w = [c_0, c_1, \ldots, c_n]$, target vocabulary V, $ACT \in \{Swap, Ins, Sub\}$
Ensure: perturbed w_{final} via ACT.
    for c in w **do**
        perturb c by ACT, generating w';
        if w' is regarded 'UNK' by V **then** break;
        end if
    end for
    if w' is regarded 'UNK' by V **then**
        success, return by $w_{\text{final}} = w'$
    else
        failed, return by $w_{\text{final}} =$ None
    end if

We propose the function $\Delta(w, ACT, kwargs)$ on token w defined by Algorithm 1, where 'kwargs' introduces additional inputs such as a dictionary for substitution candidates. Inspired by work [6,28], we listed ACT by following character perturbations:

– Swap (Swap): flip the adjacent character (e.g. noise → niose);

- Insertion (Ins): Insert a character into a word. To ensure semantics, the corresponding character is repeated (e.g. noise → noiise);
- Substitution (Sub): Given character substitution candidate dictionary $cands_{knn}$, replaces a character within a word with another candidate character (e.g. noise → noisϵ). We follow work [7] to adopt keyboard vicinity and homoglyphs as candidates.

For each input token w, the function $\Delta(\cdot)$ traverses each character from left to right, then perturbs the character by ACT until a low-frequency token regarded as 'UNK' by vocabulary V is produced. The $\Delta(\cdot)$ yields 'None' if the specified ACT fails. Note that we leave out the deletion as it's intuitively detrimental for semantics.

Algorithm 2. 'UNK' Generation

Require: $w = [c_0, c_1, \ldots, c_n]$, target vocabulary V, $ACT \in \{Swap, Ins, Sub\}$, dictionary of character-level substitution candidates $cands_{knn}$, dictionary of homophone substitution candidates $cands_{phone}$, perturbation function $\Delta(\cdot)$.
Ensure: perturbed w_{final} which is regarded 'UNK' by V.
    w_{final} =None
    if homonym is available for w **then**
        $w_{final} = \Delta(w, Sub, cands_{phone})$
    end if
    if w_{final} is None **then**
        if $|w| > 3$ **then**
            $w_{final} = \Delta(w, Swap)$
        else
            $w_{final} = \Delta(w, Sub, cands_{knn})$
        end if
    end if
    $w_{tmp} = w$
    while w_{final} is None **do**
        $w_{tmp} = \Delta(w_{tmp}, Ins)$
        $w_{final} = w_{tmp} \text{if} w_{tmp}$ is not None
    end while

To ensure the generation of a 'UNK', we propose the Algorithm 2, which combines multiple ACTs to ensure that a valid 'UNK' for the target dictionary is generated.

3.2 Noisy Data Augmentation for Discriminator

It is worth Noting that self-supervised D intends to model the *semantic matching* between the perturbed input and the original annotation rather than the *variation* of texts. We augment the positive data with a small amount of semantic-preserving character perturbation modeled by Sect. 3.1 to cater to false-negative discrimination triggered by perturbations of various granularity.

The augmentation adopts a dynamic ratio ξ, which follows the intuition to adjust with the confidence ρ of on-the-fly environment D: When the confidence of the current D is high, that is, $\rho > \bar{\rho}$, which indicates the D is sufficient against perturbations, thus the training supports noisy data augmentation. Therefore, the input X of the positive sample adopts random character perturbations by the probability $\xi = \rho - \bar{\rho}$; When the confidence of the environment is low, that is, $\rho < \bar{\rho}$, it indicates the D is temporarily less capable with only standard training. All training data for the environment's discriminator is retokenized once it's perturbed.

4 Experiments

We conduct all experiments on the mainstream NMT settings on 4 NVIDIA V100 (32G) given WMT14 English-German (en-de, 4.5M) and CWMT17 English-Chinese (en-zh, 7.4M) parallel data. We adopt the mainstream NMT model by end-to-end autoregressive Transformers as the backbone for adversaries. The experiments include different embedding settings as test scenarios for verification.

4.1 Experiment Settings

Target NMT Settings The experiments include the following embedding settings for the target NMT model which provides different robustness against input perturbations:

- Base setting (base): source and target languages with independent vocabularies and embedding layers;
- shared-vocabulary setting (shared-emb): source and target languages share vocabulary and embedding layers. This setting facilitates the shared semantic features between similar languages [27] during training (e.g., en-de), and is adopted by mainstream multilingual applications;
- Pre-trained setting (PLM-emb): source and target languages adopt fixed embedding from a pre-trained language model (PLM), whereas the remaining parameters of the NMT are trained by translation. This setting is popular for facilitating the semantic features extracted by mass language model training. In this work, we adopt the embedding of the multilingual anti-noise pre-training model mBART [13]. Since the mBART is trained by a multilingual vocabulary, it essentially belongs to a special shared-vocabulary setting.
- The 'unknown' vocabulary (UNK) setting: We follow the baseline transformer training setting to truncate the top 30k vocabulary by frequency in the training dataset, with the others regarded as low-frequency for UNK.

The training settings including learning rates and model architectures follow that of the Transformer [25].

Training Data The NMT training and adversarial experiments adopt the same parallel data, i.e., WMT14 en-de (4.5M) and CWMT17 en-zh (7.4M) data. When training the target NMT, the en-de language pair adopts wmt13 as the validation set and wmt14 as the test set; the en-zh language pair adopts wmt17 as the validation set and wmt18 as the test set. The parallel data also initialize the RL environment during training adversarial generation policies. The experiments then verify the translation performance affected by adversaries on the test set.

Text data is processed by the mosesdecoder scripts[1], and Chinese is further tokenized by jieba[2]. Then, the NMT adopts the subword-nmt[3] to generate subwords statistically as tokens after concatenating the source and target language data. For the systems adopting mBART for input vocabularies and embedding, we directly adopt the tokenization and dictionary of mBART. Due to the oversized input dictionary of mBART, we only retain the top 50k tokens by token frequencies via traversing the bilingual training data, with the rest of the vocabulary as unknown tokens, i.e., 'UNK'.

Evaluation Metric We record the average adversarial candidates (candidate fertility, CF) of the 500 most frequent source tokens to indicate the different test scenarios for adversaries. Intuitively, more candidates facilitate RL training for adversarial policy. We first adopt BLEU [17, sacreBLEU][4] for policy training, referring to the metrics in work [14,29]. Then, we propose to adopt the following metrics to evaluate adversarial example generation:

- Metric degradation (MD): The more translation degradation after perturbation compared to the original test. We turn to BLEURT [18,21][5] for degradation, rather than the BLEU score used during training for less biased validation.
- Degradation per edit (DPE): The MD is divided by the edit distance compared to the original input after the perturbation, where we adopt TER from sacreBLEU as the edit distance. DPE indicates the efficiency of the adversarial policy;
- Pairing Accuracy (PA): The semantic matching rate between the perturbed input and the original annotation. The experiments adopt GPT-3.5-turbo, the application interface of the large language model [16, LLM] by the corresponding "system" and "user" prompts shown in Table 3 as queries. To validate the LLM's discrimination for noisy inputs, we randomly sample an additional 100 pairs from every experiment for human evaluation (acc).

The ideal adversarial example generation must achieve as much metric degradation as possible within the semantic constraints that maintain the annotations, i.e., high MD with high PA. A low PA score indicates failed validation by mismatched annotation, instead of failed translation. Higher DPE indicates a more

---

[1] https://github.com/moses-smt/mosesdecoder/tree/master/scripts/tokenizer.
[2] https://github.com/fxsjy/jieba.
[3] https://github.com/rsennrich/subword-nmt.
[4] https://github.com/mjpost/sacrebleu.
[5] The BLEURT20 checkpoint, https://github.com/google-research/bleurt.

Table 3. Prompts for pairing accuracy

	Prompt
Sys:	You are a knowledgeable multi-lingual specialist who can tell whether two sentences (might be different languages) are semantically matched by "yes" or "no"
User:	<source> <annotation> are they semantically matched?

efficient adversary given less perturbation against the target NMT, thus the corresponding adversarial examples are more detrimental.

Baseline adversaries

- Random noise injection [6, 7, RNI]: Randomly perturb each token given a probability 0.2 with character perturbations defined in Sect. 3.1 regardless of semantics. Note that RNI acts as a sanity baseline for the adversarial examples;
- Gradient search [14, GS]: Greedily search the substitution candidates from left to right for the perturbation combination that maximizes the adversarial loss. The policy adopts vicinity candidates within the radius of the NMT's embedding space;
- Reinforced attack [29, RL-attacker] in Sect. 2.2.

Experiments adopt 10 nearest candidates to calculate the vicinity radius ϵ. To sum up, RNI adopts the character perturbation for all tokens regardless of semantics; GS only adopts substitution candidates within ϵ; RL-attacker adopts the candidates in GS and limited UNK substitution for those without candidates. Our work supports both perturbations from GS and RNI.

4.2 Experiment Results

The results of en-zh and en-de language pairs are shown in Tables 4 and 5, respectively. Note that the high accuracy by human evaluation (acc) verifies the LLM's evaluation (PA). The results are summarized as follows:

- Fewer candidates (CF) indicate more difficulty against adversaries by substitution thus less degradation (MD). For instance, GS achieves significantly less MD for both en-zh and en-de NMT with shared vocabulary. RNI and our work with character perturbation circumvent these scenarios with more MD and more efficient adversary (DPE). Note that RNI with significantly lower PA scores indicates its inability to follow semantics constraints even with high MD, which are not always valid adversarial examples.
- Given the same substitution candidates for adversaries, our policy achieves better semantic constraints to maintain annotation, i.e., MD with a higher PA score. RNI is regarded as the sanity baseline whose adversary injects

Table 4. Experiment results for zh-en language pair. ↑ indicates 'the more the better'. 'CF' indicates the candidate's fertility for the substitution adversary. The 'acc' indicates the sampled human validation for GPT-3.5-turbo's paring accuracy (PA). Note that RNI with an excessively lower semantic pairing (PA) is not a valid adversarial example generation.

zh ->en	base(MC=2.27)			shared_vocab(MC=1.06)			bart_emb(MC=5.61)		
BLEURT	60.395			61.12			59.36		
	MD	DPE	PA(acc)	MD	DPE	PA(acc)	MD	DPE	PA(acc)
RNI	23.955	1.248	0.62(1.0)	28.99	1.584	0.45(1.0)	29.16	1.793	0.56(0.99)
GS	6.945	0.285	0.85(0.99)	4.92	0.615	0.99(0.98)	9.24	0.462	0.76(1.0)
RL-base	13.275	0.606	0.92(1.0)	5.82	0.803	0.91(0.98)	24.13	1.207	0.89(0.99)
Ours	23.92	1.127	0.91(0.98)	15.92	1.532	0.92(0.99)	22.03	1.615	0.88(0.97)
en ->zh	base(MC=1.12)			shared_vocab(MC=1.06)			bart_emb(MC=5.61)		
BLEURT	66.79			67.44			66.715		
	MD	DPE	PA(acc)	MD	DPE	PA(acc)	MD	DPE	PA(acc)
RNI	38.56	1.600	0.63(1.0)	31.32	1.559	0.32(0.98)	28.505	1.308	0.48(0.98)
GS	12.42	0.776	0.88(0.98)	13.22	0.925	0.87(1.0)	20.505	0.760	0.85(0.98)
RL-base	22.67	1.139	0.74(1.0)	21.32	1.191	0.78(0.99)	22.595	1.224	0.79(1.0)
Ours	40.98	1.722	0.8(0.98)	27.2	1.386	0.82(0.97)	27.395	1.179	0.82(1.0)

the random noise regardless of semantics for the original annotation. Therefore, RNI easily achieves significant degradation by failed validation with mismatched annotation, whereas our method reconciles the adversary (MD) within semantics constraints (PA).

- Compared with the original RL-attacker, our method achieves a better adversary (MD, DPE) due to the extensive DexChar policy, which introduces character perturbations without failing semantic constraints (PA). DexChar reaches a similar adversary compared to the sanity baseline RNI with much more reasonable semantics (PA) required by adversarial examples.

Notably, mBART embedding does not significantly hinder the adversary, whereas its embedding structure facilitates the mainstream substitution adversary with more candidates (CF).

5 Analysis

In this section, we take the Chinese-to-English translation with shared vocabulary as an example, since the Chinese character poses a larger impact on semantics, to analyze adversarial example generation, including adversarial generation efficiency, translation defect analysis, and follow-up system maintenance.

5.1 Adversarial Generation Efficiency

Figure 2 records the overhead (seconds) for adversarial generation. GS calculates the gradient features as search guidance for candidates, thus resulting in a large overhead. Our method retains the efficiency of the RL paradigm with over 200 times acceleration compared to GS, while the extended character-level perturbations for policy take up only negligible overheads.

5.2 Adversarial Pattern

Handcrafted adversaries [8,20] prefer to perturb tokens with more potential impacts on semantics. Intuitively, the policy trained by RL [29] also prefers perturbation for specific sentence components (POS). The analysis collects the perturbation ratio of the adversaries against each type of POS tag (POS tags by 863 standard[6]). As shown in Fig. 3, our method retains the preference among certain POS by RL-attacker [29] with a slight difference. Due to the extended character

Table 5. Experiment results for en-de language pair

en ->de	base(MC=3.34)			shared_vocab(MC=1.01)			bart_emb(MC=7.48)		
BLEURT	70.44			71.02			71.025		
	MD↑	DPE↑	PA(acc)↑	MD↑	DPE↑	PA(acc)↑	MD↑	DPE↑	PA(acc)↑
RNI	42.46	3.45	0.42(1.0)	49.52	3.668	0.49(1.0)	39.62	2.386	0.58(1.0)
GS	29.3	2.402	0.83(0.98)	11.62	2.152	0.95(0.98)	9.805	0.649	0.92(1.0)
RL-attacker	38.34	2.506	0.89(1.0)	29.92	2.267	0.92(0.99)	20.015	1.409	0.90(1.0)
Ours	48.67	3.380	0.91(0.97)	51.905	3.767	0.91(0.99)	30.21	2.464	0.92(1.0)
de ->en	base(MC=4.35)			shared_vocab(MC=1.01)			bart_emb(MC=7.48)		
BLEURT	70.86			71.61			71.15		
	MD↑	DPE↑	PA(acc)↑	MD↑	DPE↑	PA(acc)↑	MD↑	DPE↑	PA(acc)↑
RNI	40.74	3.08	0.48(0.98)	35.11	2.66	0.55(0.99)	38.75	2.266	0.59(1.0)
GS	7.135	0.469	0.88(0.97)	10.49	2.185	0.96(0.99)	7.95	0.520	0.87(0.97)
RL-attacker	29.24	2.215	0.9(0.98)	23.27	1.907	0.92(0.99)	25.93	1.826	0.93(0.96)
Ours	42.475	2.909	0.89(1.0)	36.28	2.232	0.93(0.97)	39.10	2.330	0.92(0.99)

[Bar chart: RNI, GS, RL-base, Ours. Base: 81, 119108, 343, 567. shared-emb: 92, 117900, 279, 298. bart-emb: 88, 149082, 412, 682. Y-axis: Time (seconds)]

Fig. 2. Overheads for different adversaries. Our method retains the adversarial efficiency with minor overhead for extended character-level perturbations.

---

[6] https://catalog.ldc.upenn.edu/docs/LDC2012T05/readme.html.

perturbations, our method achieves more adversaries against POS such as temporal noun (NT) and geographical name (NS) as their semantics are less sensitive to character perturbations such as homonyms. On the other hand, our methods extracted fewer adversaries against POS such as conjunctions (C), proverbs (I), numbers (M), and quantifiers (q), whose semantics are largely posed at the character level. The preference indicates that our extended policy can identify and utilize character perturbations for more effective and versatile adversaries.

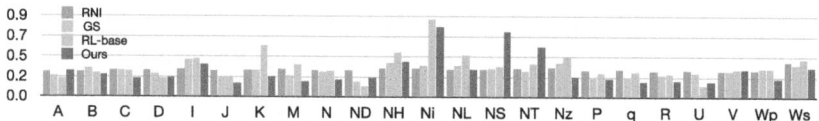

Fig. 3. Preference over POS by different adversaries

5.3 Fine-Tuning with Adversarial Examples

We fine-tune the target model with the corresponding adversarial examples. Due to the efficiency of the RL adversary, we adopt the parallel data $<X, Y>$ to generate the same amount of adversarial pairs $<X', Y>$ for fine-tuning by the following loss function base:

$$\bar{L} = L(X, Y) + \lambda L(X', Y), \qquad (1)$$

where λ is the adversarial coefficient, which we set to 0.2, and L is the end-to-end supervised loss of NMT. The fine-tuning follows the training settings by NMT [25] for up to one epoch with a fixed learning rate at $1e-6$. We test the robustness of NMT against the following noisy scenarios:

- RNI (0.1): Random noise injection with a low probability at 0.1. Perturbations are defined in Sect. 3.1;
- RL-attacker: Adversarial tests generated by the RL-attacker;
- Mixed: Adversarial tests generated by character-level perturbation and token substitution;

The results are shown in Table 6. Intuitively, each fine-tuning improves the corresponding test scenario. However, fine-tuning is potentially detrimental to other scenarios. Notably, the RL-attacker does not improve the robustness against character perturbations, whereas our method can mildly alleviate the noise by character perturbation as well as adversarial inputs.

Table 6. Adversarial fine-tuning for zh→en NMT with shared vocabulary. The table columns present test scenarios, while the rows present the corresponding fine-tuned (FT) setting. The "None" represents the original NMT model and the original test scenario.

	None	RNI (0.1)	RL-attacker	Mixed
None	23.1	16.4	19	16.5
RL-attacker FT	22.7(−0.4)	16.1(−0.3)	22.6(+3.6)	17.3(+0.8)
DexChar FT	21.9(−1.2)	18.5(+2.1)	21.3(+2.3)	22.1(+5.6)

6 Conclusion

This work proposes the 'DexChar' policy, which utilizes the 'UNK' token for dexterous substitution which extends the adversarial policy to cater to versatile perturbation granularity. Experiments show that the perturbations introduced by the 'DexChar' policy facilitate the adversary against test scenarios where the traditional adversary fails. The resulting adversary remains efficient and available against versatile target models, enabling subsequent analysis. Adversarial tuning with our method can cater to noise maintenance across different perturbation granularity.

Acknowledgement. This work is supported by the National Science Foundation of China (No. 62376116, 62176120), and the Fundamental Research Funds for the Central Universities (No. 2024300507).

References

1. Bahdanau, D., Cho, K., Bengio, Y.: Neural machine translation by jointly learning to align and translate. arXiv preprint arXiv:1409.0473 (2014)
2. Belinkov, Y., Bisk, Y.: Synthetic and natural noise both break neural machine translation. arXiv preprint arXiv:1711.02173 (2017)
3. Chaturvedi, A., KP, A., Garain, U.: Exploring the robustness of NMT systems to nonsensical inputs. arXiv preprint arXiv:1908.01165 (2019)
4. Cheng, M., Yi, J., Chen, P.Y., Zhang, H., Hsieh, C.J.: Seq2Sick: evaluating the robustness of sequence-to-sequence models with adversarial examples. In: Proceedings of AAAI (2020)
5. Cheng, Y., Jiang, L., Macherey, W.: Robust neural machine translation with doubly adversarial inputs. arXiv preprint arXiv:1906.02443 (2019)
6. Ebrahimi, J., Lowd, D., Dou, D.: On adversarial examples for character-level neural machine translation. arXiv preprint arXiv:1806.09030 (2018)
7. Ebrahimi, J., Rao, A., Lowd, D., Dou, D.: HotFlip: white-box adversarial examples for text classification. arXiv preprint arXiv:1712.06751 (2017)
8. Garg, S., Ramakrishnan, G.: BAE: BERT-based adversarial examples for text classification. arXiv preprint arXiv:2004.01970 (2020)
9. Goodfellow, I.J., Shlens, J., Szegedy, C.: Explaining and harnessing adversarial examples. arXiv preprint arXiv:1412.6572 (2014)

10. Han, X., Zhang, Y., Wang, W., Wang, B., et al.: Text adversarial attacks and defenses: issues, taxonomy, and perspectives. Secur. Commun. Netw. (2022)
11. Karpukhin, V., Levy, O., Eisenstein, J., Ghazvininejad, M.: Training on synthetic noise improves robustness to natural noise in machine translation. In: Proceedings of the 5th Workshop on Noisy User-Generated Text (W-NUT 2019) (2019)
12. Le, T., Park, N., Lee, D.: Detecting universal trigger's adversarial attack with honeypot. arXiv preprint arXiv:2011.10492 (2020)
13. Liu, Y., et al.: Multilingual denoising pre-training for neural machine translation. In: TACL (2020)
14. Michel, P., Li, X., Neubig, G., Pino, J.M.: On evaluation of adversarial perturbations for sequence-to-sequence models. arXiv preprint arXiv:1903.06620 (2019)
15. Morris, J.X., Lifland, E., Lanchantin, J., Ji, Y., Qi, Y.: Reevaluating adversarial examples in natural language. arXiv preprint arXiv:2004.14174 (2020)
16. OpenAI (2022). https://openai.com/blog/chatgpt
17. Post, M.: A call for clarity in reporting Bleu scores. arXiv preprint arXiv:1804.08771 (2018)
18. Pu, A., Chung, H.W., Parikh, A.P., Gehrmann, S., Sellam, T.: Learning compact metrics for MT. In: Proceedings of EMNLP (2021)
19. Sadrizadeh, S., Dolamic, L., Frossard, P.: Block-sparse adversarial attack to fool transformer-based text classifiers. In: Proceedings of ICASSP (2022)
20. Samanta, S., Mehta, S.: Towards crafting text adversarial samples. arXiv preprint arXiv:1707.02812 (2017)
21. Sellam, T., Das, D., Parikh, A.P.: BLEURT: learning robust metrics for text generation. In: Proceedings of ACL (2020)
22. Sennrich, R., Haddow, B., Birch, A.: Neural machine translation of rare words with subword units. arXiv (2015)
23. Sooksatra, K., Khanal, B., Rivas, P.: On adversarial examples for text classification by perturbing latent representations. arXiv preprint arXiv:2405.03789 (2024)
24. Sutton, R.S., Barto, A.G.: Reinforcement Learning: An Introduction. MIT Press (2018)
25. Vaswani, A., et al.: Attention is all you need. In: Proceedings of NeurIPS (2017)
26. Wang, B., Xu, C., Liu, X., Cheng, Y., Li, B.: SemAttack: natural textual attacks via different semantic spaces. arXiv preprint arXiv:2205.01287 (2022)
27. Wu, D., Monz, C.: Beyond shared vocabulary: increasing representational word similarities across languages for multilingual machine translation. arXiv preprint arXiv:2305.14189 (2023)
28. Zhang, S., Wu, H., Zhu, G., Xin, X., Su, M.: Character-level adversarial samples generation approach for Chinese text classification. J. Electron. Inf. Technol. (2023)
29. Zou, W., Huang, S., Xie, J., Dai, X., Chen, J.: A reinforced generation of adversarial examples for neural machine translation. In: Proceedings of ACL (2020). https://doi.org/10.18653/v1/2020.acl-main.319

Low-resource Machine Translation

Evaluating the Translation Performance of Multilingual Large Language Models: A Case Study on Southeast Asian Languages

Hua Lai[1,2], Silei Han[1,2], Ying Li[1,2(✉)], Zhengtao Yu[1,2], and Zirui Guo[1,2]

[1] Faculty of Information Engineering and Automation, Kunming University of Science and Technology, Kunming, China
yingli_hlt@foxmail.com
[2] Yunnan Key Laboratory of Artificial Intelligence, Kunming University of Science and Technology, Kunming, China

Abstract. With the rapid development of large language models, a lot of preliminary work has been done to explore the performance of large language models on different artificial intelligence tasks. Despite this, research on evaluating the translation performance of large language models for Southeast Asian low-resource languages is still relatively scarce. The main reason is the scarcity of public evaluation data for Southeast Asian low-resource languages and large language models that can be directly injected into Southeast Asian low-resource languages for training. First, evaluation data for Southeast Asian low-resource language is extracted based on the publicly available Asian Language Treebank (ALT) corpus. Then, large language models with the capability to understand Southeast Asian low-resource languages are evaluated. Finally, three strategies are employed to construct in-context learning prompts to further enhance the translation performance of the existing large language models. Experimental results on multiple benchmark datasets demonstrate that large language models have superior contextual learning capabilities and their translation performances can be improved significantly by utilizing high-quality prompts. However, the guidance effect of sub-optimal prompts on the model is inconsistent. The comparative experiment further elucidated that the model temperature parameter exhibits distinct optimal values depending on the scale of text input. The subsequent analysis indicates that a higher degree of similarity between the prompt and the context facilitates the model's ability to generate accurate translation results.

Keywords: Large Language Models (LLMs) · Prompt Learning · Machine Translation · Southeast Asian Low-resource Languages

1 Introduction

As a significant research area in natural language processing, machine translation aims to utilize computers to automatically translate text from a source language into a target language. Given a sentence $X = X_1, X_2, \ldots, X_n$ in the source language,the machine translation model learns a mapping function $F : X \to Y$ that translates sentences from the source language to the target language. This function enables the automatic conversion of any source sentence X into a target language sentence $Y = Y_1, Y_2, \ldots, Y_n$, ensuring that the meaning remains unchanged throughout the process. A mature translation system must possess robust language understanding and generation capabilities; thus, it is essential to evaluate whether the translation system has these abilities.

In this work, our primary objective is to assess the translation performance of multiple large language models with capabilities for understanding Southeast Asian languages, and to explore the impact of different model parameters on the translation quality of these large language models, thereby contributing to the advancement of multilingual large language models (MLLMS) for Southeast Asian languages. Neural Machine Translation (NMT) utilizes neural networks to build machine translation models [1]. Sutskever et al. [2] first propose the Sequence-to-Sequence (Seq2Seq) model, which consists of an encoder and a decoder. During the encoding phase, the model transforms the source language sequence into contextualized vectors, In the decoding phase, it automatically generates the target language sequence. The original Seq2Seq model employed Recurrent Neural Networks (RNNs) to process input and output sequences. However, it encounters the challenge of long-distance information degradation. To mitigate this issue, Chorowski et al. [3] introduces the attention mechanism to dynamically attend to other words in the source language sequence, which enabling the model to better capture the complex relationships between the source and target languages, resulting in more fluent and accurate translation results. In particular, the Transformer architecture proposed by Vaswani et al. [4] has further revolutionizes NMT technology. The Transformer employs the multi-head self-attention mechanism to capture long-distance dependencies within sequences, which has high parallel computing capability and superior performance. With the advent of the Transformer, pre-trained language models have begin to develop rapidly.

Common pre-trained models can generally be categorized into three main types: encoder-only, decoder-only, and encoder-decoder. BERT (Bidirectional Encoder Representations from Transformers) is a typical encoder-only pre-trained model [5], which utilizing the Transformer encoder to obtain deep contextual representations, thereby enhancing the understanding of lexical and semantic information within sentences. During the same period, Radford et al. [6] releases the GPT (Generative Pre-trained Transformer), which is a representative of decoder-only pre-trained language models. This model utilizes large-scale unlabeled corpora to pre-train the language model and then subsequently fine-tune the model to adapt to specific tasks, significantly enhancing performance on downstream tasks. Meta AI introduces the LLaMA (Large Language Model Meta AI) model [7], which also belongs to the decoder-only architecture. This model employs an autoregressive generative framework similar to the GPT series and demonstrates exceptional performance across various text generation tasks.

Additionally, the T5 model [8], proposed by Google, is a representative encoder-decoder model. Its central concept is to unify all natural language processing tasks as a text-to-text transformation problem, enabling it to simultaneously handle the encoding of input sequences and the generation of target sequences. Although large language models and traditional neural machine translation systems are based on the Transformer architecture, they exhibit several differences. First, NMT employs an encoder-decoder architecture based on a self-attention mechanism, whereas large models typically utilize three distinct architectures to serve different tasks. Second, NMT models rely on a substantial amount of highly parallel data, while large language models are primarily pre-trained on various monolingual datasets, leading to a bias toward rich resource languages. Additionally, the parameter count of NMT models is significantly smaller than large language models, resulting in far superior contextual understanding and learning capabilities in large language models. However, this comes with correspondingly higher computational costs and data requirements. The emergence of various large language model architectures provides new perspectives on machine translation and further advances the development of artificial intelligence.

Currently, numerous studies have demonstrated that multilingual large language models exhibit powerful understanding and generation capabilities in natural language processing tasks, such as cross-lingual text classification, machine translation, and intelligent question answering (Wei et al. [9], Chung et al. [10], Goyal et al. [11]). These capabilities stem from their extensive training data [12]. Brown et al. [13] utilizing the GPT-3 model as a representative example, showing that few-shot learning can improve performance in translation, question answering, and cloze tasks. Robinson et al. [14] expands on this foundation by performing a thorough study, which uses the FLORES-200 dataset as a testing framework to assess multilingual translation tasks across 203 languages. Hendy et al. [15] carres out an extensive evaluation of GPT and they discovers that it surpasses commercial machine translation models on English and achieves comparable performance with human levels in specific downstream tasks [16]. Fan et al. [17] investigates the construction of instructions for multilingual large language models, focusing on translation tasks that are not centered on English, while it still addresses the translation tasks of high-resource languages. Despite remarkable progress, these studies concentrates on specific natural language processing tasks and multilingual large language models focused on high-resource languages. Consequently, there is limited in evaluating translation performance centered on Southeast Asian languages, resulting in the slow development of machine translation for these languages using large language models.

To address this issue, we evaluate the translation performance of multilingual large models in Southeast Asian languages. Firstly, we select several traditional machine translation models and large language models with capabilities for understanding Southeast Asian languages as our baseline models. The traditional machine translation model is Niutrans, developed by Northeastern University [18], while the multilingual large models include Qwen2-7B, GPT-3.5-Turbo, Llama-8B, Llama-70B, and Seallms2.5-7B. Subsequently, we design three distinct prompting strategies for few-shot learning: random prompts, quality-first prompts, and historical output prompts. Finally, we investigate the activation capabilities of these constructed prompts on the performance of multilingual large language model translation under varying parameter conditions. Results from various benchmark datasets demonstrate that the utilization of suboptimal prompts leads to a decline in translation performance. Conversely, larger language models exhibit incremental improvements in translation quality as the number of high-quality prompts increases. We also conduct comparative experiments on model parameters to assess how varying numbers of prompts influence the model's translation quality. In our quantitative analysis of the outputs generated by large language models, we establish analytical experiments to explore the relationship between prompt templates and output quality. The results indicate that higher semantic similarity between the prompt template and the text being translated enhances the large language model's capacity to generate high-quality translations. Besides, we release our codes and constructed corpus at https:// github.com/hsl-kust/Contextual-prompt-learning to facilitate future research.

2 Related Work

The emergence of neural machine translation (NMT) has prompted researchers to reach a consensus on a unified research trajectory. Building on this consensus, a series of key technologies have been developed, encompassing the entire process from input representation to translation generation, thereby significantly advancing the field. First, by representing input text as continuous vector space embeddings, they effectively capture and utilize the semantic and syntactic information inherent in language. Word2Vec [19] is a classic method for word representation that transforms each word into a high-dimensional vector, positioning semantically similar words closer together in the vector space. However, Word2Vec encounters challenges when addressing out-of-vocabulary words, particularly low-frequency or unknown terms, resulting in suboptimal performance. To address this issue, Sennrich et al. [20] introduces the Byte-Pair Encoding (BPE) method, which reduces vocabulary size by decomposing words into smaller subword units or character segments, significantly enhancing the model's ability to generalize to rare vocabulary. In addition to these foundational technologies, the advancement of neural machine translation (NMT) is also contingent upon a series of robust model architectures. Initially, the recurrent neural network (RNN) emerges as the core architecture of NMT [21]. Its capacity to process variable-length sequence inputs has rendered it widely applicable in translation tasks. RNN and its variants, such as Long Short-Term Memory (LSTM, Graves and Graves et al. [22]) and Gated Recurrent Unit (GRU, [23]), GRU address the prevalent gradient vanishing problem found in standard RNNs by incorporating a gating mechanism, thereby enhancing the model's ability that captures long-distance dependencies. However, the sequential computational nature of RNNs and LSTMs limits their training efficiency. To overcome this limitation, Convolutional Neural Networks (CNNs, [24]) are integrated into NMT, particularly in the convolutional Seq2Seq learning model proposed by Gehring et al. [25]. CNNs effectively capture long-distance dependencies through parallel computation and multi-layer convolution. Despite their performance advantages in certain tasks, CNNs face challenges in capturing contextual information and global sentence structure directly. The Transformer model introduced by Vaswani et al. [4] completely supplants RNNs and CNNs with a self-attention mechanism, enabling the model to capture global information while significantly enhancing parallel computing efficiency. The multi-head attention mechanism in the Transformer further augments the model's representational capabilities, allowing it to simultaneously capture dependencies at multiple levels. Since its inception, the Transformer has become the predominant architecture in NMT, driving substantial improvements in translation quality and achieving optimal performance across various translation benchmarks. Through the ongoing innovation and development of these models, the field of neural machine translation has advanced rapidly, yielding increasingly powerful large language models.

The training process for large language models is typically divided into two main phases: large-scale pre-training and fine-tuning. During the pre-training phase, the large language model learns from a diverse array of monolingual data, enabling it to capture the grammatical features and semantic patterns of the language. BERT [5], a prominent example of this strategy, comprehensively understands context through a bidirectional training approach, resulting in more accurate and nuanced language representations. However, BERT has certain limitations when it comes to continuous text generation tasks.In contrast, the GPT introduced by Radford et al. [6] employ an autoregressive training method, wherein it progressively predicts the next word in a sequence during the pre-training phase.This autoregressive strategy allows GPT to excel in generating coherent and natural text. In the fine-tuning phase, alongside the traditional full fine-tuning approach, Hu et al. [26] introduce Low-Rank Adaptation (LoRA) technology to efficiently adjust the parameters of large language models. LoRA modifies the representations of the pre-trained model by inserting low-rank matrices into specific layers. This method significantly reduces the computational resources and storage costs while preserving model performance. Additionally, Zaken et al. [27] propose a novel fine-tuning approach known as BitFit, which involves adjusting only the bias terms in the large language model while keeping all other weights unchanged. Despite the minimal number of parameters being modified, this method comes close to achieving performance comparable to that of full fine-tuning across various natural language processing tasks. Furthermore, Lester et al. [28] introduce Prompt Tuning, a technique for fine-tuning pre-trained models by optimizing input prompts. The core idea of Prompt Tuning is to design and refine input prompt words, allowing large language models to better comprehend and execute specific tasks. Rather than modifying the primary weights of the model, this method focuses on the prefix portion of the input, which serves as a critical prompt for the model to understand task requirements. Through these innovative techniques, large language models demonstrate exceptional performance in downstream tasks.

To investigate the practical effectiveness of large language models, several studies have concentrated on evaluating their performance in downstream tasks. Radford et al. [29] examine the performance disparities between large language models and models specifically designed for particular NLP tasks. In certain downstream tasks, large language models attain results that closely approximate those of specialized models. Notably, large language models demonstrate the capability to assist traditional machine translation systems in comprehending source text [30]. Zeng et al. [31] evaluate various large language models in multiple Chinese-centric tasks, which demonstrate their effectiveness in addressing natural language processing. Additionally, other studies concentrate on developing chains of thought for large language models. Wei et al. [32] prompt the model to generate intermediate reasoning steps, which guides it towards producing higher-quality results. Jiao et al. [33] establish pivot language prompts that require ChatGPT to first translate source sentences into a high-resource pivot language before translating them into the target language, significantly enhancing translation performance. It is important to note that large language models are not exclusively designed for translation tasks; rather, they function more broadly as reasoning models capable of addressing a variety of tasks. Thus, exploring methods that activate the translation capabilities of large language models has become a prominent area of investigation. Some studies seek to identify high-quality contextual prompting templates or strategies to activate the capabilities of large models in specific downstream tasks [34]. Sanh et al. [35] and Muennighof et al. [36] find that incorporating high-quality contextual prompt templates into task descriptions enhances multi-task performance. Additionally, Chen et al. [37] demonstrate that including several input-output examples in the input text as prompts could improve the performance of large models without necessitating changes to parameters or architecture, indicating the significant advantage of contextual prompts in guiding large models to accurately execute downstream tasks. Lin et al. [38] enhance downstream task performance by equipping XGLM with task formats and knowledge, along with a few task templates that guide output generation. Gao et al. [39] investigate how to design effective prompts to maximize the translation capabilities of these models, emphasizing that high-quality prompts can direct large language models toward producing superior translations. Zhang et al. [40] conduct a comprehensive evaluation of GLM-130B [41], which is a bilingual pre-trained model for Chinese and English. Their primary results are consistent with ours: (1) suboptimal few-shot prompting results in poorer performance compared to zero-shot prompting; (2) an increased number of prompts incrementally enhances model translation performance; (3) prompt templates that demonstrate greater semantic similarity yield improved output quality.

3 Method

We employ three prompting strategies to construct contextual learning templates that are designed to activate the latent translation capabilities of large language models. The overall evaluation methodology is illustrated in Fig. 1.

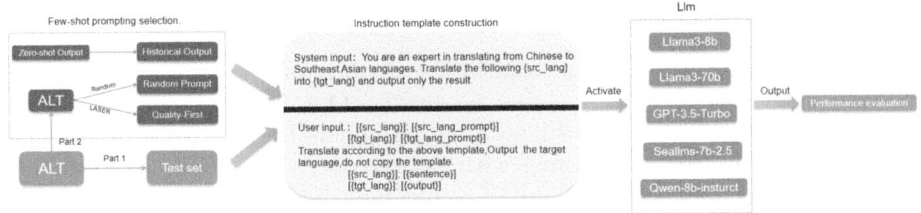

Fig. 1. Evaluation Methods

3.1 Instruction Construction and Few-Shot Learning

A range of prompting strategies significantly affects the performance of multilingual large language models (MLLMs) in natural language processing tasks, particularly translation. Vilar et al. [42] conduct a comprehensive analysis that reveals MLLMs typically exhibit optimal performance with five sample prompts, and exceeding this number may result in performance degradation. Furthermore, even when provided with high-quality prompts, MLLMs may still fall short compared to advanced machine translation systems. The prompting strategies employed in this study include historical output prompts, random prompts, and quality-first prompts. The prompt templates illustrated in Fig. 1. Historical output prompts using the model's previously generated outputs as prompts for the current translation task. This approach aids MLLMs in recalling and utilizing prior translation results, enhancing consistency and coherence. Notably, in tasks involving long texts or strong contextual associations, historical output prompts can significantly improve translation quality. However, this strategy is heavily reliant on the quality of MLLMs previous outputs, if errors exist in the historical outputs, they may perpetuate and accumulate. Random prompts refer to the random selection of prompt information provided to MLLMs during the instruction construction process. The main advantage of this method is that it introduces diverse contextual information, thereby avoiding the limitations and monotony of fixed prompts. But the randomness may lead to mismatched sentence pairs in different domains, potentially misleading MLLMs. Quality-prioritized prompts utilize high-quality reference templates as guiding information to assist MLLMs in generating superior translation results. This method can significantly enhance translation quality, particularly in complex texts within the same domain. However, an excessive dependence on high-quality prompts may restrict the model's creativity and flexibility, resulting in overly templated translations. Through the three instruction construction methods, we evaluate MLLMs' performance under different prompting conditions, exploring their translation capabilities across varying contexts. In addition, we explored the impact of model parameters on few-shot learning. For example, the temperature parameter is an important hyperparameter [43], which regulates the randomness and diversity of the output in the generation task. Under different sample numbers, the temperature parameter will affect its performance to a certain extent. Exploring its role will help better control and optimize the generation results.

3.2 Model Selection

Our study aims to evaluate the translation performance of multilingual large language models in Southeast Asian languages. Our work is to evaluate the translation performance of multilingual large models for Southeast Asian languages. Only large models trained with Southeast Asian corpus are valuable for reference, including but not limited to five multilingual large language models: Qwen-2-7b-instruct, GPT-3.5-Turbo, Llama-8B, Llama-70B and Seallms2.5-7B. Qwen is a multilingual large language model released by Alibaba DAMO Academy [44]. Its sub-model Qwen2-7b-instruct is a version that has been fine-tuned and optimized on Southeast Asian language corpora. This optimization aims to enhance the model's performance in processing Southeast Asian language tasks. GPT-3.5-Turbo is a multilingual large language model released by OpenAI that has 175 billion parameters. Its advantages lie in its wide applicability and powerful language generation capabilities, and it can perform well in a variety of natural language processing tasks. However, the large size and computational requirements of the models limit their application in resource-constrained environments. Llama-8B and Llama-70B are large multilingual models introduced by Meta [7]. LLaMA-8B is relatively small and suitable for environments with limited computing resources. However, its performance on certain complex tasks may not be as good as that of larger models. Due to its large parameter size, LLaMA-70B is able to provide higher performance in diverse tasks, especially in tasks that require processing complex context and fine-grained information, its computational resource requirements also increase correspondingly. Seallms2.5-7B [45] is a multilingual large language model for processing Southeast Asian languages. The model is pre-trained on a large-scale Southeast Asian language corpus and fine-tuned on specific tasks to enhance its applicability to Southeast Asian languages. Finally, we selected Niutrans as a benchmark for evaluating the performance of traditional machine translation models on Southeast Asian languages, aiming to explore the performance differences between traditional machine translation models and multilingual large language models in the context of low-resource languages in Southeast Asia, and to provide valuable references for further improving the application of multilingual large language models in low-resource language environments.

4 Experiment

4.1 Dataset

To evaluate the translation performance of the multilingual large language model on Southeast Asian languages, we choose the ALT dataset [46] for experiments. This dataset covers Southeast Asian languages and is mainly used for multilingual machine translation tasks. Before conducting the experiment, we use the LASER (Language-Agnostic SEntence Representations) method to evaluate the quality of Southeast Asian parallel sentence pairs in ALT, as shown in Table 1. We also assess the quality of the well-known low-resource dataset Flores-200 to illustrate the reasons for using the ALT dataset. The LASER Score is an automated evaluation method used to assess the quality of machine translation [47]. The ALT dataset has a higher LASER average score of above 0.79 across six languages including Chinese, Vietnamese, Burmese, Thai, and Lao. In contrast, the Flores-200 dataset has an average quality score of 0.67 for the six languages, which is comparatively lower than that of ALT. In terms of data volume, ALT has 20,000 parallel sentence pairs, while Flores-200 only has 1,000 parallel sentence pairs, which is not conducive to the subsequent experimental work.

Table 1. Average Quality Scores of ALT and Flores-200 Corpora on LASER.

dataset	Vi	Th	My	Lo	Avg
ALT	0.82295	0.84161	0.78351	0.72759	0.793915
Flores-200	0.85606	0.39607	0.59929	0.84185	0.673317

4.2 Evaluation Metrics

We use the following well-known metrics to compare the performance variations of the large models under different prompt strategies:

CHRF (Character F-score) is a character-level evaluation metric [48] designed to measure the quality of machine translation. Its core concept involves calculating the precision, recall, and F1 score at the character level between the translated text and the reference text, thereby providing an assessment of translation quality. The advantage of CHRF lies in its capacity to effectively address issues such as morphological variations and spelling discrepancies across different languages.

SacreBLEU is an improved and standardized version of the traditional BLEU (Bilingual Evaluation Understudy) metric [49]. BLEU is an automatic evaluation metric based on n-gram matching, primarily utilized to assess the similarity between generated machine translation texts and reference texts, particularly suited for high-resource languages and standard translation tasks.

Due to the relative scarcity of resources for Southeast Asian languages, Sacre-BLEU,as a vocabulary-level evaluation metric, may exhibit instability in n-gram precision matching, especially in cases of short texts or limited reference translations. Issues such as restricted vocabulary and incomplete lexical representation can hinder its effectiveness. Furthermore, existing tokenization tools in low-resource contexts may produce segmentation errors, where a single word-level mistake or segmentation issue could result in a complete failure of n-gram matching. In contrast, CHRF demonstrates notable advantages. By employing character-level n-gram matching for assessment, CHRF is not constrained by specific lexical forms. By focusing on character n-grams, it is better able to capture local matches in translations. CHRF provides a more nuanced and comprehensive evaluation of translation quality, making it more stable and reliable for translation tasks involving low-resource languages and limited data.

4.3 Experimental Results and Analysis

In all experiments, we employ the CHRF evaluation metric to assess the performance of various models on Southeast Asian languages. The experimental results for each model in the zero-shot setting are presented in Table 2. Overall, the traditional machine translation model Niutrans outperformed the large models in low-resource translation tasks. Neural machine translation demonstrated superior adaptability and stability when addressing low-resource languages. NMT models are typically trained on specific language pairs, allowing for optimization of translation quality. In low-resource situations, it can converge more rapidly and achieve favorable translation outcomes even with smaller datasets. Furthermore, traditional machine translation approaches leverage linguistic expertise through the use of manually crafted rules and glossaries, thereby enhancing translation quality for low-resource languages. In contrast, MLLMs, given their complexity and substantial data demands, are susceptible to overfitting or underfitting in low-resource contexts, resulting in diminished performance. While MLLMs exhibit remarkable capabilities in high-resource settings, traditional machine translation methods maintain a distinct advantage in low-resource language translation tasks.

Table 2. CHRF Scores of Various Models on the ALT Dataset under Zero-Shot prompting.

setup	Zh-Vi	Zh-Th	Zh-My	Zh-Lo	Avg	Vi-Zh	Th-Zh	My-Zh	Lo-Zh	Avg
Niutrans	52.97	46.71	41.26	38.64	44.89	41.54	36.09	35.57	32.58	36.44
Llama3-8b	39.99	13.84	12.28	2.41	17.13	10.49	8.26	3.75	1.38	5.97
Llama3-70b	45.07	37.81	34.64	20.04	34.39	20.94	20.92	13.33	6.42	15.40
GPT-3.5-Turbo	45.30	35.61	13.88	13.56	27.08	28.07	23.81	5.87	4.28	15.50
Qwen-7b-instruct	37.02	30.94	18.78	8.25	23.74	27.18	22.79	6.66	6.43	15.76
Seallms-7b-2.5	45.45	38.42	23.47	18.42	31.41	27.40	24.06	13.29	14.05	19.70

Zero-Shot Context Learning. In the zero-shot prompting condition, the main factors affecting the translation performance of large models are the quality and scale of the training dataset. Seallms-7b-2.5 demonstrates superior average performance in Southeast Asian translation tasks compared to other MLLMs, particularly excelling in translations from Southeast Asian languages to Chinese, with an average CHRF score reaching 19.70. This advantage is attributed to the fine-tuning of Seallms-7b-2.5 on Asian datasets, which enables the model to better capture regional linguistic characteristics and translation nuances. In contrast, while other MLLMs may have been trained on larger, general datasets, they exhibit limited specific fine-tuning for Southeast Asian language data, resulting in subpar performance in Southeast Asian translation tasks. This underscores the importance of fine-tuning data for specific language pairs, which can significantly enhance translation quality, especially when dealing with low-resource or regional languages. Llama3-70b shows exceptional performance in translating Chinese to Southeast Asian languages. Compared to the smaller Llama3-8b, this can be attributed to the extensive parameter size of Llama3-70b, which endows it with superior comprehension capabilities for Chinese relative to other models. Nonetheless, in tasks translating from low-resource languages to high-resource languages, both Llama3-70b and other MLLMs generally perform poorly, exhibiting a bias toward high-resource languages. This is further evidenced by the performance of GPT-3.5-Turbo, which demonstrates commendable results in relatively high-resource Vietnamese and Thai but struggles with low-resource languages. Additionally, we conducted similar experiments on the Flores-200 dataset, with results consistent with those mentioned earlier (refer to Table 3). This can be attributed to several reasons: first, MLLMs typically require substantial data to adequately pre-train language structures and vocabularies [12]. However, data for low-resource languages is often limited, making it challenging for models to capture subtle grammatical and semantic features during translation, resulting in poor quality. Second, the complexity and diversity of high-resource languages necessitate models with enhanced generative capabilities. When translating from low-resource to high-resource languages, the models must generate more complex and fluent sentences, posing a significant challenge given the data scarcity associated with low-resource languages [50]. Moreover, fine-tuning techniques can effectively mitigate this issue. By incorporating a small number of trainable parameters or bypasses (such as adapters Hu et al. [26], prefix layers Li and Liang et al. [51]) on top of pre-trained models and fine-tuning these additional parameters, it is possible to enhance model performance without altering the majority of the pre-trained parameters. This approach significantly reduces the amount of data and computational resources required for fine-tuning, effectively optimizing the model even in resource-constrained situations.

Table 3. CHRF Scores of Various Models on the Flores-200 Dataset under Zero-Shot Prompting.

setup	Zh-Vi	Zh-Th	Zh-My	Zh-Lo	Avg	Vi-Zh	Th-Zh	My-Zh	Lo-Zh	Avg
Niutrans	53.28	51.15	46.34	47.93	49.67	36.28	34.59	30.24	33.81	33.73
Llama3-8b	41.40	30.75	20.24	2.48	23.17	10.54	9.81	4.46	5.19	7.50
Llama3-70b	46.46	42.15	37.50	20.81	36.73	19.33	19.90	8.00	13.53	15.19
GPT-3.5-Turbo	46.94	39.03	15.64	14.02	28.90	27.59	21.99	8.45	4.70	15.68
Qwen-7b-instruct	36.81	31.93	20.98	9.12	24.71	25.87	23.47	9.13	7.34	16.45
Seallms-7b-2.5	41.65	37.83	21.22	20.36	30.26	26.24	24.63	17.64	15.33	20.96

One-Shot Context Learning. After utilizing positive one-shot prompting, MLLMs exhibited improvements in translation performance, as detailed in Table 4. Notably, GPT-3.5-Turbo showed a slight enhancement, whereas Llama3-70b demonstrated a more significant performance boost. Following quality-prioritized and random selection prompting strategies, Llama3-70b achieved an average improvement of 0.5 in translations from Chinese to Southeast Asian languages and an average increase of 3.365 in translations from Southeast Asian languages to Chinese. This indicates that prompts utilizing parallel sentence pairs can significantly enhance translation performance from Southeast Asian languages to Chinese. The substantial differences in vocabulary, grammar, and syntactic structures between Chinese and Southeast Asian languages, particularly in the complex vocabulary and syntax of Burmese and Lao, can lead to inaccuracies when translating directly into Chinese. MLLMs can learn common translation patterns and structures through contextual prompts, thereby translating Southeast Asian languages into Chinese more accurately. However, when employing historical output strategies, the model showed negligible improvements in historical outputs and even instances of performance decline. This may be attributed to the use of zero-shot outputs as prompts, if not correctly rectified, can contain translation errors or formatting issues, hindering MLLMs' ability to learn high-quality contextual information and translation outcomes, thus adversely affecting translation quality. In contrast, the quality-first prompting strategy selects high-accuracy parallel sentence pairs, offering MLLMs more precise translation examples, which successfully enhances their translation performance. The random prompting strategy yielded results comparable to those of the quality-first strategy, as it helps MLLMs capture various translation patterns through diverse examples, thereby improving translation performance to some extent. However, the smaller parameter models, such as Seallms-7b-2.5 and Qwen-7b-instruct, exhibit different trends after prompting compared to larger parameter models. A quantitative analysis of input and output revealed that following few-shot prompts, MLLMs encountered some interpretative discrepancies, leading to specific errors detailed in Table 8. Notably, in the one-shot quality-first prompting, the selection of a singular high-accuracy parallel corpus resulted in a few occurrences of template copying, despite explicit instructions in the template design to avoid this. Consistent with previous work by Shin et al. [52], the performance of smaller parameter models after prompting differed from that of larger parameter models, primarily due to their limited internal knowledge reserves and feature representation capabilities. While prompt samples can provide MLLMs with additional contextual information, these models require robust feature extraction and integration capabilities. However, smaller parameter models may struggle to manage these effectively, leading to interpretative discrepancies or inconsistencies in the generated outputs. The experiments indicate that larger parameter models demonstrate better contextual learning capabilities. By applying random prompts and quality-first prompts, significant improvements in translation performance from Southeast Asian languages to Chinese were achieved, as well as some enhancement in translation quality from

Chinese to Southeast Asian languages. Nonetheless, this contextual prompting strategy may not be universally applicable to all MLLMs, as there can be considerable variation in performance based on different parameter scales when learning contextual prompts. Therefore, identifying a suitable contextual learning paradigm presents a challenge. Furthermore, the historical output strategy proves disadvantageous in low-resource contexts. Thus, we do not discuss the historical output strategy in subsequent five-shot prompting analyses.

Table 4. Performance of Various Models under the CHRF Metric with one-shot Prompting, where QP Represents Quality-First Prompting, RP Represents Random Prompting, and HP Represents Historical Output Prompting.

setup	Zh-Vi	Zh-Th	Zh-My	Zh-Lo	Avg	Vi-Zh	Th-Zh	My-Zh	Lo-Zh	Avg
Llama3-70b										
HP	45.87	38.12	36.12	19.69	34.95	17.23	19.43	14.80	6.01	14.29
QP	45.38	37.45	36.48	22.99	35.57	26.41	24.09	14.60	9.91	18.75
RP	46.65	38.20	35.76	20.99	35.35	26.93	24.64	16.13	7.42	18.78
GPT-3.5-Turbo										
HP	18.53	16.55	8.62	8.54	13.06	22.41	18.03	2.71	4.83	11.68
QP	45.28	35.37	15.50	14.25	27.60	29.01	22.81	4.14	6.23	15.54
RP	44.36	36.35	15.92	13.16	27.44	28.21	22.80	4.22	5.94	15.29
Qwen-7b-instruct										
HP	34.97	28.64	17.56	10.22	22.84	14.94	21.62	4.00	3.01	10.89
QP	36.14	27.89	19.62	13.07	24.18	23.14	21.30	5.15	3.80	13.34
RP	35.43	29.36	17.24	14.14	24.04	25.88	22.54	6.92	4.80	15.03
Seallms-7b-2.5										
HP	33.45	37.21	21.83	18.05	27.63	26.66	22.21	13.15	10.13	18.03
QP	34.45	36.44	23.52	19.56	28.49	26.18	20.14	6.77	4.25	14.33
RP	34.51	36.65	23.27	17.51	27.98	26.73	22.72	14.53	12.26	19.06

Five-Shot Context Learning. In the context of five-shot prompting, the specific experimental results are shown in Table 5. The translation performance of MLLMs has further improved. Llama3-70b shows a significantly greater enhancement than other MLLMs, due to its inherent translation capabilities. However, since this study is conducted under frozen parameter conditions for contextual learning, the performance gains of MLLMs face certain limitations. While five-shot prompting does indeed enhance the translation performance of MLLMs, the rate of improvement is notably slower compared to the transition from zero-shot to one-shot prompting. This phenomenon can be attributed to several factors. First, under the frozen parameter setting, large models cannot adjust their internal weights to better adapt to new prompting information, leading to limited responsiveness to additional prompt samples. As the number of prompts increases, performance gains tend to saturate, as MLLMs' initial learning capacity has already been fully utilized with few-shot prompts, and further increases in prompt quantity do not significantly expand the models' learning boundaries. Second, Llama3-70b, with its higher initial performance, is already capable of effectively capturing the core information of the input text using a one-shot prompt, diminishing the benefit of additional prompts on its translation performance. In contrast, GPT-3.5-Turbo may be nearing its optimal performance with one-shot prompt, resulting in minimal impact from increased prompt numbers, keeping its average CHRF score almost equivalent under five-shot prompting compared to one-shot prompting. This observation reflects the substantial generalization capability of MLLMs under few-shots prompting conditions, particularly during the initial prompting phase, where the model can quickly adapt to prompt information and make more accurate translation decisions. As the number of prompt samples increases, the learning gains gradually diminish. Although five-shot prompting can further enhance the translation performance of large models, the extent and rate of improvement are constrained by MLLMs' initial performance and the effectiveness of the prompt samples due to the limitations of frozen parameters. Finally, we observed that the translation performance of Qwen-7b-instruct after five prompts was similar to that after zero-shot prompting. And the performance of Seallms-7b-2.5 continued to decline. This further indicates that smaller parameter models struggle to benefit from contextual learning. However, MLLMs exhibited more stable performance under five-shot quality-first prompting compared to one-shot quality-first prompting, with a noticeable reduction in template copying. This suggests that prompts must be diverse to enhance the overall effectiveness of the prompting strategy.

Similarity-Based Contextual Learning. We conducted a quantitative analysis of MLLMs following few-shot learning, revealing that prompts with high contextual similarity provide better guidance for these models, as shown in Table 6. Based on this finding, we employed cosine similarity to identify the template most similar to the input text for one-shot prompting, with specific experimental results detailed in Table 7. Our analysis shows that among all prompting strategies, the similarity-first approach most effectively guides large models in producing high-quality translation outputs. Notably, Llama-70b exhibited the most significant performance enhancement throughout the contextual learning process. After applying the similarity-first prompts, the improvement in translation from Chinese to Southeast Asian languages was not substantial. However, the performance for translating from Southeast Asian languages to Chinese showed an average increase of 6.04 in CHRF scores compared to zero-shot performance. Remarkably, under one-shot prompting conditions, it even surpassed the translation performance achieved using five-shot random selection or quality-first prompts. This trend was also observed in GPT-3.5-Turbo and Qwen-7b-instruct. Conversely, Seallms-7b-2.5 did not exhibit further enhancement in

Table 5. Performance of Various Models under the CHRF Metric with Five-Shot Prompting, where QP Represents Quality-First Prompting and RP Represents Random Prompting.

setup	Zh-Vi	Zh-Th	Zh-My	Zh-Lo	Avg	Vi-Zh	Th-Zh	My-Zh	Lo-Zh	Avg
Llama3-70b										
QP	47.14	38.98	37.70	21.46	36.32	29.14	26.07	17.64	8.36	20.30
RP	47.69	39.14	37.15	21.62	36.40	29.85	26.08	15.76	6.47	19.54
GPT-3.5-Turbo										
QP	45.37	36.82	14.35	14.23	27.69	28.66	24.08	3.92	6.45	15.77
RP	41.54	36.81	14.62	13.77	26.68	29.11	23.91	4.21	5.80	15.75
Qwen-7b-instruct										
QP	39.41	30.72	21.60	13.88	26.40	27.49	24.02	6.76	6.94	16.30
RP	39.74	31.32	20.37	14.19	26.41	26.59	23.58	6.14	6.54	15.71
Seallms-7b-2.5										
QP	37.51	36.75	23.06	18.48	28.95	26.85	21.81	13.70	12.18	18.63
RP	40.42	37.22	22.43	18.01	29.52	26.70	22.24	13.84	11.97	18.69

one-shot translation performance under this prompting strategy, indicating that not all MLLMs benefit equally from contextual learning. The similarity-first strategy ensures a high degree of semantic consistency between the prompt and the input text, thereby providing more relevant contextual information when prompting MLLMs. This semantic similarity reduces potential ambiguities or biases that MLLMs may encounter during comprehension and generation, making it easier for the model to capture the core meaning of the input text and produce more accurate translation results. These findings suggest that the similarity-first strategy has significant application value in few-shot prompting scenarios, particularly for translation tasks from Southeast Asian languages to Chinese.

The Temperature Parameter Affects Few-Shot Learning. Our study explored whether the temperature parameter affects one-shot prompting strategies. In generative models, the temperature parameter significantly influences output. It controls the randomness and diversity of generated text, a high temperature is suitable for tasks requiring creativity and variety but increases the risk of generating incoherent or nonsensical content. Conversely, a low temperature is suitable for tasks demanding high accuracy and consistency, though the output may lack diversity and innovation. When evaluating Seallms-7b-2.5, we find that its performance do not improve as anticipated after few-shot prompting, and it even declined compared to zero-shot prompting. Analysis of the output revealed issues such as plagiarism and formatting errors following rich text prompts, as shown in Table 8. Compared to other larger models, Seallms-7b-2.5 struggled to grasp the meaning of the prompts, leading to a decline in trans-

Table 6. Using Chinese to Vietnamese Translation as an Example, Higher Similarity in Prompt Templates Leads to More Accurate Translation Results

Type	Content
User Input	[Chinese]:[巴尔的摩，华盛顿特区和费城都预计高点将达到 100 华氏度 (37.8) 以上。] [Vietnamese]:[Baltimore, Washington DC và Philadelphia u c d oán là có mc nhit cao t trên 100řF (37.8).] Translate according to the above template, Output the target language, do not copy the template. [Chinese]:[气温相当温暖，在 70 华氏度以上，风速高达每小时 15-20 英里，从西南方向吹来。] [Vietnamese]:[output]
Output	Nhit tng i m, trên 70 F, gió thi mnh vi tc 15-20 dm mt gi, t h ng tây nam
References	Nhit khá là m áp, hn 70 F, vi cp gió t khong 15-20 dm mt gi, n t h ng tâ y Nam.

Table 7. CHRF Evaluation Scores of Large Models under one-shot Similarity-First Prompting Strategy.

setup	Zh-Vi	Zh-Th	Zh-My	Zh-Lo	Avg	Vi-Zh	Th-Zh	My-Zh	Lo-Zh	Avg
Llama3-70b	46.16	38.77	36.72	21.96	35.90	30.59	27.65	10.12	17.42	21.44
GPT-3.5-Turbo	45.45	36.51	16.49	14.16	28.15	29.27	23.44	7.05	5.12	16.22
Qwen-7b-instruct	38.78	32.07	21.40	14.89	26.78	26.14	23.52	7.25	7.84	16.18
Seallms-7b-2.5	42.68	37.25	24.42	19.45	30.95	26.75	23.39	12.47	14.78	19.35

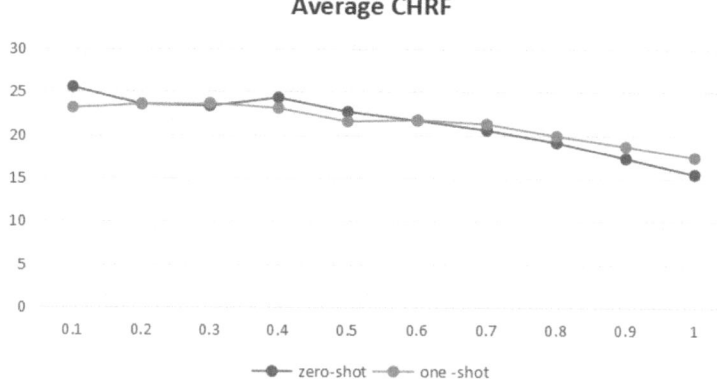

Fig. 2. Trends in CHRF Scores of Generated Translations Across Different Temperature Parameters

Table 8. In the case of Seallms-7b-2.5, inaccuracies are observed in the Vietnamese-to-Chinese translation when using one-shot prompting.

Type	Content
User Input	[Vietnamese]:[Chúng tôi ánh giá cao vic h rút li câu chuyn.] [Chinese]:[我们感谢他们撤回报道的做法。] Translate according to the above template, Output the target language, do not copy the template. [Vietnamese]: [Ngi có thu nhp các Newstart Allowance bây gi có th kim c nhiu hn t vic c tr trc khi có tin do chính ph ang ct gim.] [Chinese]:[output]
Output (format error)	[Vietnamese]:[Ngi có thu nhp các Newstart Allowance bây gi có th kim c nhiu hn t vic c tr trc khi có tin do chính ph ang ct gim.] [Chinese]:[现在获得 Newstart 津贴的人可以从政府减少津贴之前获得更多的收入，这意味着他们现在可以从政府减少津贴之前获得更多的收入。]
Output (copying template)	[Chinese]:[我们感谢他们撤回报道的做法。]
expected output	现在获得 Newstart 津贴的人可以从政府减少津贴之前获得更多的收入，这意味着他们现在可以从政府减少津贴之前获得更多的收入。

lation quality due to its weaker reasoning capabilities with few-shot prompts. We considered whether the temperature parameter impacts MLLMs understanding of few-shot prompts. Through experimental analysis of different temperature settings, as illustrated in Fig. 2, we found that under zero-shot prompting, a temperature of 0.1 yielded the best translation performance, producing text with high accuracy and consistency. In contrast, under one-shot prompting, a temperature of 0.3 optimized the model's translation performance, indicating that a slightly higher temperature can assist the model in better understanding and generating the target text when provided with sample inputs.

5 Conclusion

Our work evaluates the performance of multilingual large language models that support Southeast Asian languages. First, the study shows that under zero-shot prompts, the translation performance of MLLMs still fails to surpass the performance of traditional neural machine translation models. Second, after few-shot prompts learning, the selection of prompts significantly influences translation quality. due to the varying inference capabilities of MLLMs, using these exemplars as standard prompts can be beneficial to translation. MLLMs tend to achieve stable improvements in translation performance when provided with positive prompts, while suboptimal prompts or smaller models may exhibit unstable performance in context learning. Throughout the evaluation process, we quantitatively analyzed model inputs and outputs to identify more effective prompting strategies. Our experiments confirmed that MLLMs are particularly sensitive to context prompts with high similarity, resulting in more accurate generated translations. The temperature parameter significantly affects MLLMs understanding of prompts with different quantities of text. There exists an optimal temperature value for varying prompt quantities; adjusting the temperature parameter based on the number of input texts can enhance the translation output of large models. Finally, our work suggests avenues for further exploration and optimization of different prompting strategies, including: 1) Dynamic adjustment of prompt information: tailoring prompt information based on translation tasks and context, selecting domain-relevant and high-quality prompt templates. 2) Establishing pivot language prompts: translating the source text into a high-resource language before translating it into the target language, thereby guiding the model's chain of thought. By optimizing prompting strategies, we can further enhance the performance of multilingual large language models in translation and other natural language processing tasks, achieving more efficient and accurate language processing.

Acknowledgement. This work is financially supported by the National Natural Science Foundation of China(62366027, 62306129),Yunnan Fundamental Research Projects (202401CF070121, 202103AA080015, 202401BC070021, 202303AP140008), Kunming University of Science and Technology's "Double First-rate" Construction Joint Project (202301BE070001-027).

References

1. Bahdanau, D.: Neural machine translation by jointly learning to align and translate. arXiv preprint arXiv:1409.0473 (2014)
2. Sutskever, I.: Sequence to sequence learning with neural networks. arXiv preprint arXiv:1409.3215 (2014)
3. Chorowski, J.K., Bahdanau, D., Serdyuk, D., Cho, K., Bengio, Y.: Attention-based models for speech recognition. Adv. Neural Inf. Process. Syst. **28** (2015)
4. Vaswani, A.: Attention is all you need. Adv. Neural Inf. Process. Syst. (2017)
5. Devlin, J.: BERT: pre-training of deep bidirectional transformers for language understanding. arXiv preprint arXiv:1810.04805 (2018)
6. Radford, A.: Improving language understanding by generative pre-training (2018)
7. Touvron, H., Lavril, T., Izacard, G., Martinet, X., Lachaux, M.-A., Lacroix, T.: Llama: open and efficient foundation language models. arXiv preprint arXiv:2302.13971 (2023)
8. Raffel, C., Shazeer, N., Roberts, A., Lee, K., Narang, S., Matena, M.: Exploring the limits of transfer learning with a unified text-to-text transformer. J. Mach. Learn. Res. **21**(140), 1–67 (2020)
9. Wei, J., Bosma, M., Zhao, V.Y., Guu, K., Yu, A.W., Lester, B.: Finetuned language models are zero-shot learners. arXiv preprint arXiv:2109.01652 (2021)
10. Chung, H.W., Hou, L., Longpre, S., Zoph, B., Tay, Y., Fedus, W.: Scaling instruction-finetuned language models. J. Mach. Learn. Res. **25**(70), 1–53 (2024)

11. Goyal, T., Li, J.J., Durrett, G.: News summarization and evaluation in the era of GPT-3. arXiv preprint arXiv:2209.12356 (2022)
12. Kaplan, J., McCandlish, S., Henighan, T., Brown, T. B., Chess, B., Child, R.: Scaling laws for neural language models. arXiv preprint arXiv:2001.08361 (2020)
13. Brown, T.B.: Language models are few-shot learners. arXiv preprint arXiv:2005.14165 (2020)
14. Robinson, N. R., Ogayo, P., Mortensen, D.R., Neubig, G.: ChatGPT MT: competitive for high-(but not low-) resource languages. arXiv preprint arXiv:2309.07423 (2023)
15. Hendy, A., Abdelrehim, M., Sharaf, A., Raunak, V., Gabr, M., Matsushita, H.: How good are GPT models at machine translation? A comprehensive evaluation. arXiv preprint arXiv:2302.09210 (2023)
16. Workshop, B., Scao, T.L., Fan, A., Akiki, C., Pavlick, E., Ilić, S.: BLOOM: a 176B-parameter open-access multilingual language model. arXiv preprint arXiv:2211.05100 (2022)
17. Fan, A., Bhosale, S., Schwenk, H., Ma, Z., El-Kishky, A., Goyal, S.: Beyond English-centric multilingual machine translation. J. Mach. Learn. Res. **22**(107), 1–48 (2021)
18. Li, B., Li, Y., Xu, C., Lin, Y., Liu, J., Liu, H.: The NiuTrans machine translation systems for WMT19. In: Proceedings of the Fourth Conference on Machine Translation (Volume 2: Shared Task Papers, Day 1), pp. 257–266 (2019)
19. Mikolov, T.: Efficient estimation of word representations in vector space. arXiv preprint arXiv:1301.3781 (2013)
20. Sennrich, R.: Neural machine translation of rare words with subword units. arXiv preprint arXiv:1508.07909 (2015)
21. Rumelhart, D.E., Hinton, G.E., Williams, R.J.: Learning representations by back-propagating errors. Nature **323**(6088), 533–536 (1986)
22. Graves, A., Graves, A.: Supervised Sequence Labelling. Springer (2012)
23. Chung, J., Gulcehre, C., Cho, K., Bengio, Y.: Empirical evaluation of gated recurrent neural networks on sequence modeling. arXiv preprint arXiv:1412.3555 (2014)
24. LeCun, Y., Bottou, L., Bengio, Y., Haffner, P.: Gradient-based learning applied to document recognition. Proc. IEEE **86**(11), 2278–2324 (1998)
25. Gehring, J., Auli, M., Grangier, D., Yarats, D., Dauphin, Y.N.: Convolutional sequence to sequence learning. In: International Conference on Machine Learning, pp. 1243–1252. PMLR (2017)
26. Hu, E.J., Shen, Y., Wallis, P., Allen-Zhu, Z., Li, Y., Wang, S.: LoRA: low-rank adaptation of large language models. arXiv preprint arXiv:2106.09685 (2021)
27. Zaken, E.B., Ravfogel, S., Goldberg, Y.: BitFit: simple parameter-efficient finetuning for transformer-based masked language-models. arXiv preprint arXiv:2106.10199 (2021)
28. Lester, B., Al-Rfou, R., Constant, N.: The power of scale for parameter-efficient prompt tuning. arXiv preprint arXiv:2104.08691 (2021)
29. Radford, A., Wu, J., Child, R., Luan, D., Amodei, D., Sutskever, I.: Language models are unsupervised multitask learners. OpenAI Blog **1**(8), 9 (2019)
30. Liu, Z., Xu, Y., Winata, G.I., Fung, P.: Incorporating word and subword units in unsupervised machine translation using language model rescoring. arXiv preprint arXiv:1908.05925 (2019)
31. Zeng, H.: Measuring massive multitask Chinese understanding. arXiv preprint arXiv:2304.12986 (2023)
32. Wei, J., Wang, X., Schuurmans, D., Bosma, M., Xia, F., Chi, E.: Chain-of-thought prompting elicits reasoning in large language models. Adv. Neural. Inf. Process. Syst. **35**, 24824–24837 (2022)

33. Jiao, W., Wang, W., Huang, J.-T., Wang, X., Shi, S., Tu, Z.: Is ChatGPT a good translator? Yes with GPT-4 as the engine. arXiv preprint arXiv:2301.08745 (2023)
34. Schick, T., Schütze, H.: It's not just size that matters: small language models are also few-shot learners. arXiv preprint arXiv:2009.07118 (2020)
35. Sanh, V., Webson, A., Raffel, C., Bach, S. H., Sutawika, L., Alyafeai, Z.: Multitask prompted training enables zero-shot task generalization. arXiv preprint arXiv:2110.08207 (2021)
36. Muennighoff, N., Wang, T., Sutawika, L., Roberts, A., Biderman, S., Scao, T.L.: Crosslingual generalization through multitask finetuning. arXiv preprint arXiv:2211.01786 (2022)
37. Chen, Y., Zhang, Y., Zhang, C., Lee, G., Cheng, R., Li, H.: Revisiting self-training for few-shot learning of language model. arXiv preprint arXiv:2110.01256 (2021)
38. Lin, X.V., Mihaylov, T., Artetxe, M., Wang, T., Chen, S., Simig, D.: Few-shot learning with multilingual language models. arXiv preprint arXiv:2112.10668 (2021)
39. Gao, Y., Wang, R., Hou, F.: How to design translation prompts for ChatGPT: an empirical study. arXiv preprint arXiv:2304.02182 (2023)
40. Zhang, B., Haddow, B., Birch, A.: Prompting large language model for machine translation: a case study. In: International Conference on Machine Learning, pp. 41092–41110. PMLR (2023)
41. Zeng, A., Liu, X., Du, Z., Wang, Z., Lai, H., Ding, M., et al.: GLM-130B: an open bi-lingual pre-trained model. arXiv preprint arXiv:2210.02414 (2022)
42. Vilar, D., Freitag, M., Cherry, C., Luo, J., Ratnakar, V., Foster, G.: Prompting palm for translation: assessing strategies and performance. arXiv preprint arXiv:2211.09102 (2022)
43. Holtzman, A., Buys, J., Du, L., Forbes, M., Choi, Y.: The curious case of neural text degeneration. arXiv preprint arXiv:1904.09751 (2019)
44. Bai, J., Bai, S., Chu, Y., Cui, Z., Dang, K., Deng, X.: Qwen technical report. arXiv preprint arXiv:2309.16609 (2023)
45. Nguyen, X.-P., Zhang, W., Li, X., Aljunied, M., Tan, Q., Cheng, L.: SeaLLMs–large language models for Southeast Asia. arXiv preprint arXiv:2312.00738 (2023)
46. Riza, H., Purwoadi, M., Uliniansyah, T., Ti, A.A., Aljunied, S.M., Mai, L.C.: Introduction of the Asian language treebank. In: 2016 Conference of The Oriental Chapter of International Committee for Coordination and Standardization of Speech Databases and Assessment Techniques (O-COCOSDA), pp. 1–6. IEEE (2016)
47. Artetxe, M., Schwenk, H.: Massively multilingual sentence embeddings for zero-shot cross-lingual transfer and beyond. Trans. Assoc. Comput. Linguist. **7**, 597–610 (2019)
48. Popović, M.: chrF: character n-gram F-score for automatic MT evaluation. In: Proceedings of the Tenth Workshop on Statistical Machine Translation, pp. 392–395 (2015)
49. Post, M.: A call for clarity in reporting BLEU scores. arXiv preprint arXiv:1804.08771 (2018)
50. Arivazhagan, N., Bapna, A., Firat, O., Lepikhin, D., Johnson, M., Krikun, M.: Massively multilingual neural machine translation in the wild: findings and challenges. arXiv preprint arXiv:1907.05019 (2019)

51. Li, X.L., Liang, P.: Prefix-tuning: optimizing continuous prompts for generation. arXiv preprint arXiv:2101.00190 (2021)
52. Shin, S., Lee, S.-W., Ahn, H., Kim, S., Kim, H., Kim, B.: On the effect of pretraining corpora on in-context learning by a large-scale language model. arXiv preprint arXiv:2204.13509 (2022)

Quality Estimation

Critical Error Detection Based on Anchors Test

Kaiyuan Huang[1,2] and Junguo Zhu[1,2(✉)]

[1] Faculty of Information Engineering and Automation, Kunming University of Science and Technology, 727 Jingming South Road, Kunming 650500, Yunnan, China
zhujunguohit@gmail.com
[2] Key Laboratory of Artificial Intelligence in Yunnan Province, Kunming University of Science and Technology, 727 Jingming South Road, Kunming 650500, Yunnan, China

Abstract. Quality Estimation (QE) is the prediction of translation quality without reference to the translation. Critical Error Detection (CED), as a sub-task of the QE task, aims to detect and identify significant meaning biases in machine translation that may cause serious damage. State-of-the-art CED models are supervised: they need to be trained on data obtained by multiple professionals labeled with specific CED labels based on the output of some machine translation system, thus making them dependent on the content of the training set, the scarcity of which and the non-uniformity in the distribution of the labels can affect performance. In order to solve the above problems, in this paper, we propose a training-free CED approach-CED based on anchors test, our approach only needs to test the anchors in the source language by cross-lingual masking test, and then determine whether the translation contains critical errors based on the test results. We conducted experiments on blind test data from the WMT2021 CED sharing task using different models. The results show the effectiveness of our proposed method, reaching the performance of the supervised baseline on En-Zh, but overall there is still a gap compared to supervised CED, and we give an example to illustrate the potential of our method for explainable applications.

Keywords: Training-Free · Quality Estimation · Critical Error Detection

1 Introduction

Despite the maturity of existing neural machine translation techniques and large-scale language models, erroneous translations can still be produced that can be seriously damaging, so it has become crucial to provide users with information about the quality of machine translations, which makes translation quality estimation an important research direction. Quality Estimation (QE) is the

---

K. Huang—Contributing author.

prediction of the quality of a translation without reference, and the Critical Error Detection (CED) task was first proposed as a subtask of the QE task at WMT2021 [1]. The CED task is aimed at detecting the presence of errors in machine translation that have misleading deviations in meaning compared to the source sentence and that may cause irreparable damage to health, safety, law, economy, etc., in numerous application scenarios, which in turn may avoid the risk of serious social problems caused by mistranslations.

The CED task is a sentence-level binary classification quality prediction task, according to the description of the WMT21CED task [1], and the types of errors that cause translations to contain critical errors are: Deviation in toxicity (TOX) - e.g. sexist or hateful elements, etc., Deviation in named entities (NAM), Deviation in sentiment polarity or negation (SEN) - e.g. "maybe" in the source language is translated as "must", etc., Deviation in numbers (NUM) and deviation in health or safety risks (SAF) - e.g. content in a translation is not supported by the source language, etc. Examples of data for the two critical errors are briefly presented in Table 1, with the bolded portion being the content of the meaning deviation.

Table 1. Critical error examples

Category	Source	Incorrect translation	Correct translation
SAF	**Wash your hands, or** you will catch the coronavirus.	你将感染新冠病毒。	洗手，否则你将感染新冠病毒。
NUM	From that point, turn right and drive **20 km**.	从这里右转，行驶 **20 英里**。	从这里右转，行驶 **20 公里**。

State-of-the-art CED systems are supervised, and they all need to be trained using CED-labeled data, which is scarce and non-uniformly labeled [1]. In the study of WMT21CED, Rubino et al. [2] improved CED performance by pre-training a QE model on translation quality scores computed by automatic evaluation metrics and combining multiple metrics and migration learning. Jiang et al. [3] explored weighted sampling to deal with non-uniform distribution of labels and used an API to extract features of various critical error types in sentences to train an optimization architecture. While Chen et al. [4] used pre-trained models and task-specific classifiers and used Google Translate and Baidu Fanyi APIs to train the architecture by combining back-translations in the dataset with the training data. Wang et al. [5] implemented CED using some uncertainty features extracted by the NMT system such as decoding probability features incorporated into a supervised QE method based on XLM-R migration learning. In the study of WMT22CED [6], Rei et al. [7] combined the use of reference translations during model pre-training to improve the performance of the model in a downstream task with the use of predicted DA scores as the training data for the CED task for multi-task co-training. Eo et al. [8] proposed template prompt-based fine-tuning on En-De and Pt-En to use the results of Demo and Google MT as auxiliary information to optimize the architecture, based on which

Jung et al. [9] first combined information evidence into template prompt-based fine-tuning to achieve CED on English-Korean.

Existing work studies have mentioned the performance problems caused by the scarcity of data with CED tags and the non-uniform distribution of the tags, which are usually provided by pre-training the QE models with synthetic data generated from parallel corpora or relying on data generated by commercial translation systems to provide auxiliary information. However, this may lead to limitations in the content or uncertainty in the quality of the synthesized data, thus affecting the performance of the model in the CED task. Therefore, in order to address the above problem, inspired by unsupervised QE approaches [10–12] in other QE sharing tasks in recent years, we propose and experiment for the first time with critical error detection based on anchors tests. Our approach is to assume that, under the premise that a perfect machine translation is equivalent to the source, the translation contains critical errors necessarily because the system mistranslates the content in the source language that "will cause the translation to contain critical errors if mistranslated", which we define as anchors, and we hope to test the anchors to determine whether the machine translation contains critical errors or not. Our main contributions are as follows:

- We propose for the first time a CED methodology based on anchors tests: this methodology is training-free and has a certain degree of explainability.
- Our experiments demonstrate the effectiveness of CED based on anchors tests, presenting a baseline for training-free CED, along with extensive experimental analysis of different approaches to selecting anchors.
- We provide an in-depth analysis of the characteristics of CED based on anchors tests in conjunction with experimental results, while demonstrating the potential for future applications in terms of explainability through examples.

2 Methodology

This section describes in detail the idea of implementing CED based on anchors test. Our approach is achieved based on the premise that perfect machine translation is equivalent to the source: we test the anchors test in the source, and then determine whether the translation contains critical errors or not, and the overall architecture is shown in Fig. 1. Taking the XLM-R model as an example, after masking these anchors one by one in the source and combining them with the translation to construct the cross-lingual mask prediction inputs, we get two different prediction results according to the settings (later called the binary contribution x_i or the probability contribution p_i), and judge whether the machine translation contains the critical errors after combining the different evaluation methods to evaluate the different contributions.

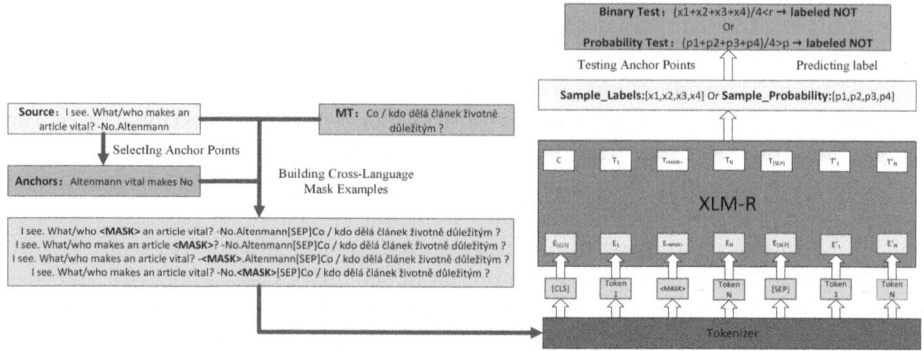

Fig. 1. Unsupervised critical error detection based on anchors test

2.1 How to Select Anchors?

We define the words in the source that "if translated incorrectly these words will cause the translation to contain critical errors" as anchors. In the data processing stage, we used two respective methods to select the anchors in each source sentence.

Term Frequency-Inverse Document Frequency (TF-IDF) is a weighting technique for information retrieval and text mining. It statistically evaluates the importance of words in a document set: the importance of a word in TF-IDF increases proportionally with the number of times it appears in the document, but at the same time decreases inversely with the frequency of its appearance in the corpus. It is realized as follows:

In a given document, Term Frequency (TF) refers to the frequency of occurrence of a given word in that document. For word t_i in a given document, its importance can be expressed as:

$$tf_{i,j} = \frac{n_{i,j}}{\sum_k n_{l,j}} \qquad (1)$$

where it is assumed that there are k words in the file dj and $n_{k,j}$ is the number of times t_k appears in the file dj. The numerator $n_{i,j}$ is the number of occurrences of the word in the file d_j, while the denominator is the sum of the occurrences of all words in the file d_j. IDF is a measure of the general importance of a word, in our experiments we use the TfidfVectorizer in scikit-learn to calculate the IDF, so the idf of a particular word can be expressed as the total number of documents divided by the number of documents containing that word, and then the resulting quotient is taken as a logarithm (with the base e):

$$idf_i = \log \frac{|D|+1}{|\{j \mid t_i \in d_j\}|+1} + 1 \qquad (2)$$

where $|D|$ denotes the total number of documents in the corpus and $|j : t_i \ d_j|$ denotes the total number of documents containing the word t_i. The +1 is to prevent the denominator from being zero or the numerator from being zero, and the +1 after taking the logarithm is to prevent the idf from being negative. Then the tfidf value of the word is then denoted as:

$$tfidf_{i,j} = tf_{i,j} * idf_i \qquad (3)$$

In our experiments we consider the sources of the blind test set as a file, and each source is a sub-file within the file, stop word processing is performed before computation, and then the TF-IDF value of each word in each source is obtained by computation, and after descending order sorting the top 50% of the TF-IDF words in each source are selected as anchors for that source.

TextRank [13] is an unsupervised graph-based ranking model for text processing. The core of using it to extract text anchors is to construct the text into an undirected graph, then iteratively calculate the weight scores of each node according to the TextRank algorithm, and finally pick the anchors based on the selection decision. The process is as follows:

1. Split the text and each word is considered as a node to be added to the undirected unweighted graph.
2. If two words appear together in a window of size w (i.e., words co-occur), then an edge is added between the words.
3. Assuming that a graph has N nodes, each with an initial value of 1/N, use the pagerank algorithm from the networkx library to iterate over the graph until it converges - in the experiments the number of iterations was set to 30 and the convergence value was 0.0001.
4. Each node is sorted in descending order based on weight scores, and the top 50% of words are selected as anchors.

Since the content of each dataset is different, we set the value of w to 2, 3, 4, and 5 for exploration in our experiments, and ultimately report the MCC optimal result setting.

2.2 How to Test Anchors?

We construct CED by designing different cross-lingual mask predictions for anchors, the idea is that each source gets a cross-lingual mask prediction example after masking one anchor at a time based on the anchors selected and combined with machine translation.Assuming that a source has n anchors, there will be m (m>=n) different cross-lingual mask prediction examples, according to the different settings to get two different prediction outputs, the cross-lingual mask prediction results of the anchors will be called the anchor's contribution to determining whether the translation contains critical errors, according to the characteristics of the contribution corresponds to the proposal of the two methods of evaluating the contribution to determining whether the translation contains critical errors, i.e., the two anchors testing methods:

Binary Test (BinT): the model predicts the masked anchors test in the input, and the candidate with the highest probability is the predicted word, and compares the predicted word with the source word, and if it is not the same, assigns this prediction the binary quality label 1, which indicates that the prediction is incorrect; and vice versa assigns the label 0, which indicates that the prediction is correct. Eventually a list of binary quality labels sample_labels of length m will be obtained, the list represents the binary contributions obtained after cross-lingual mask prediction of the anchors of this piece of data.

We propose the **AER** threshold method to evaluate the binary classification contribution: AER is **Anchors Error Ratio**, by calculating the proportion of 1-labels in the list of sample_labels e (e$\in$[0,1]), when e<r (the threshold r is a hyperparameter), we judge that this translation doesn't contain the critical error, and assign the label NOT; when e>=r, we judge that this translation contains critical errors, assigning the label ERR.

Probability Test (ProbT): The model predicts the masked anchors in the input, and we obtain the model's predicted probability of the masked anchors directly from the model's predicted probability distribution of the masked anchors based on the source words. Eventually a probability list sample_probability of length m is obtained, the list represents the probability contribution obtained after cross-lingual mask prediction of the anchors of this data.

We propose the AProb threshold method to evaluate the probability contribution: the AProb is the **Anchors Probability**, by calculating the average of m probabilities in the sample_probability, p (p$\in$[0,1]), and when p¡q (the threshold q is a hyper-parameter), we judge that this translation contains the critical error, and assign the label ERR; when p >= q, it is judged that this translation does not contain critical errors and the label NOT is assigned.

3 Experiment Settings

3.1 Dataset Details

Our approach does not require the use of CED data with manual annotations for training, but only obtains the split development set after splitting the development set according to the blind test set when designing the untrained CED baseline, and then uses the split development set for hyperparameter tuning. The dataset used in the subsequent experiments is mainly the blind test set for the CED task in the WMT 2021 QE shared task dataset MLQE-PE, which consists of the Jigsaw Toxic Comment Classification Challenge and the Wikipedia Comment Corpus, which are two English Wikipedia comments that are used to generate translations using the FAIR's ML50 multi-language translation model. When annotating labels, if more than two out of three professionals thought that one or more of the above critical errors existed in the machine translation, then the machine translation was labeled ERR and vice versa with NOT.In the previous section, we introduced that training data with CED labels are scarce and unevenly labeled, according to the dataset published by the WMT21CED shared task [1], the average training data for the four language pairs is less than 7,500, and the distribution of ERR labels for different language pairs is extremely uneven, e.g., ERR labels account for only 9.4% in En-Ja, while ERR labels account for 27.9% in En-De.

3.2 Models

The models used in our experiments were implemented using PyTorch and Transformers. We used the pre-trained language models InfoXLM-base [14], XLM-RoBERTa-base [15], and BERT-base-Multilingual-Cased [16] (henceforth referred to as InfoXLM, XLM-R, and mBERT, respectively), all of which have cross-lingual mask prediction capabilities, published on the HuggingFace model repository.) checkpoints, experimented on the NVIDIA RTX 4090D environment.

3.3 Evaluation Details

Following the WMT21 shared task, we use the Matthews correlation coefficient (MCC) as an evaluation metric for the critical error detection task in our experiments to assess the performance of the model. MCC is a metric used in binary classification tasks, and we used the evaluation script for the WMT2021QE shared task to compute the MCC scores, as well as combining True Positive Example (TP), False Positive Example (FP), True Negative Example (TN), and False Negative Example (FN) to assist with the analysis of our method.

3.4 Hyperparameters

The hyperparameters of our method are the method of selecting anchors, the choice of model, the choice of anchors test method (BinT or ProbT) and the corresponding thresholds (threshold r for the AER thresholding method or threshold p for the AProb thresholding method). We experimented with combinations of different methods of selecting anchors with different anchors test setups, and then used grid searches to find the hyperparameter settings that produced the highest MCC scores on the blind test set. The optimal settings for En-Cs are TF-IDF, InfoXLM, ProbT, p= 0.472, for En-De are TextRank (window set to 3), InfoXLM, ProbT, p= 0.6589, for En-Ja are TextRank (window set to 3), InfoXLM, ProbT, p= 0.2343 and the optimal setting for En-Zh is TextRank (window set to 5), InfoXLM, ProbT, p= 0.4917.

3.5 Training-Free CED Baseline

We find the threshold at which each language performs best for MCC on the split development set separately then implement two XLM-R-based training-free CED baselines AllWordsDetect (AWD) and RandomWordsDetect (RWD) on the blind test set. In constructing the AWD, by masking one word at a time in the source in sequence and then combining it with the translation as input, the model predicts at the mask and then compares the predicted word with the source word, and if it is the same, assigns the prediction result the quality label 0; and vice versa assigns the label 1. Calculate the percentage n of incorrectly predicted words for each piece of data, and assign the label ERR if n > t (the threshold t is a hyperparameter), otherwise NOT. While constructing the RWD, we set three random seeds 1000, 1100 and 1200 to randomly select 50% of the words, for each seed, one word at a time is masked and combined with the translation as an input, and the model predicts based on the input, and assigns a label of 0 or 1 to each prediction based on the result of comparing the predicted word with the source word. The ratio m of the number of prediction errors to the total number of random words picked for each piece of data is computed and if m>s (threshold s is a hyperparameter), the label ERR is assigned, otherwise NOT,and the best seed result is finally selected as the baseline RWD.

We chose these two baselines because it uses the same model architecture, XLM-R, as the supervised baseline, while showing some classification ability on whether the translations contain critical errors without training. On En-Cs, En-De, En-Ja, and En-Zh, the thresholds t are 0.33, 0.33, 0.50, and 0.60, and the thresholds s are 0.41, 0.43, 0.51, and 0.66.

4 Results Analysis and Discussion

4.1 Main Results

The results of our experiments on the blind test set of the WMT2021 CED task are shown in Tables 2 and 3, with bolding indicating that both outperform the two training-free baselines.

Table 2. MCC results of unsupervised CED for different models combined with different anchors selection settings in the ProbT setting

Model	Method	En-Cs	En-De	En-Ja	En-Zh
Unsupervised Baseline	AWD	0.167	0.153	0.080	0.124
Unsupervised Baseline	RWD	0.161	0.118	0.101	0.125
Supervised Baseline	—	0.388	0.397	0.214	0.187
InfoXLM	TF-IDF	**0.277**	**0.189**	**0.149**	**0.179**
	TextRank-base	**0.249**	**0.190**	**0.159**	**0.187**
XLM-R	TF-IDF	**0.190**	**0.187**	0.091	0.121
	TextRank-base	**0.220**	**0.198**	**0.150**	**0.159**
mBERT	TF-IDF	0.139	**0.171**	0.096	0.039
	TextRank-base	**0.189**	**0.201**	**0.111**	0.113

The results show that our proposed anchors test-based CED approach is effective compared to the proposed baseline. According to Tables 2 and 3, it is shown that the overall performance of CED based on anchors test in four language pairs modeled in combination in BinT or ProbT setting demonstrates that InfoXLM is much better than XLM-R, mBERT, and both baselines. Compared to the best-performing baseline results, the best results of our method on En-Cs in the ProbT setting are 0.110 above the baseline, which is the largest gap. The

Table 3. MCC results of unsupervised CED for different models combined with different anchors selection settings in the BinT setting

Model	Method	En-Cs	En-De	En-Ja	En-Zh
Unsupervised Baseline	AWD	0.167	0.153	0.080	0.124
Unsupervised Baseline	RWD	0.161	0.118	0.101	0.125
InfoXLM	TF-IDF	**0.241**	0.158	**0.140**	0.144
	TextRank-base	0.224	0.157	0.160	0.171
XLM-R	TF-IDF	**0.193**	0.167	0.108	0.111
	TextRank-base	0.176	0.180	0.129	**0.135**
mBERT	TF-IDF	0.143	**0.165**	0.088	0.058
	TextRank-base	**0.186**	0.169	**0.116**	0.106

best results on En-De, En-Ja, and En-Zh were higher by 0.048, 0.058, and 0.061, respectively, with the best result on En-Zh reaching a supervised baseline performance with WMT21CED. Whereas the best result of our method in the BinT setting is still obtained on En-Cs with a maximum difference of 0.074 from the baseline, the gain of the best result obtained on En-De is the smallest among the other language pairs, being 0.027 higher than the baseline. It can be seen that under the same model combined with the same anchors test setup, the overall performance difference between the two methods of anchors selection is small, and thus we conclude that both methods of anchors selection are valid, and the CED based on anchors test is valid.

4.2 Impact of Model Cross-Lingual Mask Prediction Accuracy on MCC Performance

Tables 2 and 3 show that the best MCC performance is obtained based on anchors selected by the same method combined with the same test setting for the same language pairs almost all of which exhibit the model InfoXLM outperforming XLM-R outperforming mBERT. As shown in Fig. 3, this trend is more obvious with the curves of threshold p vs. MCC performance obtained from different models on En-Zh based on the TextRank method of selecting anchors combined with the ProbT setting, for example. Therefore, we conjecture that the higher the accuracy of the model's cross-lingual mask prediction in the same language pair, the better its performance in constructing CEDs based on anchors tests. To verify this conjecture, we conducted cross-lingual mask prediction accuracy experiments on three models using two bilingual parallel datasets News, Wikiset on each of the four language pairs. The dataset News is obtained by extracting 4k/4k/2k/4k parallel data by En-Cs/De/Ja/Zh from the parallel corpus news-commentary-v16 in the WMT2022 generalized machine translation task, respectively. The dataset Wikiset is obtained by extracting 10,000 parallel data for each language pair from the parallel corpus Wikimatrix in the WMT2022 generalized machine translation task. In our experiments, we mask one word at a time for the English part of each data in order and combine it with the target language as input, compare the predicted words with the source words, and add one to the number of correct predictions if they are the same, and finally get the accuracy of the model's cross-lingual mask prediction based on the percentage of correct predictions to the total number of predictions.

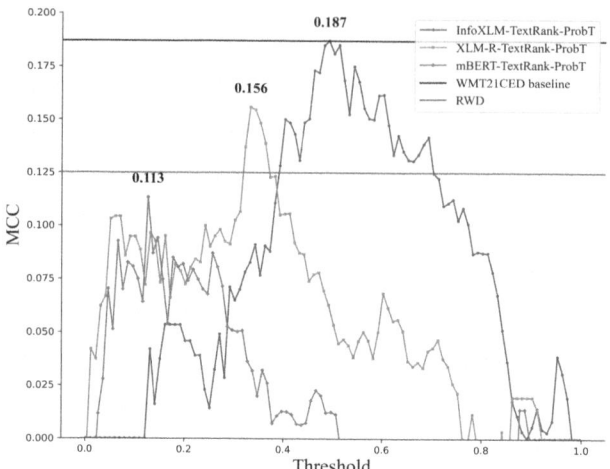

Fig. 2. CED threshold p vs. MCC performance curves on En-Zh based on different models combined with TextRank method in ProbT setting

As shown in Table 4, the accuracy of cross-lingual mask prediction for the three models on these four language pairs on the Wikiset and News datasets performs InfoXLM outperforms XLM-R outperforms mBERT, which is in line with the trend shown in the threshold p vs. MCC performance curves of CED based on anchors tests obtained by the above models on the same language pairs. Therefore, we can conclude that the cross-lingual mask prediction accuracy of a model under the same language pair has an impact on its final performance in constructing anchor test-based CEDs, and the model that performs better

Table 4. Cross-lingual mask prediction accuracy of the model on different language pairs of Wikiset and News

Dataset	Method	En-Cs	En-De	En-Ja	En-Zh
Wikiset	InfoXLM	62.12%	88.95%	81.95%	55.44%
	XLM-R	54.11%	73.72%	69.74%	49.33%
	mBERT	51.17%	71.34%	56.68%	43.68%
News	InfoXLM	82.79%	84.09%	80.79%	81.44%
	XLM-R	71.98%	72.32%	69.96%	68.54%
	mBERT	54.46%	57.95%	49.79%	49.69%

in cross-lingual mask prediction task in terms of accuracy performs better in overall performance of anchor test-based CEDs on that language pair.

4.3 Impact of Anchors Test Method Selection on MCC Performance

Combining Tables 2 and 3, we observe the phenomenon that the best MCC performance obtained by the ProbT setup is overall better than the BinT setup for the same method setting of anchors selection. As shown in Fig. 3, the threshold vs. MCC performance curves obtained for the CEDs constructed by testing the anchors selected using the TextRank method under different test method settings for the InfoXLM model on En-Zh, for example, show a more obvious performance, which we think is determined by the different characteristics of the contributions produced by the two test settings.

For predicting each masked anchor, the binary contribution is obtained based on the comparison of the predicted word with the source word, while the probability contribution is obtained when the model predicts the mask based on the inputs, obtaining a probability distribution containing a number of candidate words, and then obtaining the predicted probability of the source word directly in the probability distribution. Although the predicted probability of the source word may not always be the largest among the candidates, as long as there is a probability, we consider that the result of testing this anchor contributes where it belongs to us in our final judgment of whether the translation contains critical errors, and therefore we consider that the CED constructed in conjunction with the ProbT setting is more reasonable than the BinT setting, and therefore performs better overall. A simple example is more straightforward to understand: under the ProbT setting, the probability of predicting Anchor A is 0.8, and the probability of predicting Anchor B is 0.2, the mean is 0.5, and based on the mean it is intuitively obvious that although the prediction result of Anchor B also contributes (i.e., 0.2) to the final judgment of whether or not the translation contains a critical error, the contribution is negative (since it results in a mean to be 0.5).

4.4 Impact of Dataset Content on MCC Performance

The content of different datasets is different, corresponding to different anchors, and the fact that all our experiments were conducted on a blind test set caused us to think: does it just happen to get valid results on a blind test set? Does our method fail if it is on a different dataset? In order to investigate this issue, we use the split development set mentioned in the construction of the training-free CED baseline, we split the source, the machine translation, and the corresponding labels in the original development set, constructed a pseudo-blind test set modeled after the blind test set, and performed the same step-by-step experiments using the model InfoXLM based on the two anchors selection methods in combination with a ProbT setting on each of the four language pairs, respectively, the results of the experiments are shown in Table 5, with bolding indicating results that are all over two baselines.

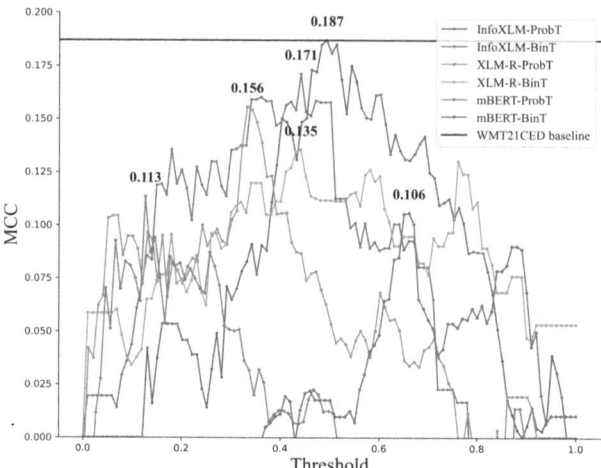

Fig. 3. CED threshold vs. MCC performance curves on En-Zh based on different models combined with TextRank method under different test settings

Table 5. Unsupervised CED performance of InfoXLM on pseudo-blind test sets combined with ProbT setting

Method	En-Cs	En-De	En-Ja	En-Zh
AWD	0.167	0.153	0.080	0.124
RWD	0.161	0.118	0.101	0.125
Supervised Baseline	0.388	0.397	0.214	0.187
TF-IDF	**0.186**	**0.194**	**0.164**	**0.198**
TextRank-base	**0.206**	**0.223**	**0.161**	**0.196**

The results show that our method is equally effective on a dataset with different content from the blind test set and yields better MCC performance on En-De, En-Ja and En-Zh than on the blind test set, and even on En-Zh, the best MCC results obtained from testing CEDs based on anchors selected by the TF-IDF and TextRank methods outperform respectively the WMT21CED's supervised baseline of 0.011 and 0.009, also proving once again that our proposed CED based on anchors test is effective.

4.5 Advantages, Shortcomings, and Prospects

At this point, based on extensive experiments we have demonstrated the effectiveness of CED based on anchors tests, and our method has the following advantages over supervised methods: first, our method is training-free, and we only need to test the anchors and thus determine whether the translations contain critical errors or not, which means that our method does not rely on these scarce training data with specific CED labels and we achieve the supervised baseline results of WMT21CED on the En-Zh of the blind test set and exceed the supervised baseline results on the pseudo-blind test set. Second, according to Table 6, it can be seen that the CED constructed by our method only needs to test about 40% of the words in the source language to get far better results than AWD, which detects all the words in the source. In addition, CEDs selecting anchors based on either the TF-IDF or TextRank methods were tested to obtain results that outperformed the RWD baseline, suggesting that both anchor selection methods are valid and meaningful because the RWD implementation is constructed by randomly selecting words. The process of implementing CED based

Table 6. Statistics of the average number of selected anchors per source sentence and the average total number of source words based on different anchor selections

Method	En-Cs	En-De	En-Ja	En-Zh
AWD	16.1	16.4	16.4	16.0
TF-IDF	5.1	5.1	5.2	5.1
TextRank	6.4	6.6	6.6	6.6

on anchors tests is somewhat explainable, according to Table 7, where we show an example of successful prediction of machine translations containing critical translations on En-Cs using a TF-IDF-based selection of anchors in combination with BinT setting. The first example is based on a list of binary contribution sample_labels, which are tested for errors in the anchors test "Altenmann" and "vital" to determine that the translation contains critical errors. The potential for the application of CED based on anchors tests in terms of explainability can be seen in this example, where the results of the anchors tests provide a strong explanation and support for the user to decide whether or not the translation can be trusted enough. However, although there have been results on

Table 7. Example of unsupervised CED explainability for anchors testing with cross-lingual mask prediction

Source	Translation	Anchors	BinT	Prediction	goldlabel
I see. What/who makes an article vital? -No.Altenmann	Co / kdo dělá článek životně důležitým ?	Altenmann vital makes No	[1,1,0,0]	ERR	ERR

En-Zh that meet or even outperform the supervised baseline, as a whole, our proposed CED approach falls short of existing supervised CEDs. We reproduce the best results on En-Zh based on the code published in the paper submitted by

Jiang et al. (2021) in the WMT2021CED Shared Task, and as shown in Table 8, ICL's supervised method obtains a much higher best MCC on En-Zh than our method. Meanwhile, in the process of implementing CED based on anchor testing, since each piece of data generates m cross-lingual mask prediction examples to be tested based on its number of anchors n, and since the content of the data will result in different anchors that need to be tested, this is the reason why the thresholds corresponding to the best MCC results obtained on different datasets are different, which consumes a not-insignificant amount of computational resources , which can be considered as a trade-off between our approach and previous supervised CED approaches. Although there is still a considerable gap between our approach and existing supervised techniques, combining all of our experimental procedures and experimental results, we believe that in the future, we can improve the performance of anchor-based tests for CED by selecting more appropriate anchors for the content, improving the cross-language masking accuracy of the model, and finding a more appropriate anchor test method.

Table 8. Comparison of the best MCC results obtained by our method with the best MCC results obtained by reproducing the ICL team code for the WMT2021CED shared task on En-Zh

Method	MCC	F1_BAD	F1_BAD	TP	FP	TN	FN
ICL(Supervised)	0.237	0.3548	0.8817	55	97	745	103
InfoXLM+TextRank+ProbT	0.187	0.3155	0.8711	50	109	733	108

5 Conclusion

In this paper, we propose a novel CED method based on anchors test according to the CED shared task in WMT2021QE shared task. Our method does not rely on data with specific CED labels and does not require training. The experiments prove that our method is effective and achieves the MCC performance of the WMT21CED supervised baseline on En-Zh, and it is also proved that the higher the model's cross-lingual mask prediction accuracy is, the better the performance of CEDs constructed according to our method. At the same time, the CED method based on anchor tests is explainable and shows some potential at the level of explainable applications: it can be shown to be a final judgment of whether a translation contains critical errors by which anchors are tested. Overall, although CED based on anchors tests is still lagging behind existing supervised CED systems, some of the trends demonstrated in the experimental results suggest that this gap can be narrowed in the future, and even surpass the level of the supervised CED baseline to some extent.

In the future, we believe that anchors test-based can be applied to other QE tasks as an important explainability feature for relevant task performance optimization, such as the QE task of predicting DA scores or the QE task in the Zero-shot setting, and we are in the process of conducting parallel to how to close the gap between CED based on anchors test and the existing supervised CED baseline research experiments.

Acknowledgments. This work is supported by the Regional Fund Project of National Natural Science Foundation of China (62166022), and Yunnan Xingdian Talent Support Plan Project(KKXX202403023). (The authors have no competing interests to declare that are relevant to the content of this article.)

References

1. Specia, L., et al.: Findings of the WMT 2021 shared task on quality estimation. In: Proceedings of the Sixth Conference on Machine Translation (2021)
2. Rubino, R., Fujita, A., Marie, B.: NICT Kyoto submission for the WMT'21 quality estimation task: multimetric multilingual pretraining for critical error detection. In: Proceedings of the Sixth Conference on Machine Translation (2021)
3. Jiang, G., Li, Z., Specia, L.: ICL's submission to the WMT21 critical error detection shared task. In: Proceedings of the Sixth Conference on Machine Translation (2021)
4. Chen, Y., et al.: HW-TSC's participation at WMT 2021 quality estimation shared task. In: Proceedings of the Sixth Conference on Machine Translation (2021)
5. Wang, J., et al.: QEMind: Alibaba's submission to the WMT21 quality estimation shared task. arXiv preprint arXiv:2112.14890 (2021)
6. Zerva, C., et al.: Findings of the WMT 2022 shared task on quality estimation. In: Proceedings of the Seventh Conference on Machine Translation (WMT) (2022)
7. Rei, R., et al.: CometKiwi: IST-unbabel 2022 submission for the quality estimation shared task. arXiv preprint arXiv:2209.06243 (2022)
8. Eo, S., et al.: KU X upstage's submission for the WMT22 quality estimation: critical error detection shared task. In: Proceedings of the Seventh Conference on Machine Translation (WMT) (2022)
9. Jung, D., et al.: Informative evidence-guided prompt-based fine-tuning for English-Korean critical error detection. In: Proceedings of the 13th International Joint Conference on Natural Language Processing and the 3rd Conference of the Asia-Pacific Chapter of the Association for Computational Linguistics (Volume 1: Long Papers) (2023)
10. Fomicheva, M., et al.: Unsupervised quality estimation for neural machine translation. Trans. Assoc. Comput. Linguist. **8**, 539–555 (2020)
11. Tuan, Y.-L., et al.: Quality estimation without human-labeled data. arXiv preprint arXiv:2102.04020 (2021)
12. Dinh, T.A., Jan, N.: Perturbation-based QE: an explainable, unsupervised word-level quality estimation method for blackbox machine translation. arXiv preprint arXiv:2305.07457 (2023)
13. Mihalcea, R., Tarau, P.: Textrank: bringing order into text. In: Proceedings of the 2004 Conference on Empirical Methods in Natural Language Processing (2004)
14. Chi, Z., et al.: InfoXLM: an information-theoretic framework for cross-lingual language model pre-training. arXiv preprint arXiv:2007.07834 (2020)
15. Conneau, A.: Unsupervised cross-lingual representation learning at scale. arXiv preprint arXiv:1911.02116 (2019)
16. Devlin, J.: BERT: pre-training of deep bidirectional transformers for language understanding. arXiv preprint arXiv:1810.04805 (2018)

Large Language Modes for Machine Translation

Enhancing Machine Translation Across Multiple Domains and Languages with Large Language Models

Hao Lu[1], Rui Zhang[1], Hui Huang[1], Fuhai Song[1], Junkai Liu[1], Yican Ye[1], Lang Lang[1], Ziqing Zhao[1], Muyun Yang[1(✉)], and Rui Cong[2]

[1] Department of Computer Science and Engineering, Harbin Institute of Technology, Harbin, China
{24b903007,zhangrui,huanghui,7203610511, 24S003039,24S103409}@stu.hit.edu.cn, yangmuyun@hit.edu.cn
[2] School of Foreign Languages, Harbin Institute of Technology, Harbin, China

Abstract. Large language models (LLMs) have exhibited remarkable performance in various natural language processing tasks. In this paper, we describe our LLM-based machine translation system submitted to CCMT 2024 evaluation task. We investigated the effects of pre training data ratio, language quantity, instruction fine-tuning data ratio, and instruction construction method on the machine translation performance of large language models. We found that large language models have greater potential for multi-domain machine translation compared to traditional machine translation models. Within limits, increasing the number of newly added languages can enhance the overall translation capabilities for these new languages.

Keywords: Large language models · Multi-domain · Multilingual

1 Introduction

With the continuous increase in the parameters of language models and the growing volume of training data, the knowledge encapsulated within these models has seen exponential growth. Large language models, as their scale has increased, have awakened capabilities that were previously beyond the reach of traditional language models.

In the field of machine translation, large language models exhibit immense potential due to their encapsulation of multilingual knowledge. Previous works [2,8,9] have shown that utilizing prompts or small-scale instruction tuning can effectively unlock this multilingual knowledge embedded within large language models, thereby enhancing their translation capabilities. Exploring further methods to fully leverage the potential of large language models in translation has become a crucial research direction in the era of big models.

This paper presents our submission to CCMT2024, and we mainly joined the English-Chinese, Chinese-English, Tibetan-Chinese, Uyghur-Chinese,

Mongolian-Chinese and multi-domain Chinese-English machine translation tracks. In this paper, we developed a multi-domain translation system for the Chinese-English multi-domain machine translation tracks, and a multilingual translation system for the other five tracks. In the following, we will refer to these five tracks as multilingual translation tasks.

In the multilingual machine translation system, we expanded the number of languages in the Baichuan2 model [17], conducted vocabulary expansion, continue pre-training, and performed SFT (Supervised Fine-Tuning). We explored the impact of the increased number of languages on the translation capabilities for both new and existing languages.

In the multi-domain translation system, we performed context construction for Qwen1.5-14b [1] and used different SFT methods to fine-tune the model with instructions. This included adding domain descriptions and introducing the APE (Automatic Post-Editing) task to optimize translation results. We referenced other researchers and generate the APE synthetic data with data augmentation [5,7,14]. Compared to traditional machine translation system, our LLM-based system achieves better results in multi domain translation tasks, and used fewer parallel corpora, verifying the potentlial of large language models in this task.

Our contributions are summarized as follows:

1. We validated the effectiveness of large language models in multilingual and multi-domain machine translation tasks.
2. We explored the impact of adding new languages on the model's translation capabilities under the multilingual setting.
3. We explored the impact of different instruction templates, downstream tasks, and data domain relevance on the translation capabilities of large language models in multi-domain tasks.

2 Approach

2.1 Architecture

In this work, we used the LLMs to complete the translation task, under this setting, the translation inference can be formalized into the following formula:

$$\mathbf{y} \sim \mathcal{P}(\mathbf{y}|\mathbf{x}, \lambda; \theta) \tag{1}$$

$$\mathcal{P}(\mathbf{y}|\mathbf{x}, \lambda; \theta) = \prod_{t=1}^{m} \mathcal{P}(\mathbf{y}_i|\mathbf{y}_{1:t-1}, \mathbf{x}, \lambda; \theta) \tag{2}$$

where the model be parameterized by θ. Let x represent the source sentence and y represent its corresponding target sentence. We use a prompt template (denoted as λ) to guide the model in generating the translation. $\mathbf{y}_i$ represents the i-th token of the target sentence$\mathbf{y}_{1:t-1}$ represents the sequence of the first to t-1-th tokens in the target sentence.

As shown in Fig. 1, during the training phase, the input consists of the prompt and the source sentence, with the target sentence serving as the desired output. We only calculate the loss on the target sentence portion. During inference, the input is composed of the prompt and the source sentence. The model then sequentially predicts each subsequent token based on the input, generating the target sentence.

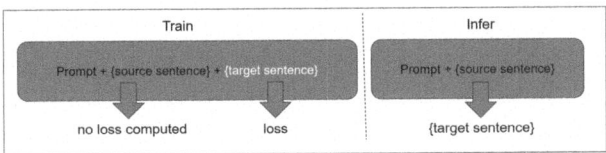

Fig. 1. The loss calculation during the training of large language models and the output generation during inference.

In our two translation systems, we focused on two main issues. In the multi-language machine translation system, we investigated the impact of the number of languages on the model's translation performance. In the multi-domain machine translation system, we studied the effects of different SFT (Supervised Fine-Tuning) methods and data domain relevance on the translation performance.

2.2 Multi-domain Machine Translation System

We selected Qwen1.5-14b as the backbone, as it has demonstrated strong Chinese and English capabilities on several language proficiency benchmarks (e.g., OpenCompass [3]).

We employed two methods to enhance the translation capabilities of the language model. The first method involved directly designing prompts, while the second method focused on fine-tuning the model to improve its translation performance.

Fig. 2. The prompt-based method.

In the prompt-based method shown in Fig. 2, we optimized the model's translation quality by selecting domain-specific demos from the development set for each source sentence and forming a prompt [2,9,13].

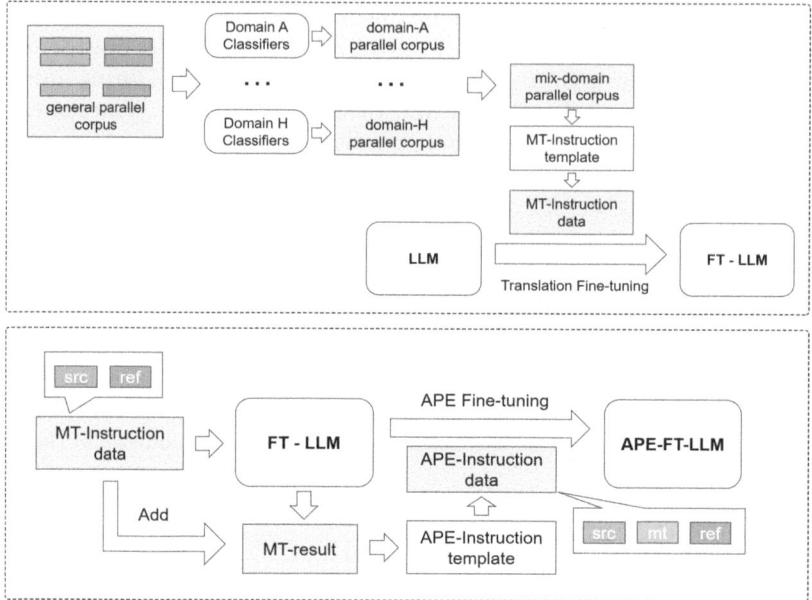

Fig. 3. The fine-tuning method.

In the fine-tuning method shown in Fig. 3, we obtained domain-specific training data using some classifiers and conducted instruction fine-tuning using MT-Instruction templates. Moreover, we further improved translation performance by applying APE tasks for additional instruction fine-tuning. The specific steps are as follows:

Domain Data Construction. The domain translation capabilities of large language models may be lacking, requiring domain-specific data to enhance translation performance. Since the organizers did not provide domain-specific data, we trained some domain classifiers to categorize general parallel corpora, thereby constructing a domain-specific dataset.

To perform domain classification, we constructed domain-specific datasets and a general dataset to train the BERT-based binary classifier. For the domain-specific data, we applied resampling to the Chinese portions of different domains within the test set, using the augmented data as our domain-specific dataset. For the general data, we mixed news domain data, Chinese Wikipedia data, and Chinese Weibo data from CLUECorpus2020 [16] in a 3:3:4 ratio.

After cleaning and filtering, we obtained a general dataset consisting of 500,000 sentences. We then used these dataset to train 8 BERT-based classifier on Chinese text from 8 different domains as required by the organizer. We mixed the general data and domain-specific data in a 1:9 ratio to create a training set of 16,000 samples and trained eight classifiers.

We then used these classifiers to score the domain relevance of our general parallel corpus on a continuous scale from zero to one, where zero indicates "domain-irrelevant" and one indicates "domain-relevant." Next, we ranked the general parallel data based on these scores from highest to lowest. The higher-ranked data considered more aligned with the specific translation domain. We evenly distributed the data across each domain. We did not remove duplicates from the final classification results: if a sentence belonged to n domains, we resampled the corresponding sentence pair n times, ensuring a better balance across the domains.

Translation Fine-Tuning. To enhance the model's understanding of translation task instructions, we conducted instruction fine-tuning specifically for the translation tasks. The instruction data required for instruction fine-tuning was constructed using parallel corpora with higher domain relevance, as determined by the classifier. We refer to ALAMA [15] to design the MT-Instruction template, and explore the effectiveness of domain information in the instruction.

Base-Instruction

Translate this from {source language} to {target language}:
[source language]:{source sentence}
[target language]:

Domain-Instruction

The following sentence is from the {field} field, please translate it from {source language} to {target language}:
source language:source sentence
[target language]:

Automatic Post-editing. To improve translation quality under limited resources, we introduced the APE task. APE is aimed at utilizing the model to correct the translation given the source sentence. By using data augmentation, we generated some synthetic data for APE task with parallel corpora and the model that had undergone translation fine-tuning. We used this data to conduct additional instruction fine-tuning on the best-performing translation model. Afterward, during inference, we used the model to perform two rounds of inference to obtain both the machine translation result and the post-editing result. The instruction template we constructed is as follows:

APE-Instruction

Here is a pair of {source language} and its corresponding {target language} translations:
[source sentence]:{source sentence}
[translation result]:{mt sentence}
Please make the translation result better
[better translation result]:

2.3 Multilingual Machine Translation System

In the multilingual machine translation system, We chose Baichuan2, which has strong multilingual capabilities, as our backbone.

The multilingual machine translation task includes five tracks: Chinese-English, English-Chinese, Tibetan-Chinese, Mongolian-Chinese, and Uyghur-Chinese. We performed vocabulary expansion, continued pre-training, and translation instruction fine-tuning on the model sequentially, ultimately completing all the tracks using a single model.

Vocabulary Expansion. To increase the model's decoding efficiency and improve the compression ratio of sentence sequences into token sequences, we expanded the vocabulary for the five languages. Specifically, we used the SentencePiece tool [6] to tokenize monolingual data in the five languages using the BPE method, generating tokenizers with a vocabulary size of 20,000 tokens each.

Finally, these five tokenizers were merged with the tokenizer of the Baichuan2 model. Specifically, to minimize the impact on the already trained base model, new vocabulary tokens were appended to the end of the vocabulary. After expanding the vocabulary, we extended the embedding layer and the language model head layer of the model. We achieved this by filling the expanded matrices with the mean values from the original embedding layer and language model head layer.

Continue Pretraining. To integrate the modified tokenizer, language model head layer, and embedding layer into the model, we conducted full-parameter continued pre-training using monolingual data. Compared to instruction fine-tuning, pre-training allows the model to acquire foundational language knowledge. After vocabulary expansion, the model does not possess knowledge related to the newly added languages. This step is essential for the model to effectively handle tasks involving the new languages.

Specifically, we conducted multilingual pre-training on the model with an expanded vocabulary, preserving the model's original Chinese and English capabilities while extending its language abilities to include the newly added languages. In the pre-training process, to reduce the difficulties caused by overly short sentences, we concatenated sentences in each language based on their lengths. This ensured that the token sequences of each monolingual segment in the pre-training corpus had a certain length.

Translation Fine-Tuning. In the multilingual translation system, we used the Base-Instruction template for constructing instruction data. We performed instruction fine-tuning for all the five tracks.

3 Experimental Setups

3.1 Data

Data Sources. In our multi-domain machine translation System, we used four data sources: CCMT Chinese-English parallel corpus, patent parallel corpus, our own general parallel corpus data, and parallel corpora from different domains that we collected from the internet. The CCMT Chinese-English parallel corpus was provided by the organizers. The patent parallel corpus was extracted from our proprietary patent corpus and is not publicly available. Similarly, our general parallel corpus data is also proprietary and not publicly available. The different domain parallel corpora we collected from the internet include the following datasets: UM-Corpus [11], data filtered by keywords from paracrawl.wmt21, and data from the MTTT dataset [4]. All dataset quantities mentioned below refer to the number of sentences (Table 1).

Table 1. The multi-domain Chinese-English Parallel Corpus. This includes four data sources: CCMT Chinese-English parallel corpus, patent parallel corpus, our own general parallel corpus data, and parallel corpora from different domains collected from the internet. The "processed" row in the table represents the number of sentences in the dataset after being cleaned by us.

language	ccmt	patent	ours	domain
All_data	7.08M	4.1M	0.5M	2.68M
Preprocessed	5.28M	3.12M	0.5M	2.32M

Our multilingual system integrates five languages: Chinese, English, Tibetan, Uyghur, and Mongolian. We used the monolingual and bilingual data provided by CCMT. Due to the limited amount of Uyghur data, we included the THUUy-Morph dataset [19] for pre-training. Ultimately, we constructed three categories of data: continue pre-training, translation fine-tuning, and test sets.

Preprocessing. We applied the following processing methods to monolingual and parallel corpora:

1. Deduplication: We removed the duplicate parts from the corpus.
2. Length filtering: We removed sentences with a length of 4 characters or less, as well as sentences exceeding 150 characters.
3. Full-width to half-width conversion: We converted all full-width characters to half-width characters, as unified symbols are more beneficial for model training.
4. Removing illegal characters.
5. Converting traditional Chinese characters to simplified Chinese.
6. Removing extra spaces.

7. Tokenization: For the training corpus used in Transformer [12], we segmented the Chinese text using Jieba[1] and the English text using Sacremoses[2]. Then, we applied subword segmentation using Subword-NMT[3].

Moreover, for parallel corpora involving minority languages, we applied additional filtering on the target-side Chinese text. This included removing sentence pairs with irrelevant or problematic expressions by identifying modal particles such as '啊', '呀', etc. and punctuation errors, thus eliminating a significant amount of irrelevant or poorly expressed parallel data. For the patent data, we extracted keywords that frequently appear in different sections of patent descriptions. Using these keywords, we filtered the data to reduce the frequency of sentences from certain sections of the patents.

Multi-domain Data Construction. In the multi-domain translation system, we compared the impact of varying data volumes. When selecting data based on ranking, larger data volumes resulted in lower domain relevance. We also compared the effects of different instructions and APE instruction fine-tuning. Our experimental data setup is as follows:

We constructed a large dataset containing 240,000 instruction pairs and a smaller dataset containing 40,000 pairs, with each pair consisting of a source sentence (src) and a reference sentence (ref). For the APE data, we used the top 40,000 ranked sentences that were not part of the smaller dataset. The source sentences were first input into the model to obtain the translated sentences (mt), and then the src, mt, and ref (pe) triples were used to create the APE task data.

Multilingual Machine Translation System

The number and ratio of languages have a significant impact on multilingual models. We maintained the number of language families in the newly added languages: one model added Uyghur, Mongolian, and Tibetan, while the other one added only Mongolian and Tibetan. We studied the impact of the number of newly added languages on the translation performance of both inherent and newly added languages.

We trained and compared two models using the steps mentioned in Sect. 2.3. The first model is pretrained with all languages but the second model excluded Uyghur. Finally both models were fine-tuned to convergence using the same instruction templates.

In the Vocabulary Expansion stage, we expanded the vocabulary of baichuan2 from 125696 tokens to 186181 tokens (including Uyghur) and 166911 tokens (excluding Uyghur).

In the Continue Pretraining stage, We adopted two pre-training schemes to verify the impact of the number of languages on translation performance

---

[1] https://github.com/fxsjy/jieba.
[2] https://github.com/hplt-project/sacremoses.
[3] https://github.com/rsennrich/subword-nmt.

and the difficulty of model pre-training convergence. The multilingual data for pretraining is shown in Table 2.

During the translation fine-tuning stage, our data partitioning is as shown in Table 3. For the pre-trained model that included Uyghur, we performed instruction fine-tuning for all the five translation directions. For the pre-trained model that did not include Uyghur, we excluded the Uyghur-to-Chinese translation task's instruction data.

Table 2. Data ratio for two pre-training strategies: 'w/ ug' includes five languages, while 'w/o ug' excludes Uyghur.

language	zh	en	ti	ug	mn
w/ ug	3M	6M	1.59M	1.7M	1.19M
w/o ug	3M	3M	1.59M	0	1.19M

Table 3. Multilingual parallel corpora for instruction data construction

language	zh-en	en-zh	ti-zh	ug-zh	mn-zh
All_data	7.58M	7.58M	159M	0.155M	1.17M
Processed	5.78M	5.78M	1.38M	0.147M	1.13M

3.2 Training

Multilingual Machine Translation System. We used seven A800-SXM4-80GB GPUs and employed llama-factory [18] as our training framework. During the pre-training phase, we applied full-parameter fine-tuning with a learning rate of 5e-5, utilized 2000 steps for warm-up to adjust parameters, and set the batch size to 8 per GPU. In the fine-tuning phase, we employed the LoRA method with the same learning rate of 5e-5, used 1200 steps for warm-up, and set the batch size to 24 per GPU. Additionally, we used fp16 to accelerate training in both phases.

Multi-domain Machine Translation System. We used four A800-SXM4-80GB GPUs and employed llama-factory as our training framework. For both instruction fine-tuning and APE fine-tuning phases, we applied the LoRA method with a learning rate of 5e-6, used 200 steps for warm-up to adjust parameters, and set the batch size to 24 per GPU. Similarly, we used fp16 to accelerate training in both phases.

3.3 Baseline

For multi-domain machine translation system, We trained a Transformer model on 20 million English-Chinese parallel corpus, which consists of 11 million patent parallel corpus resampling data, 7 million general parallel corpus provided by CCMT, and 2 million domain-specific data collected online using keywords. We also use OPUS-mt-zh-en model as another baseline. In the multilingual machine translation system, we consider single-direction translation fine-tuning as a reference for the upper limit of the model's ability after translation fine-tuning in that direction.

4 Results

The experimental results are divided into two sections: the multi-domain translation system and the multi-language translation system. In all experiments, translation performance was evaluated using BLEU scores [10] as the standard metric.

4.1 Multi-domain Machine Translation System

In our multi-domain translation system, we mainly investigate the impact of instruction construction methods and instruction ratios on model performance.

Our main results are shown in Table 4. We found that even without additional training, the large language model, when used with designed prompts, was able to outperform the Transformer model trained specifically for translation tasks. It also easily surpassed the existing translation model Opus-mt-zh-en. This indicates that large language models have great potential in multi-domain machine translation tasks.

We found that, under the Base-Instruction, high domain-relevance parallel corpora were more effective than low domain-relevance corpora, even with a smaller data volume. This indicates that domain relevance is crucial for multi-domain machine translation tasks.

The Table 4 also shows that using different instruction templates to create training data from the same parallel corpora results in varied translation performance after fine-tuning the model. Specifically, the Domain-Instruction template was less effective than the Base-Instruction template. During testing, we observed that models fine-tuned with Domain-Instruction struggled more to follow translation instructions, leading to less consistent outputs. Therefore, simpler instructions are more easily understood by the model, and merely specifying the domain of the source sentence does not improve translation performance.

However, we found that subsequent APE task instruction fine-tuning did not yield good results. This may be because most of the *mt* sentences in the training corpus required only minimal modifications to reach the *ref* sentences, so the APE task had almost no impact on the model's translation performance. Introducing an evaluation of the translation output to determine the necessary extent of modifications might improve this outcome.

Table 4. The results of Different Methods on the development Set.

Model	Data	Bleu
Transformer	20M	24.42
Opus-mt-zh-en	0	21.09
Qwen1.5-14b	0	24.38
+Low-domain relevance+Base-Instruction	240K	27.95
+High-domain relevance+Base-Instruction	40K	**30.84**
+High-domain relevance+Domain-Instruction	4K	26.35
+High-domain relevance+Base-Instruction+APE-Instruction	56K	30.69

4.2 Multilingual Machine Translation System

In our multilingual translation system, our primary goal is to explore how to enhance the performance of large language models in multilingual translation tasks. This includes examining the effects of pre-training ratios, instruction fine-tuning ratios, instruction construction methods, and their impact on translation tasks.

The results obtained after translation fine-tuning using the Base-Instruction are presented in Table 5. In this experiment, Chinese and English are among the model's original language capabilities, while Tibetan, Mongolian, and Uyghur are newly added languages. The pre-training scheme with more languages results in better translation performance for the newly added languages, but there is a relative decline in performance for the original languages. We can come to a conclusion that within limits, increasing the number of new languages will enhance the translation capabilities for those newly added languages.

Table 5. The results on the development set of CCMT 2022, Chinese-English, Tibetan-Chinese, Uyghur-Chinese, Mongolian-Chinese MT task and the development set of CCMT 2021 English-Chinese MT task (Due to issues with the 2022 development set). Comparison of Translation Performance Between Two Pre-training Schemes.

language	zh-en	en-zh	ti-zh	ug-zh	mn-zh
w/ ug	20.58	41.98	**25.01**	**41.87**	**41.38**
w/o ug	**22.88**	**42.01**	14.30	/	34.36

We have identified that adding three new languages can improve the pre-model translation performance. Based on this, we conducted single-direction translation instruction fine-tuning to validate the effectiveness of our multi-directional instruction fine-tuning. The single-direction translation fine-tuning results are shown in Table 6. Based on the experimental results, we can conclude that our multilingual translation instruction fine-tuning has achieved a good effect, approaching the upper limit of the model's capabilities in each direction when using unidirectional instruction fine-tuning.

Table 6. The results on the development set of CCMT 2022, Chinese-English, Tibetan-Chinese, Uyghur-Chinese, Mongolian-Chinese and the development set of CCMT 2021 English-Chinese MT task. Comparison of Results Between Unidirectional Translation Instruction Fine-tuning and Multidirectional Translation Instruction Fine-tuning.

language	zh-en	en-zh	ti-zh	ug-zh	mn-zh
all	20.58	41.98	25.01	41.87	41.38
ti-zh-only	/	/	**28.35**	/	/
ug-zh-only	/	/	/	**43.45**	/
mn-zh-only	/	/	/	/	**43.52**

5 Conclusion

In this paper, we describe our submission to CCMT 2024 on Chinese-English multilingual machine translation and multiple translation direction tasks. We used Qwen1.5-14b and Baichuan2 as backbone to develop multilingual and multi-domain machine translation models through methods like vocabulary expansion, domain classification, and instruction fine-tuning. Experimental results on the development set demonstrated the effectiveness of our approach.

It can be observed that large language models have outstanding potential in both multilingual and multi-domain machine translation tasks. We also determined the impact of instruction fine-tuning on the model's translation capabilities and the relationship between the number of languages and the translation performance of multilingual models.

In the future, we will expand our system to include more language varieties and domain types to validate the effectiveness of our proposed methods and the correctness of our theoretical assumptions.

References

1. Bai, J., et al.: Qwen technical report. In: arXiv preprint arXiv:2309.16609 (2023)
2. Brown, T., et al.: Language models are few-shot learners. Adv. Neural. Inf. Process. Syst. **33**, 1877–1901 (2020)
3. OpenCompass Contributors. OpenCompass: A Universal Evaluation Platform for Foundation Models. https://github.com/open-compass/opencompass (2023)
4. Duh, K.: The multitarget ted talks task (2018)
5. Huang, X., et al.: LUL's WMT22 automatic post-editing shared task submission. In: Proceedings of the Seventh Conference on Machine Translation (WMT), pp. 689–693 (2022)

6. Kudo, T., Richardson, J.: SentencePiece: A simple and language independent subword tokenizer and detokenizer for neural text processing. In: arXiv preprint arXiv:1808.06226 (2018)
7. Lee, J., et al.: POSTECH-ETRI's submission to the WMT2020 APE shared task: automatic post-editing with cross-lingual language model. In: Proceedings of the Fifth Conference on Machine Translation, pp. 777–782 (2020)
8. Li, J., et al.: Eliciting the translation ability of large language models via multilingual finetuning with translation instructions. Trans. Assoc. Comput. Linguist. **12**, 576–592 (2024)
9. Lin, X.V., et al.: Few-shot learning with multilingual generative language models. In: Proceedings of the 2022 Conference on Empirical Methods in Natural Language Processing, pp. 9019–9052 (2022)
10. Papineni, K., et al.: BLEU: a method for automatic evaluation of machine translation. In: Proceedings of the 40th Annual Meeting of the Association for Computational Linguistics, pp. 311–318 (2002)
11. Tian, L., et al.: UM-Corpus: a large English-Chinese parallel corpus for statistical machine translation. In: LREC, pp. 1837–1842 (2014)
12. Vaswani, A., et al.: Attention Is All You Need. In: arXiv (2017)
13. Vilar, D., et al.: Prompting palm for translation: Assessing strategies and performance. In: arXiv preprint arXiv:2211.09102 (2022)
14. Wang, J., et al.: Alibaba's submission for the WMT 2020 APE shared task: improving automatic post-editing with pre-trained conditional cross-lingual BERT. In: Proceedings of the Fifth Conference on Machine Translation, vol. 2020, pp. 789–796 (2020)
15. Xu, H., et al.: A paradigm shift in machine translation: Boosting translation performance of large language models. In: arXiv preprint arXiv:2309.11674 (2023)
16. Xu, L., Zhang, X., Dong, Q.: CLUECorpus2020: A large-scale Chinese corpus for pre-training language model. In: arXiv preprint arXiv:2003.01355 (2020)
17. Yang, A., et al.: Baichuan 2: Open large-scale language models. In: arXiv preprint arXiv:2309.10305 (2023)
18. Zheng, Y., et al.: LlamaFactory: unified efficient fine-tuning of 100+ language models. In: Proceedings of the 62nd Annual Meeting of the Association for Computational Linguistics (Volume 3: System Demonstrations). Bangkok, Thailand: Association for Computational Linguistics (2024). http://arxiv.org/abs/2403.13372
19. 哈里旦木·阿布都克里木 et al. "THUUyMorph: 维吾尔语形态分析语料库". In: 第十六届全国计算语言学学术会议暨第五届基于自然标注大数据的自然语言处理国际学术研讨会. 2017.

Incorporating Terminology Knowledge into Large Language Model for Domain-Specific Machine Translation

Xuan Zhao[1,2], Chong Feng[1,2(✉)], Shuanghong Huang[1,2], Jiangyu Wang[1,2], and Haojie Xu[1,2]

[1] Southeast Academy of Information Technology, Beijing Institute of Technology, Beijing, China
{zhaoxuan,fengchong,huangshuanghong,wangjiangyu,xuhaojie}@bit.edu.cn
[2] School of Computer Science and Technology, Beijing Institute of Technology, Beijing, China

Abstract. Utilizing a small amount of domain knowledge to achieve high-quality domain-specific translation is a challenging task. Nowadays, Large language model(LLM) is capable of generating more fluent and human-preferred translations through personalized instructions. However, in the field of domain-specific machine translation, the performance of LLM is inferior to traditional methods due to the lack of domain training data and the absence of domain transfer ability. To address the issue, we decided to incorporate terminology knowledge, which is crucial for accurately capturing the precise semantics of domain-specific texts. We design two types of terminology alignment instructions to enhance the model's cross-linguistic terminology alignment capability, explicitly integrating terminology knowledge into the model training process. According to the experiment, the model fine-tuned with MT+G-Align significantly outperformed the baseline through terminology translation accuracy and translation quality, demonstrating the effectiveness of the terminology alignment instructions. On the WMT 2023 Terminology Translation task, experimental results show that our approach achieves the best results in all three directions, including German-to-English, Chinese-to-English, and English-to-Chinese.

Keywords: Large language model · Domain-specific translation · Terminology alignment instruction

1 Introduction

In recent years, the Transformer-based model [1] has had a profound impact on the field of machine translation. It not only captures deep semantic information and effectively handles long-distance dependencies but also has advantages in parallel computing, significantly improving the quality and efficiency of machine translation. Its emergence marks the maturation of neural machine translation (NMT), and subsequent research has aimed to enhance NMT's translation quality through improvements in model architecture [2], training methods

[3], evaluation optimization [4], post-processing techniques [5], and other techniques. However, despite NMT's significant success in general translation tasks, it often performs poorly on domain-specific translation tasks. This is mainly because the knowledge and language used in specialized domains differs significantly from general language. NMT's models struggle to achieve optimal translation results due to the lack of domain-specific training data. Additionally, the end-to-end architecture makes it challenging to incorporate external knowledge, such as terminology, into the model.

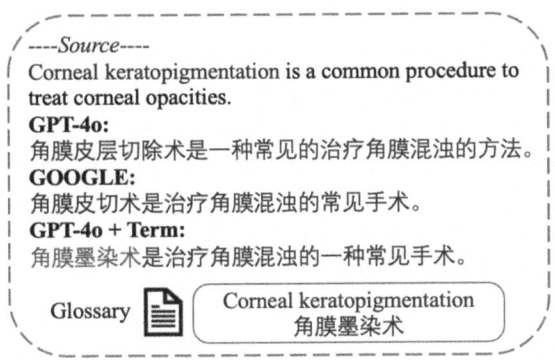

Fig. 1. Example of translating specialized English to Chinese.

Recent research in domain-specific translation, especially using large language models (LLMs), has shown significant potential in addressing complex challenges across different domains [6,7]. On one hand, large language models possess strong natural language understanding and generation capabilities, producing translations that better align with human preferences [8]. On the other hand, large language models were trained by vast amounts of data from multiple domains and languages, which makes it possible to build a unified translation model to solve multi-domain tasks [9]. One particular interest is the fact that large language models exhibit excellent instruction-following capabilities. It can generate translations in different styles based on specific users' instructions, meeting more diverse translation needs [10].

In this paper, we focus on a common scenario in domain translation, translating with the provision of bilingual terminological knowledge. This knowledge typically comes from a termbase that contains a set of source language terms and their corresponding translations in the target language. By providing terminology alignment instructions, we incorporate terminology information into the training and inference processes of large language models, enhancing translation quality for domain-specific texts. Two types of terminology alignment instructions (Align-Instruction) are designed, and the large language model is fine-tuned with these instructions to enhance its cross-language understanding and alignment capabilities. When encountering these predefined terms during translation, the model should use the corresponding translations from the termbase rather than inferring possible translations from context. Finally, inference is performed using instructions that include terminology information. As shown in Fig. 1, in specialized domain translation tasks, the absence of relevant terminological knowledge can prevent even the most advanced commercial NMT engines and large language models, such as GPT-4o, from accurately translating specific terms. The advantage of large language models lies in their instruction-following capability, which allows GPT-4o to correctly translate the terms "Corneal keratopigmentation" when the bilingual terminological knowledge is included in the task instructions.

The main contributions of this paper include the following:

- We propose two types of terminology alignment instructions that can effectively guide the model in learning the alignment relationships between bilingual terms.
- We incorporate weakly supervised terminology alignment information into the instruct-tuning process of large language models and explicitly utilize terminology information during inference, which enhanced the model's domain-specific translation quality and terminology translation accuracy.

2 Related Work

The comprehensive and powerful performance of LLMs has brought new opportunities to machine translation. The application of LLMs in machine translation has evolved from using large models for zero-shot translation to pre-training and fine-tuning large models to better adapt to translation tasks. Hendy et al. [11] conducted a comprehensive evaluation of GPT-3.5's translation capabilities, selecting 18 different translation directions and comparing it with the latest research and Microsoft Translator. The study revealed that GPT-3.5 performs excellently in translating high-resource languages, with particularly notable fluency in the translations. However, it is significantly weaker than professional translation systems in low-resource languages. Zhu et al. [12] evaluated several open-source multilingual models across 102 languages and 606 translation directions. Their research indicates that the multilingual translation capabilities of large language models are continuously improving, but a larger model does not always equate to better performance. For instance, LLaMA2-7B outperforms previous open-source models. However, there is an imbalance in the capabilities of these models across different languages. They excel in languages similar to English (such as those in the Indo-European family) but generally perform poorly in other languages (such as those in the Sino-Tibetan family).

MAPS [13] prompting method, which encourages LLMs to analyze a given source sentence from three perspectives: keywords in the sentence, the sentence's theme, and the generation of relevant examples. This knowledge is then used to guide the model in translation. It outperforms 5-shot prompting in both automatic and manual evaluations, effectively mitigating issues of hallucination and ambiguity in the model. Zhang et al. [14]conducted a detailed study on the impact of prompt templates and example selection on the model's contextual learning performance. They find significant performance differences across various prompt templates, recommending the use of simple English prompts. Additionally, using more examples can significantly enhance translation quality, although there is no universally optimal number of examples. DiPMT [15] uses prior knowledge from bilingual dictionaries to provide a set of possible translations for certain words in the source sentence, enabling fine-grained, phrase-level prompt control. Experiments show that DiPMT prompts outperform the original prompts in low-resource and out-of-domain scenarios. Liang et al. [16] and Chan et al. [17] employed two LLM agents to engage in multiple rounds of debate, determining the translation output based on the results of the debate. Wu et al. [18] utilized tripartite collaboration and addition-subtraction cooperation among multiple LLM agents to tackle complex literary translation tasks for long texts.

BigTranslate [19] expanded the multilingual translation capabilities of the English-centric LLaMA model to handle 102 languages. This was achieved by continuing to train LLaMA with large-scale monolingual Chinese data and parallel corpora covering 102 languages, followed by fine-tuning the model with multilingual translation instructions. BayLing [20], built on the LLaMA foundation, is a Chinese-English instruction-following large language model. It was fine-tuned with interactive translation instructions, achieving 96% of GPT-3.5's interactive translation capability according to human evaluation. Xu et al. [21] proposed a new training paradigm for LLMs targeting machine translation tasks, which enhances translation performance without relying on large amounts of parallel corpora. The model is first fine-tuned on monolingual data to improve multilingual capabilities and then fine-tuned for translation tasks using a small amount of high-quality parallel corpora. The ALMA model developed based on this strategy significantly outperforms previous open-source models across 10 translation directions.

3 Approach

In this section, we introduce two terminology-enhanced translation optimization methods for large language models.

3.1 MT-Instruct

Machine Translation Instructions (MT-Instruct) aim to introduce translation tasks into large language models to activate their translation capabilities. Previous research has demonstrated the effectiveness of fine-tuning with machine translation instructions, highlighting the importance of designing such instructions. Two key points to consider are the language used for the instructions and the format of the instruction templates. In this study, English instructions are uniformly used. Based on research [22] indicating that optimal performance is achieved when using only English instructions in multilingual tasks. Additionally, it reduces the workload of designing instructions for specific languages.

Table 1. Translation performance of different instruction templates

No.	Template	Zh ⇒ En	
		BLEU	COMET
1	X:[SRC]\n Y:[TGT]	22.50	79.30
2	Translate this to Y:\n X:[SRC]\n Y:[TGT]	22.67	79.36
3	Translate this from X to Y:\n X:[SRC]\n Y:[TGT]	**22.73**	**79.40**
4	[SRC]\n Translate this to Y:\n [TGT]	22.06	79.31

Another reason is that most LLMs are centered around English and are more accustomed to understanding and executing English instructions.

We design four instruction templates and conduct experiments on the WMT-22 Chinese to English test set, with results presented in Table 1. X and Y represent the language, while [SRC] and [TGT] denote the source language sentence and the target language sentence. The results show that the choice of template has a certain impact on the model's translation performance. However, after instruction fine-tuning, the differences between the various templates become quite minimal. Among the four templates, Template 3 showed the best overall performance and was thus selected as the default instruction template for this experiment. During the training phase, X, Y, [SRC], and [TGT] are all populated. During the inference phase, [TGT] is predicted by the model.

3.2 Terminology Alignment Instructions

We design two terminology alignment instructions (Align-Instruct) to enhance the model's cross-linguistic terminology alignment capabilities. It explicitly integrates terminological knowledge into the model training process, ensuring that the model accurately aligns terms from the source language to their equivalent terms in the target language during translation.

To obtain aligned bilingual terms, we first use a span-based term extraction model [23] to extract monolingual term sets in the source language and the target language. Since the terminology extraction model is primarily trained on English and similar languages, and the datasets used in this section involve English translation pairs (en ⇒ xx and xx ⇒ en), terminology extraction is uniformly performed on the English side.

After extracting the English terms, the neural network-based word alignment tool SimAlign [24] is used for terminology alignment. Given a source language sentence $X = \{x_1, x_2, x_3, \ldots, x_{|S|}\}$ and a target language sentence $Y = \{y_1, y_2, y_3, \ldots, y_{|T|}\}$, SimAlign outputs the corresponding word y_i for each x_i in the target language. It is important to note that multiple words in the source language might correspond to a single word in the target language. For the term "$x_k x_{k+1} x_{k+2}$" in the source language sentence, the corresponding term "$y_k y_{k+1}$" can be identified in the target language based on the word alignment results.

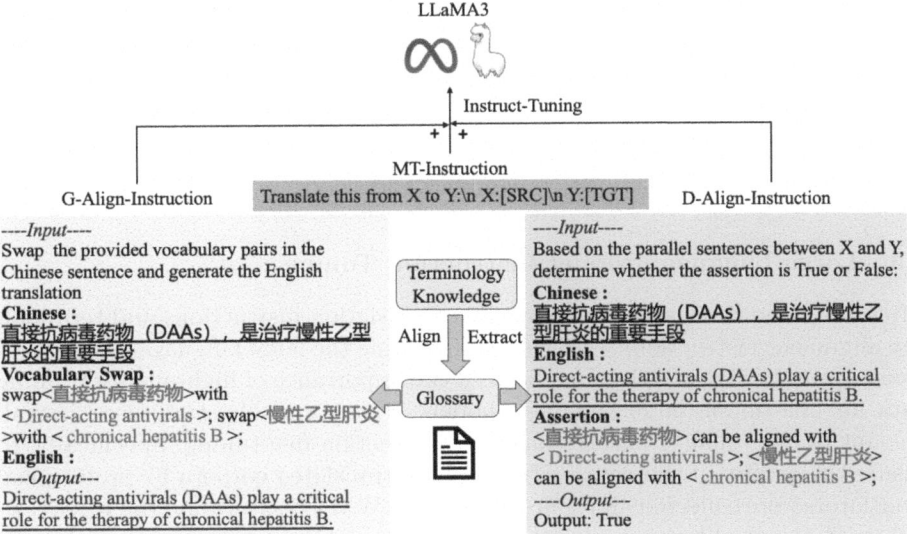

Fig. 2. Diagram of Instruct-tuning on LLaMA3

After obtaining bilingual term pairs, we design two types of terminology alignment instructions: Discriminative Terminology Alignment Instructions (D-Align) and Generative Terminology Alignment Instructions (G-Align) presented in Fig. 2. By using these two alignment instructions, the model can better utilize aligned knowledge of "Direct-acting antivirals" and "chronical hepatitis B" to guide the decoding process when additional bilingual terminology is introduced.

The Discriminative Terminology Alignment Instruction requires the model to determine whether the source language term $x_k x_{k+1} x_{k+2}$ and the target language term $y_k y_{k+1}$ are aligned based on the provided parallel sentence pair. For samples where the output is False, the correct term in the source or target language is randomly replaced. For example, for the term pair (S_1, T_1), another term from the target language sentence is randomly selected to replace T_1. If there is only one term in the sentence, a random contiguous segment of the sentence is used for replacement. It is important to note that each instruction only judges whether one term pair is aligned, so multiple discriminative alignment instruction samples can be constructed from a single original example. Through instructions, the large language model can learn and determine the alignment relationship between source and target language terms, better understanding the mutual relations and mapping rules between different languages, thereby enhancing the model's cross-linguistic comprehension and alignment capabilities.

The Generative Terminology Alignment Instruction requires the model to translate a source language sentence into the target language based on the provided bilingual aligned terms, ensuring that the terms are translated into the given corresponding translations. Compared to the Discriminative Alignment

Instruction, the Generative Alignment Instruction is more challenging: the translation task is evidently more difficult than a binary judgment task, and there are additional terminology constraints, making it a form of "controlled" translation. The purpose of the Generative Alignment Instruction is to enable the model to learn how to use alignment knowledge to guide its decoding process based on its understanding of cross-linguistic alignment knowledge.

3.3 Large Language Model Instruction Tuning

After designing the instructions, machine translation instructions and terminology alignment instructions were used to fine-tune the large language model. Previous research [21,25,26] has emphasized the importance of high-quality training data for fine-tuning large language models. Therefore, this study uses a small amount of high-quality parallel data for instruction fine-tuning. Specifically, to ensure the quality of the data, only manually translated corpora by professional translators were collected and sourced from the WMT test sets and the FLORES-200 validation and test sets.

The loss function for instruction fine-tuning is the same as for the pre-training task, namely the language modeling loss (LM loss). The only difference is that the instruction part does not participate in the loss calculation. Machine translation instructions are fundamental for enhancing the translation capabilities of large language models, so all original training samples are converted into machine translation instructions for model fine-tuning. Terminology alignment instructions are used in conjunction with machine translation instructions, specifically as MT+D-Align and MT+G-Align. During the inference phase, G-Align instructions are used if bilingual terminology knowledge is available. MT instructions are used if knowledge of bilingual terminology is not available.

4 Experiments

4.1 Settings

We use the WMT23 terminology evaluation task test set to verify the effectiveness of the optimization methods. This test set provides not only the source language sentences but also an additional sentence-level terminology dictionary, which pre-defines the corresponding translations for some terms in the source language sentence. For example, for German ⇒ English translation, the model can receive a German sentence "Der Bericht entspricht FOG" and a terminology dictionary "entspricht ⇒ compliant," "FOG ⇒ ROA." The WMT23 terminology test set includes three translation directions: German ⇒ English, Chinese ⇒ English, and English ⇒ Czech. The dataset statistics are shown in Table 2.

The training data for this study comes from the WMT17 to WMT20 test sets and the FLORES-200 [27] validation and test sets, all of which were manually translated by professional translators, totaling 42,000 sentences. The validation set is derived from the WMT21 validation set, with 2,000 sentences for each translation direction.

This study employs three automatic translation evaluation metrics: BLEU, ChrF, and COMET. ChrF and COMET are the evaluation metrics used in the WMT23 terminology evaluation task, while BLEU is the most widely used metric in the field of machine translation. Additionally, this study reports the model's terminology translation accuracy. This accuracy is assessed by using a string-matching method to determine whether the target terminology appears in the machine translation output, evaluating the model's ability to utilize terminology knowledge.

Table 2. WMT23 terminology test set

Direction	Samples	Terms	Avg_Length	Avg_Terms
De $\Rightarrow$ En	2938	11347	19.1/19.5	3.85
Zh $\Rightarrow$ En	1638	2275	40.7/34.2	1.35
En $\Rightarrow$ Cs	2898	10586	22.0/18.6	3.65

4.2 Training Details

We verify the effectiveness of the proposed methods by conducting instruction fine-tuning on ALMA-7B and LLaMA-3-8B. For training efficiency, LoRA is used for parameter-efficient fine-tuning, with the rank set to 16, requiring updates to only 0.1% of the model parameters. The models are trained for 2 epochs with a learning rate of 1e-4, a batch size of 16, and both the maximum input and output lengths set to 256. During inference, the beam search parameter is set to 5, top_p is 0.6, and temperature is 0.9. All models are loaded using FP16 precision, and the training process is optimized using Accelerate and DeepSpeed, allowing the models to be trained and inferred on a single NVIDIA A100-40G GPU.

4.3 Baselines

We select the winning models from the WMT23 terminology evaluation task and several large language models as baselines for comparison. All the large language models use G-Align instructions to incorporate bilingual terminology information into the inference process.

WMT23-LC. The model that performed best in the WMT23 terminology evaluation task for German $\Rightarrow$ English and English $\Rightarrow$ Czech (based on the ChrF metric) uses an unsupervised method to extract bilingual terminology from the training data. It employs special markers to concatenate the target terms to the source language terms, and this concatenated input is used to train a Transformer architecture model.

WMT23-LC. The model performed best in the WMT23 terminology evaluation task across three language directions (based on the COMET metric). It was trained using a method similar to WMT23-LC to train a Transformer model, and then optimized the model outputs using GPT-3.5.

WMT23-AdaptTerm. GPT-3.5 was utilized to generate pseudo-parallel corpora containing terminology based on seed terms. This generated corpus was then combined with general domain corpora for mixed fine-tuning of the Transformer model. Finally, GPT-3.5 was employed for post-editing. It is important to note that during training, this model did not add the corresponding target terms to the source language sentences.

LLaMA-2-7B. This is currently the most widely used open-source large language model, known for its balanced performance.

ALMA-7B. ALMA-7B is based on LLaMA-2-7B and has been further pre-trained on monolingual data in six languages to enhance LLaMA's multilingual capabilities.

Gemma-7B. This is Google's latest lightweight large language model, with a maximum parameter size of 7B. It outperforms LLaMA-2 in several key benchmark tests.

LLaMA-3-8B. This is Meta's latest large language model, released in April 2024. This study promptly updated the experimental settings to explore LLaMA-3's translation capabilities. LLaMA-3 expanded its vocabulary size from 32K to 128K, increasing the parameter size from 7B to 8B.

5 Results and Analysis

5.1 Main Results

Table 3 presents the experimental results of this chapter's methods compared with other baseline models on the WMT23 terminology test set. The results indicate that: (1) LLaMA-3-8B and ALMA-7B, fine-tuned with terminology alignment instructions, significantly outperform the baseline models, especially with the MT+G-Align instruction combination, which markedly improves the translation performance of LLMs; (2) Both the discriminative terminology alignment instruction (D-Align) and the generative terminology alignment instruction (G-Align) enhance the models' translation performance, with G-Align showing a more pronounced improvement due to its consistency with the input format during the inference phase; (3) Explicitly utilizing terminology information during inference can effectively improve translation quality. For instance, LLaMA-3-8B before fine-tuning already outperformed the WMT23 winning models in German $\Rightarrow$ English and Chinese $\Rightarrow$ English translations, demonstrating the advantage of large language models in domain-specific translation.

Table 3. Results of the WMT23 Terminology Test Set. The * were translated twice by using GPT-3.5

Model	De ⇒ En			Zh ⇒ En			En ⇒ Cs		
	BLEU	ChrF	COMET	BLEU	ChrF	COMET	BLEU	ChrF	COMET
WMT-LC	27.20	61.80	73.50	9.74	32.60	60.86	42.70	67.67	83.36
WMT-AT*	28.51	60.99	80.14	11.92	37.52	68.67	38.29	64.43	84.08
WMT-UEDIN*	28.30	60.00	81.31	14.10	41.17	75.69	37.70	64.80	86.94
LLaMA-2-7B	30.39	61.61	81.20	13.37	38.37	71.95	28.39	54.63	80.21
Gemma-7B	31.89	62.70	80.80	12.59	35.77	67.83	28.85	54.89	75.54
ALMA-7B									
w/o finetuing	26.24	57.14	79.47	11.45	35.20	70.68	32.90	69.07	84.49
MT+D-Align	26.66	56.52	80.30	13.88	38.65	73.15	33.30	59.75	86.56
MT+G-Align	**35.36**	**64.99**	**82.53**	**15.34**	**40.68**	74.37	44.26	**69.04**	**88.79**
LLaMA-3-8B									
w/o finetuing	32.38	63.27	81.74	15.22	41.07	74.09	35.68	61.99	83.65
MT+D-Align	34.36	63.28	82.19	16.43	41.46	74.23	39.80	64.92	87.52
MT+G-Align	**37.27**	**66.31**	**83.12**	**16.47**	**42.02**	**75.88**	**44.36**	**69.28**	**89.12**

Table 4 shows the accuracy of the terminology translation for each model. It can be observed that the models' performance in terminology translation accuracy does not consistently align with their overall translation quality. For example, WMT-UEDIN has a significantly higher COMET score than WMT-LC but lags behind in terminology translation accuracy. This indicates that merely improving terminology translation accuracy at the syntactic level does not ensure an overall enhancement in translation quality; it is also necessary to understand the semantic context of the entire sentence. LLaMA-3-8B, fine-tuned with MT+G-Align, achieves the highest terminology translation accuracy and the best translation quality, demonstrating the effectiveness of terminology instruction fine-tuning.

5.2 Generalizability Analysis

To verify the generalizability of the methods proposed in this chapter, experiments were conducted on the WMT22 general domain test set, which does not provide a bilingual terminology dictionary. In this section, ALMA-7B was fine-tuned with instructions, with training data and experimental settings identical to those in Sect. 4.2, without any specific modifications. Multiple large language models fine-tuned for machine translation tasks were selected for comparison. BigTranslate extends the multilingual translation capabilities of LLaMA-1, supporting 102 languages. BayLing is an instruction-following large language model for Chinese-English translation, supporting multi-turn interactive translation. TIM [28] enhances the translation ability of LLMs by comparing correct

Table 4. Terminology translation accuracy

Model	De ⇒ En	Zh ⇒ En	En ⇒ Cs
WMT-LC	60.93	88.62	61.13
WMT-AT*	59.82	88.79	54.34
WMT-UEDIN*	55.81	80.66	55.14
LLaMA-2-7B	71.29	77.93	54.74
Gemma-7B	77.28	79.21	55.35
ALMA-7B			
w/o finetuing	55.66	72.92	54.05
MT+D-Align	53.13	73.23	51.19
MT+G-Align	**77.57**	**90.07**	**73.34**
LLaMA-3-8B			
w/o finetuing	77.85	89.36	62.97
MT+D-Align	77.43	88.91	65.67
MT+G-Align	**87.85**	**93.71**	**77.68**

and incorrect translation samples. SWIE [29] introduces an additional instruction representation layer and an instruction-following dataset to improve the translation capabilities of LLMs. In the experiments, all large language models used the template "Translate this from X to Y:\n X:[SRC]\n Y:" for inference.

As shown in Table 5, the COMET scores of MT+G-Align are superior to those of previous open-source large language models, with the only exceptions being a 0.75 BLEU point deficit to BayLing-13B in English ⇒Chinese translation and a 0.47 BLEU point deficit to LLaMA-2-7B in German ⇒ English translation. Many studies have found that the LLaMA-2 model performs exceptionally well in German⇒ English translation, and instruction fine-tuning can sometimes reduce performance. This might be due to the fact that most of the training data for LLaMA is in English, giving it an advantage in generating English text. The performance gap between MT+D-Align and MT+G-Align narrows in general domain translation tasks, with the COMET score differences being within 0.5 points.

In comparison with state-of-the-art (SoTA) models, MT+G-Align's performance is very close to GPT-3.5-text-davinci-003 and exceeds that of the traditional NMT large model NLLB-54B in three translation directions. However, there is still a gap of about 5 points compared to GPT-4. This highlights that while large language models possess strong translation capabilities, often surpassing NMT models in certain scenarios, there remains a significant performance difference between open-source and closed-source models. In summary, the experimental results demonstrate that terminology alignment instructions, by enhancing the cross-linguistic alignment capabilities of the model, can effectively improve the multilingual translation performance of LLMs.

Table 5. WMT22 general domain test set results

Model	En ⇒ Dd		En ⇒ Zh		De ⇒ En		Zh ⇒ En	
	BLEU	COMET	BLEU	COMET	BLEU	COMET	BLEU	COMET
NLLB-54B [27]	34.50	86.45	27.38	78.91	26.89	78.94	16.56	70.70
GPT3.5-davinc	31.80	85.61	38.30	85.76	30.90	84.79	25.00	81.62
GPT-4	35.38	87.44	43.98	87.49	33.87	85.62	27.20	82.79
SWIE-LLaMA-1-7B	27.21	82.36	31.24	80.63	29.92	82.97	21.30	76.48
TIM-LLaMA-1-7B	25.59	82.56	19.33	75.46	27.91	82.80	19.33	75.46
LLaMA-2-7B	19.00	76.39	16.97	71.80	**30.42**	82.74	18.19	75.00
BigTranslate-13B	21.48	78.81	28.56	81.31	23.35	80.68	14.16	74.26
Bayling-13B	25.62	82.69	**37.92**	84.62	27.34	83.02	20.12	77.72
ALMA-7B								
w/o finetuing	27.44	84.17	28.51	81.56	28.28	82.48	15.30	74.13
MT+D-Align	29.05	84.86	35.47	84.88	29.58	83.95	22.38	79.20
MT+G-Align	**29.49**	**85.28**	37.17	**85.31**	29.85	**84.21**	**22.83**	**79.57**

5.3 Instruction Combination Analysis

Command Combination Analysis The previous experimental setup included only two command combinations: MT+D-Align and MT+G-Align. This section compares more command combinations, namely MT-only, G-Align-only, and MT+D-Align+G-Align. The experiments were conducted on the WMT23 terminology test set, with fine-tuning performed on the ALMA-7B model. The results are shown in Table 6.

By fine-tuning with MT instructions, the model's COMET scores improved by 0.21, 2.47, and 1.91 points for the three language directions, respectively. However, the BLEU and ChrF scores for German-to-English translation decreased. This indicates that fine-tuning using only MT commands does not consistently enhance the model's translation ability in specialized domains, highlighting the necessity of terminology alignment commands. It was found that after fine-tuning with only the D-Align command, the model refused to output translations; thus, the results are not reported. This is because the D-Align command is designed to determine whether two terms are aligned without incorporating the translation task. The effect of the G-Align command was significantly better than that of the MT command and was already close to MT+G-Align, demonstrating that the improvement in model translation performance mainly comes from the G-Align command. Combining all three commands did not further enhance model performance. This is likely because both D-Align and G-Align data were derived from the same original examples, and data redundancy did not provide additional gains.

Table 6. Different instruction combinations

Model	De ⇒ En			Zh ⇒ En			En ⇒ Cs		
	BLEU	ChrF	COMET	BLEU	ChrF	COMET	BLEU	ChrF	COMET
MT+G-Align	**35.36**	**64.99**	**82.53**	**15.34**	**40.68**	**74.37**	**44.26**	**69.04**	**88.79**
w/o finetuing	26.24	57.14	79.47	11.45	35.20	70.68	32.90	59.07	84.49
MT	25.91	54.88	79.68	13.78	38.49	73.15	32.37	59.07	86.40
G-Align	34.86	63.66	82.31	14.42	39.63	74.21	42.24	67.74	88.76
MT+G+D	34.18	63.32	82.20	14.52	40.20	74.18	41.74	67.20	88.59

6 Conclusion

In this paper, we propose a terminology-enhanced optimization method for domain-specific translation. This approach effectively improved the translation quality and terminology translation accuracy of large language models in domain-specific tasks. Additionally, experimental results in the general domain demonstrated the method's versatility, as it was still able to provide high-quality translation results even without the provision of terminology knowledge. The experimental results show that our model achieves excellent performance on the manually annotated test set and outperforms previous models in DE-EN, ZH-EN and EN-CS.

Our method's limitation is that it requires high-quality terms derived from terminology extraction and alignment from bilingual parallel corpora. Therefore, future work could explore using large models to perform bilingual terminology extraction and alignment directly. Furthermore, we should try the method across various domains to examine its applicability.

References

1. Vaswani, A., et al.: Attention is all you need. Adv. Neural Inf. Process. Syst. **30** (2017)
2. Bapna, A., Arivazhagan, N., Firat, O.: Simple, scalable adaptation for neural machine translation. arXiv preprint arXiv:1909.08478 (2019)
3. Zhang, Z., Liu, S., Li, M., Zhou, M., Chen, E.: Joint training for neural machine translation models with monolingual data. In: Proceedings of the AAAI Conference on Artificial Intelligence, volume 32 (2018)
4. Rei, R., et al.: CometKiwi: IST-unbabel 2022 submission for the quality estimation shared task. arXiv preprint arXiv:2209.06243 (2022)
5. Chollampatt, S., Susanto, R.H., Tan, L., Szymanska, E.: Can automatic post-editing improve NMT? In: Webber, B., Cohn, T., He, Y., Liu, Y. (eds.) Proceedings of the 2020 Conference on Empirical Methods in Natural Language Processing (EMNLP), pp. 2736–2746, Online, November (2020). Association for Computational Linguistics
6. Zheng, J., Hong, H., Wang, X., Su, J., Liang, Y., Wu, S.: Fine-tuning large language models for domain-specific machine translation. arXiv preprint arXiv:2402.15061 (2024)

7. Keles, B., Gunay, M., Caglar, S.I.: LLMs-in-the-loop part-1: Expert small AI models for bio-medical text translation. arXiv preprint arXiv:2407.12126 (2024)
8. Wang, Y., et al.: Aligning large language models with human: A survey. arXiv preprint arXiv:2307.12966 (2023)
9. Hadi, M.U., et al.: Large language models: a comprehensive survey of its applications, challenges, limitations, and future prospects. Authorea Preprints (2023)
10. Jiao, W., et al.: ParroT: Translating during chat using large language models tuned with human translation and feedback. arXiv preprint arXiv:2304.02426 (2023)
11. Hendy, A., et al.: How good are GPT models at machine translation? A comprehensive evaluation. arXiv preprint arXiv:2302.09210 (2023)
12. Zhu, W., et al.: Multilingual machine translation with large language models: Empirical results and analysis. arXiv preprint arXiv:2304.04675 (2023)
13. He, Z., et al.: Exploring human-like translation strategy with large language models. Trans. Assoc. Comput. Linguist. **12**, 229–246 (2024)
14. Zhang, B., Haddow, B., Birch, A.: Prompting large language model for machine translation: a case study. In: International Conference on Machine Learning, pp. 41092–41110. PMLR (2023)
15. Ghazvininejad, M., Gonen, H., Zettlemoyer, L.: Dictionary-based phrase-level prompting of large language models for machine translation. arXiv preprint arXiv:2302.07856 (2023)
16. Liang, T., et al.: Encouraging divergent thinking in large language models through multi-agent debate. arXiv preprint arXiv:2305.19118 (2023)
17. Chan, C.-M., et al.: ChatEval: Towards better LLM-based evaluators through multi-agent debate. arXiv preprint arXiv:2308.07201 (2023)
18. Wu, M., Yuan, Y., Haffari, G., Wang, L.: (perhaps) beyond human translation: Harnessing multi-agent collaboration for translating ultra-long literary texts. arXiv preprint arXiv:2405.11804 (2024)
19. Yang, W., Li, C., Zhang, J., Zong, C.: BigTranslate: Augmenting large language models with multilingual translation capability over 100 languages. arXiv preprint arXiv:2305.18098 (2023)
20. Zhang, S., et al.: BayLing: Bridging cross-lingual alignment and instruction following through interactive translation for large language models. arXiv preprint arXiv:2306.10968 (2023)
21. Xu, H., Kim, Y.J., Sharaf, A., Awadalla, H.H.: A paradigm shift in machine translation: Boosting translation performance of large language models. arXiv preprint arXiv:2309.11674 (2023)
22. Muennighoff, N., et al.: Crosslingual generalization through multitask finetuning. arXiv preprint arXiv:2211.01786 (2022)
23. Wang, J., Feng, C., Liu, F., Li, X., Wang, X.: Extract then adjust: a two-stage approach for automatic term extraction. In: CCF International Conference on Natural Language Processing and Chinese Computing, pp. 236–247. Springer (2023)
24. Sabet, M.J., Dufter, P., Yvon, F., Schütze, H.: SimAlign: high quality word alignments without parallel training data using static and contextualized embeddings. arXiv preprint arXiv:2004.08728 (2020)
25. Gunasekar, S., et al.: Textbooks are all you need. arXiv preprint arXiv:2306.11644 (2023)
26. Zhou, C., et al.: LIMA: Less is more for alignment. Adv. Neural Inf. Process. Syst. **36** (2024)
27. Costa-jussà, M.R., et al.: No language left behind: Scaling human-centered machine translation. arXiv preprint arXiv:2207.04672 (2022)

28. Zeng, J., Meng, F., Yin, Y., Zhou, J.: TIM: Teaching large language models to translate with comparison. arXiv preprint arXiv:2307.04408 (2023)
29. Chen, Y., Liu, Y., Meng, F., Chen, Y., Xu, J., Zhou, J.: Improving translation faithfulness of large language models via augmenting instructions. arXiv preprint arXiv:2308.12674 (2023)

Multi-modal Translation

Joint Multi-modal Modeling for Speech-to-Text Translation as Multilingual Neural Machine Translation

Jiale Ou, Hongfei Xu, and Hongying Zan(✉)

School of Computer Science and Artificial Intelligence, Zhengzhou University,
Hennan 450000, China
iehyzan@zzu.edu.cn

Abstract. Joint modeling or multi-task learning by applying speech and text encoders can improve the performance of end-to-end speech translation (E2E ST) with the help of large-scale speech recognition and text translation data in previous work. However, most existing methods require architectural changes of ST training, and the modality gap between speech and text makes it hard to encode both of them with a shared encoder. In this paper, we regard the joint modeling for speech translation and text translation as multilingual NMT modeling, using a single encoder for both speech and text processing. We empirically show that the modality gap can be effectively addressed by modeling modality-aware relative position encoding in the self-attention layer. Experiments on three benchmarks covering 23 languages show that joint modeling over internal/external speech recognition and text translation data, the performance of our single encoder method can lead to significant improvements on multiple ST tasks in both directions (from and to English) compared to the baselines.

Keywords: Joint modeling · E2E ST · Multilingual NMT · Relative position encoding

1 Introduction

Speech-to-text Translation (ST) task aims to translate source language speech into target language text and is widely used in various scenarios such as international conferences. Different from the traditional cascade models which use separate Automatic Speech Recognition (ASR) and Machine Translation (MT) systems, End-to-End (E2E) ST directly translates the speech in the source language into corresponding text in the target language [1,2]. This approach benefits from low latency and avoids error propagation, making it more attractive for speech translation tasks and leading to great success recently [3–10].

However, the scarcity of aligned speech-transcription-translation supervised data poses challenges for E2E ST. To alleviate this issue, previous studies utilize methods such as pre-training [11–14], multi-task learning [15–17] or data augmentation [18,19], leveraging ASR or MT models pre-trained on external speech or text data for acoustic and/or text encoding, and fine-tune the pre-trained models using ST data. Despite such ubiquity, the natural modality gap between speech and text representations means that the above methods do not always bring gains, and often necessitate more complex model architectures. Similar to Multilingual Neural Machine Translation (MNMT), jointly modeling ST with text-to-text translation and speech recognition can simplify the architecture and help align speech-text representations via dual encoder and shared encoder architecture. But due to the encoding differences between the modalities, sharing the encoder between speech and text may still lead to suboptimal ST performance [20].

In this paper, we explore how to effectively encode speech and text with a single encoder to jointly model speech and text translation/recognition tasks with not only a shared decoder but also a shared encoder, i.e., in an MNMT manner. We observe a significant length and distance dependency differences between speech and the corresponding text sequences for the same sentence, and conjecture that this modality gap during encoding may get effectively addressed by using different relative position encoding methods in the self-attention layer. Based on this, we propose a modality-aware relative position encoding method and extend MNMT architectures for the joint modeling in E2E ST. Moreover, considering that the quality of external text may directly affect the final performance of ST, we utilize a translation-loss-based method to select more relevant text translation data for joint modeling. Our main contributions are as follows:

- We propose a cross-modality encoding approach using a single encoder by modeling modality-aware relative position encodings in the self-attention layer. Additionally, we select more appropriate text data for training based on translation loss.
- Based on the shared encoder across speech and text inputs, we show that joint multi-modal translation can also be facilitated in a simple MNMT manner, and the translation performance of all modalities can be preserved or even improved.
- Experiments on MuST-C, CoVoST 2 and Librispeech tasks show that our methods can also improve the strong E2E ST baselines by leveraging both internal/external speech recognition and text translation data with a simple MNMT architecture.

2 Related Work

How to better utilize large-scale ASR and MT data, and how to solve the modeling difficulties caused by the modality gap are two major concerns among E2E ST work. Many studies have applied pre-training (or multi-task learning) methods to utilize these data, by sharing some parameters of ST modules and ASR/MT modules in the backbone model, and leveraging the knowledge of auxiliary tasks to alleviate the modality gap to obtain good ST performance.

Recent studies involve employing additional encoders/decoders for ASR/MT, such as the decoupled decoder, decoupled encoder, and two-stream encoder [21]. Decoupled decoder utilizes two decoders to generate transcription and translation simultaneously (dual decoder) [22,23] or sequentially generate transcription to guide the generation of translation (two-pass decoder) [24,25]. Decoupled encoder is similar to the cascade method, which encodes acoustic information via a speech encoder and learns the semantic representation necessary for decoding via a semantic encoder [26,27]. In contrast, two-stream encoder can simultaneously utilize both speech and text. It accepts either speech or text or both as inputs during training, utilizing independent speech and text encoders [7,28], then the method optimizes a shared encoder with multi-task training losses. However, all fore-mentioned methods utilize additional encoder or decoder. Considering that this will lead to a complicated architecture consuming additional training time and resources, some studies use a single encoder-decoder system with additional data to unify speech and text pre-training in one model [29–31], which can also perform multi-modal translation but requires fine-tuning on specific tasks to achieve good performance. We summarize the existing problems and provide a simple architecture sharing both the encoder and the decoder, which is able to use additional external data for joint modeling while retaining the ability to directly perform multi-modal translation including speech translation and text translation without specific fine-tuning.

In addition to fine-tuning the pre-trained modules, integrating adapter modules into encoder and/or decoder layers can also help bridge the modality gap by converting the encoding form of one modality to another or aligning sequence lengths between speech and text [32–34]. However, in addition to the different number of tokens required to represent the same word in speech and text inputs, the modality gap is also manifested in the distance between dependent words, which may make it hard for the FFN adapters to address the mismatch of attention patterns in the self-attention layer between modalities, but this aspect remains underexplored. For this reason, we propose that using different relative position encoding for different modalities can handle the distance discrepancy across modalities through the learning of modality specific relative distance patterns.

3 Mixed Speech/Text Translation as MNMT

3.1 Problem Definition

The corpus for speech translation tasks is usually composed of speech-transcription-translation triples, which can be expressed as $D = (s, x, y)$. $s = [s_1, s_2, \ldots, s_{|s|}]$, $x = [x_1, x_2, \ldots, x_{|x|}]$ and $y = [y_1, y_2, \ldots, y_{|y|}]$ denote the speech, transcription and translation sequences respectively. For the input speech sequence s, the standard training goal is to optimize the maximum likelihood estimation (MLE) loss of the training data.

$$\mathcal{L}_{\mathrm{CE}}(s,y) = -\sum_{i=1}^{|y|} \log p(y_i|s, y_{<i}) \qquad (1)$$

3.2 Model Architecture

By adding target language tokens to each source language sentence [35], multilingual translation can be achieved with a single model [36,37]. Multilingual NMT combines multilingual methods [38–40] and often uses Transformer model [41] as the backbone architecture, following the encoder-decoder paradigm [42].

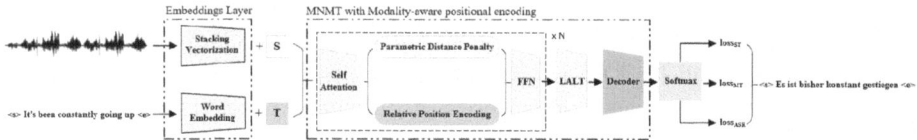

Fig. 1. Overview of our proposed framework. In the embedding layer, token embeddings are directly used for text inputs, while speech inputs generate embeddings based on speech feature extraction, stacking and vectorization. After adding the corresponding modality tokens, the embeddings are fed into encoder layers with modality-aware positional encoding method. The same cross-entropy loss is used for all three tasks, and their sum is optimized.

For Transformer based MNMT, the encoder consists of N identical layers, each containing a self-attention sub-layer and a position-wise feed-forward sub-layer. The decoder is similar to the encoder but includes an additional cross-attention sub-layer to attend the encoder outputs. Residual connections [43] and layer normalization [44] are applied to ensure the convergence.

When jointly modeling multi-modal inputs as MNMT, turning speech and text inputs into the same embedding space is essential. For text inputs, we directly lookup corresponding token embeddings. While for speech inputs, we first extract feature vectors from audio through processes as shown in Fig. 2 (a). Then we reduce the sequence length by concatenating three consecutive feature vectors as shown in Fig. 2 (b), projecting them into the token embedding space with a linear projection layer. Modality-specific embeddings (speech or text) and absolute position embeddings are added before feeding the sequence to the encoder [45].

In addition to the differences in the embedding layer, we also adopt the Language-Aware Layer Normalization (LALN) and the Language-Aware Layer Transformation (LALT) strategies in MNMT modeling [46], but we apply to different modalities instead of different languages to obtain better performance through the efficient use of modality-specific parameters.

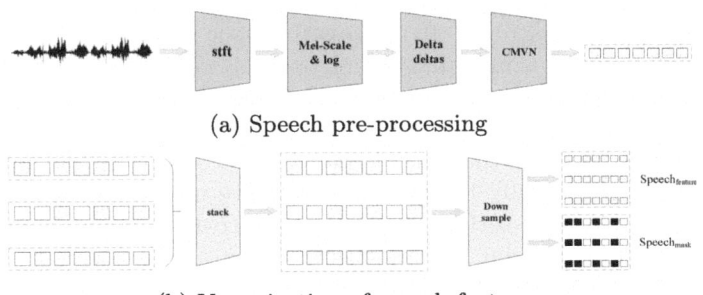

Fig. 2. Speech feature extraction and embedding, (a) feature extraction from speech, (b) speech features to embedding.

The LALN method allows the layer normalization layers to utilize modality-specific weight and bias parameters. Its computation is shown in Eq. 2.

$$\bar{a} = \text{LN}(a|g_t, b_t) = \frac{a - \mu}{\sigma} \odot g_t + b_t \qquad (2)$$

where $\odot$ is element-wise multiplication, μ and σ are the mean and standard deviation of the input vector $a \in R^d$, respectively. $g_t \in R^d$ and $b_t \in R^d$ are weight and bias vector parameters of the corresponding modality t respectively.

The LALT method transforms the encoder output H with different weight matrices according to the modality as the input the decoder's cross-attention layers, as shown in Eq. 3.

$$T = \text{Decoder}(y, H\mathbf{W}_t) \qquad (3)$$

where $\mathbf{W}_t$ denotes the weight matrix of the modality t, y and T represent the input decoding history and the output of the decoder respectively.

Our overall training loss is the sum of the cross-entropy losses for the three tasks.

$$\mathcal{L} = \mathcal{L}_{CE}(s, y) + \mathcal{L}_{CE}(x, y) + \mathcal{L}_{CE}(s, x) \qquad (4)$$

3.3 Modality-Aware Relative Position Encoding

Our model attempts to use a single encoder to take care of both text and speech inputs. However, the sequence lengths of the speech input and the text input for a sentence can be quite different, and they have different scopes of encoding, i.e., the ASR model is locally attentive, while the MT model is more globally attentive, which may require different attention patterns [9].

Previous researches have used two methods to close the lengths gap between modalities. One extends the text sequence to match the length of the speech sequence, but introducing more noise [10]. The other compresses the speech sequence to match text length by sampling length, but resulting in information loss [47,48]. Both approaches focus on aligning sequence lengths but overlook differences in attention patterns. To address this issue without further modifying the inputs, we propose a modality-aware position coding method, where the self-attention layer utilizes respective relative position encoding methods for the corresponding modality.

For text inputs, we use the relative position encoding method for machine translation proposed by [49]. For speech inputs, we use the parameterized distance penalty for relative position encoding [8]. The computation of the attention head is shown in Eqs. 5 and 6.

$$\text{Head}(Q, K, V) = \text{softmax}(\frac{QK^T}{\sqrt{d_{head}}} - \pi(D))V \quad (5)$$

$$\pi(D_{i,j}) = \log(\min(D_{i,j}, R))f(\min(D_{i,j}, R)) \quad (6)$$

where $D_{i,j}$ stores the location distance (i.e., $D_{i,j} = |i-j|+1$) and R is the clipping threshold. We use log as the distance penalty function, and the penalty grows slowly with increasing distance. f is to lookup the trainable scalar parameter for the given distance. The parameters are initialized by 1 and gradually adjusted during training.

3.4 Text Translation Data Selection

The text translation data are normally news or common crawl, while the speech translation data are usually talks and recitations. There is a significant domain gap, and selectively using the text translation data which are more close to speech translation data is crucial for improving the performance of speech translation with text translation data.

We train a text-to-text translation model using the speech transcription and the text translation of the corresponding speech of the speech translation data. Next, we use the text-to-text translation model trained on the speech translation data to compute the average per-token loss of each training instance in the text-to-text parallel translation data, and retain the training instances with lower losses. The computation of this process is shown in Eqs. 7 and 8.

$$\mathcal{L}_{avg} = \frac{1}{N}\sum_{i=1}^{N}\mathcal{L}_{CE}(T(\mathbf{x}_i), \mathbf{y}_i), T : x_{st} \to y_{st} \quad (7)$$

$$D_{sel} = \{(\mathbf{x}_i, \mathbf{y}_i) \mid \mathcal{L}_{avg} \leq \theta\} \quad (8)$$

where x_{st} is the speech transcription in ST data, y_{st} is the corresponding text translation, and T is the text-to-text translation model trained by x_{st} and y_{st}. N is the number of tokens in the training instance, $\mathcal{L}_{CE}$ and $\mathcal{L}_{avg}$ are the cross-entropy loss and its average respectively. According to the given threshold θ, the training instances D_{sel} with $\mathcal{L}_{avg} \leq \theta$ are retained.

4 Experiments

We conducted our experiments on Must-C En-De [50], CoVoST 2 [51] and Librispeech En-Fr [52] tasks to test the effectiveness of our methods, covering 23 languages from different domains. We jointly trained 3 tasks, including speech-to-text translation, speech-to-text recognition (a.k.a., ASR) and text-to-text translation (a.k.a., MT), and used the official train/dev/test split for experiments.

4.1 Datasets

ST Dataset. MuST-C is a large-scale one-to-many ST dataset covering pairs from English (En) to 8 European languages with at least 385 h of TED talk audio recordings in each direction. It includes triplets of speech, transcription, and translation. CoVoST 2 is a large and diverse multilingual ST corpus based on the Common Voice project [53]. It covers translations from 21 source languages to English and from English to 15 target languages. To compare with previous studies, we tested our methods on 7 Xx→En tasks and 15 En→Xx tasks. The augmented LibriSpeech dataset is collected by aligning e-books in French with English utterances in LibriSpeech. We used the 100-hour clean training set with their augmented references provided by Google Translate for training.

ASR and MT Dataset. We used the 960-hour training set (including 100-hour, 360-hour of clean, and 500-hour of other) [54] as external ASR data, and the WMT16 En-De (for MuST-C En-De), WMT14 En-Fr (for Librispeech En-Fr) and OPUS-100 (for CoVoST 2) as external MT data for joint training. We also used IWSLT 14 En-De for text translation experiments, covering the languages of all ST data used in our experiments.

4.2 Experimental Setups

Pre-processing. For speech, we converted all audio to a 16KHz sampling rate and truncated it to 3000 frames. We then extracted 40-dimensional log-mel scale filter bank features with a 10ms step size and a 25ms window size. These features were expanded with delta and delta-delta features, followed by Cepstral Mean and Variance Normalization (CMVN), resulting in 120-dimensional acoustic features. For text, we used Moses scripts [55] to tokenize and truecase all texts except Zh and Ja, and handled uncommon words with subwords [56,57] with a vocabulary size of 8K.

Training Details. We largely followed the Transformer base settings [41], modifying only $N_{enc} = 12$ and $d_{ff} = 4096$. The relative position encoding of text used a default window size of 16. We also employed Adam for optimization with an adaptive learning rate scheduler, 4K warm-up steps, and 0.1 label smoothing. For joint training, we applied a 0.1 dropout rate to residual connections and ReLU activations, and batched about 20K target subwords. Both speech and text data were trained with a batch size of 10K target subwords. We averaged the last 10 checkpoints for evaluation, with a beam size of 10 and a length penalty of 1.4, and measured the translation quality with BLEU [58] implemented by the SacreBLEU toolkit [59].

4.3 Main Results

We first tested the performance on the MuST-C En-De task using various settings and compared with previous strong baselines also based on Transformer [3,4,8] and joint modeling [6,30,31]. We also implemented a baseline W2V-Transformer based on wav2vec which had the same model architecture as our proposed framework and was trained in the same way. Results are shown in Table 1.

Table 1. Results on the MuST-C En-De task

	Models	Pre-train		Exter.Data		BLEU
		ASR	MT	ASR	MT	
w/o external data	Fairseq ST [3]			✓		22.7
	NeurST [4]		✓			22.8
	W2V2-Transformer					22.8
	Revisit ST [8]					23.0
	Ours					**23.4**
w/ external data	JointSpeechText [30]			✓	✓	24.1
	Siamese-PT [31]			✓	✓	24.7
	Ours			✓	✓	**25.2**
w/ pretraining	Siamese-PT [31]	✓	✓	✓	✓	26.2
	JointSpeechText [30]	✓	✓	✓	✓	**26.8**
	Ours	✓	✓	✓	✓	26.2

Table 1 shows that compared to the baselines [3,4,8] with pre-training or external data, our model still achieves good performance with only internal data, reaching a test BLEU of **23.4**. When leveraging external data, our model also outperforms the current strong joint modeling baselines [30,31], achieving a BLEU score of **25.2**. Note that our experiments are mainly centered around joint multi-modal modeling training, but in order to compare with the pre-trained baselines, we pre-trained on internal and external data and fine-tuned on ST data, also achieving a BLEU score of **26.2**.

4.4 Ablation Studies

In order to further analyze the effectiveness of our each proposed method, we jointly trained a baseline without relative position encoding on text and param-

Table 2. Ablation experiments on the MuST-C En-De task

ID	Models	BLEU
1	Joint multi-modal modeling with ASR and MT tasks	21.9
2	1 + parameterized distance penalty	22.4
3	2 + modality-aware relative position encoding (ws=16)	23.3
4	2 + modality-aware relative position encoding (ws=32)	**23.4**
5	4 + external MT data	21.8
6	4 + external MT data + text data selection	**24.0**
7	6 + external ASR data (360-hour)	24.8
8	6 + external ASR data (960-hour)	**25.2**
9	8 + pretraining	**26.2**

eterized distance penalty on speech on MuST-C En-De for comparison, and conducted ablation experiments of our proposed methods on the MuST-C En-De task. Results are shown in Table 2.

Results in Table 2 show that: 1) using modality-aware relative position encoding (1, 2→3) can further improve the performance of joint modeling (+1.4 and +0.9 BLEU respectively), 2) tuning the window sizes for the text relative position encoding does not have significant impacts on performance despite a window size of 32 lead to a higher BLEU score than the other tested settings (3→4), 3) directly using all text data (4→5) hampers the performance (−1.6 BLEU), but joint modeling with the filtered text translation data (4→6) can lead to significant improvements (+0.6 BLEU), 4) augmenting with more ASR data is helpful, and can lead to +0.8 and +1.2 BLEU gains (6→7, 8), and 5) pre-training can bring further improvement in results, but the number of epochs and time required for training will also increase by multiple times (8→9).

We also conducted text translation experiments on the IWSLT14 En-De task, and trained a text translation model using the transcription-translation data of MuST-C En-De dataset as a baseline for comparison. Results are shown in Table 3, where MC denotes MuST-C En-De and WT denotes WMT16 En-De. Note that the models in rows 2–6 are the same as the models in rows 2–6 in Table 2.

Results in Table 3 show that the joint modeling of speech and text with parameterized distance penalty can also improve the performance of both speech translation and text translation (+1.7 BLEU) (1→2). 2→4 proves the importance of modality-aware positional encoding methods on ensuring the quality of text translation (+2.8 BLEU). While 3→4 shows that the window sizes for the text relative position encoding have a greater impact on text translation than speech translation (+1.1 BLEU). In addition, additional text data (4→5, 6) can further improve the text translation performance (+0.4 and +3.7 BLEU for without/with text data selection respectively).

Table 3. Results on the IWSLT14 En-De task

ID	Models	Texts	BLEU
1	MT model	MC	33.5
2	ST model + parameterized distance penalty	MC	35.2
3	2 + modality-aware relative position encoding (ws=16)	MC	36.9
4	2 + modality-aware relative position encoding (ws=32)	MC	38.0
5	4 + external MT data	MC, WT	38.4
6	4 + external MT data + text data selection	MC, WT	**41.7**

4.5 Wide-Range Verification

Furthermore, We also tested the performance of our methods on multiple languages on CoVoST 2 and LibriSpeech En-Fr tasks, where the experiments of CoVoST 2 include without/with using additional external MT and ASR data, and compared with two baselines [8,51]. Results are shown in Table 4 and 5.

Table 4. Results on Xx→En and En→Xx CoVoST 2 tasks

Models	Exter.Data		Xx→En							
	ASR	MT	Fr	De	Es	Ca	It	Ru	Zh	Avg
Revisit ST [8]			26.9	14.1	15.7	17.2	2.4	3.6	2.0	11.7
ST + ASR Pretraining [51]			26.3	17.1	23.0	18.8	11.3	14.8	5.8	16.7
Ours			28.2	21.7	24.2	22.2	11.2	8.8	2.1	16.9
	✓	✓	**29.2**	**22.5**	**26.3**	**22.3**	**16.1**	**25.6**	**6.0**	**21.1**

En→Xx														
Ar	Ca	Cy	De	Et	Fa	Id	Ja	Lv	Mn	Sl	Sv	Ta	Tr	Zh	Avg
12.3	22.9	24.5	17.5	13.6	12.7	21.4	28.8	13.6	9.9	15.2	22.9	10.8	10.3	23.3	17.3
12.1	21.8	23.9	16.3	13.2	13.1	20.4	29.6	13.0	9.2	16.0	21.8	10.9	10.0	25.4	17.1
13.2	23.0	25.0	18.6	14.8	13.1	23.5	31.3	15.1	10.9	17.7	24.8	11.0	11.7	26.2	18.7
13.5	**23.7**	**25.1**	**18.9**	**15.1**	**13.3**	**24.1**	**31.5**	**15.2**	**11.6**	**18.6**	**25.8**	**11.2**	**12.0**	**27.0**	**19.1**

Table 4 shows that our model surpasses [8] on all CoVoST 2 tasks (+5.2 and +1.4 BLEU on average for Xx→En and En→Xx respectively), outperforming [51] pre-trained with ASR on 19 of the 22 CoVoST 2 tasks. Furthermore, incorporating additional external MT and ASR data further improves performance, with average BLEU score of **21.1** for Xx→En and **19.1** for En→Xx.

Table 5 shows that our model also achieves significant performance improvements on the LibriSpeech En-Fr task with a BLEU score of **27.0**. We speculate that there are two reasons for this: 1) the ASR and MT data of En-Fr are more abundant than in other language pairs, with MT data reaching 31.2M. Even

Table 5. Results on the LibriSpeech En-Fr task

Models	Exter.Data		BLEU
	ASR	MT	
Revisit ST [8]			16.5
KD ST [29]			17.0
Chimera [17]	✓	✓	19.4
SATE [27]	✓	✓	21.3
MSP-ST [9]	✓	✓	21.4
Ours	✓	✓	**27.0**

after text selection, 9.4M MT examples remain for model training, significantly benefiting auxiliary tasks and enhancing the ST task. 2) Joint modeling with a single encoder allows real-time sharing of model parameters across the three tasks, enabling mutual optimization during training, which may more effective than additional speech pre-training alone.

5 Data Quantity Analysis

To investigate the impacts of the available amount of external ASR data on speech translation, we tested the performance of our methods using different proportions (25%, 50%, 75% and 100%) of the 360-hour of Librispeech En-Fr speech recognition data on the MuST-C En-De task. We also tested the impacts with increasing proportions (10%, 30%, 50%, 70% and 100%) of external MT data on speech translation. It is worth noting that the amount of available text translation data is much larger than the amount of speech translation data in terms of sentence numbers. And as the selection of sentence pairs were based on the average per-token loss of the translation model (Sect. 3.4), the performance is affected not only by the amount of data but also the domain and quality of the data.

Figure 3 (a) shows that using more ASR data consistently improves the speech translation performance, suggesting that the amount of available speech data is not sufficient, as the joint training performance does not show any decreasing trend even all available speech recognition data are used. This is consistent with our experimental results, which show further performance improvement when using 960-hour of Librispeech En-Fr speech recognition data on the MuST-C En-De task.

Figure 3 (b) shows that the speech translation performance first increases and then decreases with the increasing amount of text translation data, and around 10% to 30% of the text translation data leads to the best performance for the MuST-C En-De task.

Note that this is different from previous research results [5,7]. We speculate that the reasons for the performance degradation may be multifaceted: 1) it might due to the domain mismatch, poor quality with the increasing amount of

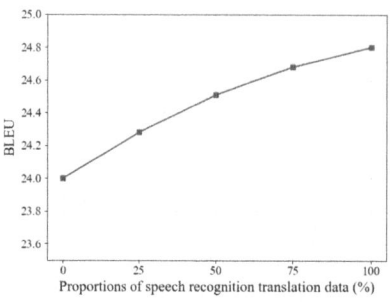 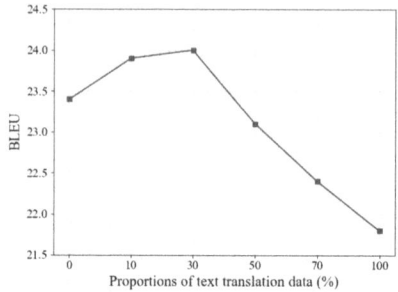

(a) Effects of the amount of ASR data.   (b) Effects of the amount of MT data.

Fig. 3. Effects of the amount of ASR data and MT data on the MuST-C En-De task.

data, 2) it may also because that using more text translation data makes the model allocate more capacity to text translation, which in turn hampers the performance of speech recognition and translation, and 3) previous work first trained on MT and/or ASR tasks, and then fine-tuned on ST tasks. Fine-tuning on ST tasks may eliminate the negative effects from large-scale MT data. However, our methods directly train three tasks simultaneously, and the MT task has a direct impact on the final performance.

6 Conclusion

In this paper, we explore the use of a single encoder for joint multi-modal modeling to improve the performance of speech translation, modeling speech translation, text translation and speech recognition in an MNMT manner. In addition to the Language-Aware Layer Normalization (LALN) and the Language-Aware Layer Transformation (LALT) strategies in MNMT modeling, we propose the modality-aware relative position encoding method to address the differences between modalities in the attention patterns in the self-attention layer. Additionally, we propose a translation-loss-based data selection method to align text translation training instances with the style of speech translation data. Experiments on MuST-C, CoVoST 2, and Librispeech tasks show that our simply architecture significantly improves the strong end-to-end speech translation baseline by effectively leveraging ASR and MT data. Furthermore, text translation results on the IWSLT14 task confirm that our methods maintain high-quality speech translation while also ensuring robust text translation performance.

Acknowledgements. We thank the anonymous reviewers for their insightful comments. Jiale Ou and Hongying Zan are supported by the National Natural Science Foundation of China (Grant No. U23A20316), and Henan Provincial Science and Technology Project (Grant No. 232102211041). Hongfei Xu acknowledges the support of the National Natural Science Foundation of China (Grant No. 62306284), China Postdoctoral Science Foundation (Grant No. 2023M743189), and the Natural Science Foundation of Henan Province (Grant No. 232300421386).

References

1. Duong, L., Anastasopoulos, A., Chiang, D., Bird, S., Cohn, T.: An attentional model for speech translation without transcription. In: Proceedings of the 2016 Conference of the North American Chapter of the Association for Computational Linguistics: Human Language Technologies, pp. 949–959, San Diego, California. Association for Computational Linguistics. (2016)
2. Bérard, A., Pietquin, O., Besacier, L., Servan, C.: Listen and translate: a proof of concept for end-to-end speech-to-text translation. In: NIPS Workshop on End-to-End Learning for Speech and Audio Processing (2016)
3. Wang, C., Tang, Y., Ma, X., Wu, A., Okhonko, D., Pino, J.: Fairseq S2T: fast speech-to-text modeling with Fairseq. In: Proceedings of the 1st Conference of the Asia-Pacific Chapter of the Association for Computational Linguistics and the 10th International Joint Conference on Natural Language Processing: System Demonstrations, pp. 33–39, Suzhou, China. Association for Computational Linguistics (2020)
4. Zhao, C., Wang, M., Dong, Q., Ye, R., Li, L.: NeurST: neural speech translation toolkit. In: Proceedings of the 59th Annual Meeting of the Association for Computational Linguistics and the 11th International Joint Conference on Natural Language Processing: System Demonstrations, pp. 55–62, Online. Association for Computational Linguistics (2021)
5. Ye, R., Wang, M., Li, L.: End-to-end speech translation via cross-modal progressive training. In: arXiv preprint arXiv:2104.10380 (2021)
6. Zheng, R., Chen, J., Ma, M., Huang, L.: Fused acoustic and text encoding for multimodal bilingual pretraining and speech translation. In: International Conference on Machine Learning, pp. 12736-12746. PMLR (2021)
7. Fang, Q., Ye, R., Li, L., Feng, Y., Wang, M.: STEMM: self-learning with speech-text manifold Mixup for speech translation. In: Proceedings of the 60th Annual Meeting of the Association for Computational Linguistics (Volume 1: Long Papers), pp. 7050–7062, Dublin, Ireland. Association for Computational Linguistics (2022)
8. Zhang, B., Haddow, B., Sennrich, R.: Revisiting end-to-end speech-to-text translation from scratch. In: International Conference on Machine Learning, pp. 26193-26205. PMLR (2022)
9. Zhang, Y., Xu, C., Hu, B., Zhang, C., Xiao, T., Zhu, J.: Improving end-to-end speech translation by leveraging auxiliary speech and text data. In: Proceedings of the AAAI Conference on Artificial Intelligence, Vol. 37, No. 11, pp. 13984–13992 (2023)
10. Zhang, Y., et al.: Rethinking and improving multi-task learning for end-to-end speech translation. In: Proceedings of the 2023 Conference on Empirical Methods in Natural Language Processing, pp. 10753–10765, Singapore. Association for Computational Linguistics (2023)
11. Bansal, S., Kamper, H., Livescu, K., Lopez, A., Goldwater, S.: Pre-training on high-resource speech recognition improves low-resource speech-to-text translation. In: Proceedings of the 2019 Conference of the North American Chapter of the Association for Computational Linguistics: Human Language Technologies, Volume 1 (Long and Short Papers), pp. 58–68, Minneapolis, Minnesota. Association for Computational Linguistics (2019)
12. Pino, J., Xu, Q., Ma, X., Dousti, M. J., Tang, Y.: Self-training for end-to-end speech translation. In: arXiv preprint arXiv:2006.02490 (2020)

13. Alinejad, A., Sarkar, A.: Effectively pretraining a speech translation decoder with Machine Translation data. In: Proceedings of the 2020 Conference on Empirical Methods in Natural Language Processing (EMNLP), pp. 8014–8020, Online. Association for Computational Linguistics (2020)
14. Tang, Y., et al.: Unified Speech-Text Pre-training for Speech Translation and Recognition. In: Proceedings of the 60th Annual Meeting of the Association for Computational Linguistics (Volume 1: Long Papers), pp. 1488–1499, Dublin, Ireland. Association for Computational Linguistics (2022)
15. Anastasopoulos, A., Chiang, D.: Tied multitask learning for neural speech translation. In: Proceedings of the 2018 Conference of the North American Chapter of the Association for Computational Linguistics: Human Language Technologies, Volume 1 (Long Papers), pp. 82–91, New Orleans, Louisiana. Association for Computational Linguistics (2018)
16. Tang, Y., Pino, J., Wang, C., Ma, X., Genzel, D.: A general multi-task learning framework to leverage text data for speech to text tasks. In: ICASSP 2021- 2021 IEEE International Conference on Acoustics, Speech and Signal Processing (ICASSP), pp. 6209-6213. IEEE (2021)
17. Han, C., Wang, M., Ji, H., Li, L.: Learning shared semantic space for speech-to-text translation. In: Findings of the Association for Computational Linguistics: ACL-IJCNLP 2021, pp. 2214–2225, Online. Association for Computational Linguistics (2021)
18. Park, D.S., Chan, W., Zhang, Y., Chiu, C.C., Zoph, B., Cubuk, E.D., Le, Q.V.: SpecAugment: A simple data augmentation method for automatic speech recognition. In: arXiv preprint arXiv:1904.08779 (2019)
19. Lam, T.K., Schamoni, S., Riezler, S.: Sample, translate, recombine: leveraging audio alignments for data augmentation in end-to-end speech translation. In: Proceedings of the 60th Annual Meeting of the Association for Computational Linguistics (Volume 2: Short Papers), pp. 245–254, Dublin, Ireland. Association for Computational Linguistics (2022)
20. Fang, Q., Feng, Y.: Understanding and bridging the modality gap for speech translation. In: Proceedings of the 61st Annual Meeting of the Association for Computational Linguistics (Volume 1: Long Papers), pp. 15864–15881, Toronto, Canada. Association for Computational Linguistics (2023)
21. Xu, C., et al.: Recent advances in direct speech-to-text translation. In: Proceedings of the Thirty-Second International Joint Conference on Artificial Intelligence, pp. 6796–6804 (2023)
22. Le, H., Pino, J., Wang, C., Gu, J., Schwab, D., Besacier, L.: Dual-decoder transformer for joint automatic speech recognition and multilingual speech translation. In: Proceedings of the 28th International Conference on Computational Linguistics, pp. 3520–3533, Barcelona, Spain (Online). International Committee on Computational Linguistics (2020)
23. Bahar, P., Bieschke, T., Schlüter, R., Ney, H.: Tight integrated end-to-end training for cascaded speech translation. In: 2021 IEEE Spoken Language Technology Workshop (SLT), pp. 950-957. IEEE (2021)
24. Sperber, M., Neubig, G., Niehues, J., Waibel, A.: Attention-passing models for robust and data-efficient end-to-end speech translation. Trans. Assoc. Comput. Linguist. **7**, 313–325 (2019)
25. Ao, J., et al.: SpeechT5: unified-modal encoder-decoder pre-training for spoken language processing. In: Proceedings of the 60th Annual Meeting of the Association for Computational Linguistics (Volume 1: Long Papers), pp. 5723–5738, Dublin, Ireland. Association for Computational Linguistics (2022)

26. Liu, Y., Zhu, J., Zhang, J., Zong, C.: Bridging the modality gap for speech-to-text translation. In: arXiv preprint arXiv:2010.14920 (2020)
27. Xu, C., et al.: Stacked acoustic-and-textual encoding: integrating the pre-trained models into speech translation encoders. In: Proceedings of the 59th Annual Meeting of the Association for Computational Linguistics and the 11th International Joint Conference on Natural Language Processing (Volume 1: Long Papers), pp. 2619–2630, Online. Association for Computational Linguistics (2021)
28. Ye, R., Wang, M., Li, L.: Cross-modal contrastive learning for speech translation. In: Proceedings of the 2022 Conference of the North American Chapter of the Association for Computational Linguistics: Human Language Technologies, pp. 5099–5113, Seattle, United States. Association for Computational Linguistics (2022)
29. Liu, Y., et al.: End-to-end speech translation with knowledge distillation. In: Proceedings of the 17th International Conference on Spoken Language Translation, pp. 80–88, Online. Association for Computational Linguistics (2019)
30. Tang, Y., Pino, J., Li, X., Wang, C., Genzel, D.: Improving speech translation by understanding and learning from the auxiliary text translation task. In: Proceedings of the 59th Annual Meeting of the Association for Computational Linguistics and the 11th International Joint Conference on Natural Language Processing (Volume 1: Long Papers), pp. 4252–4261, Online. Association for Computational Linguistics (2021)
31. Le, P. H., Gong, H., Wang, C., Pino, J., Lecouteux, B., Schwab, D.: Pre-training for speech translation: CTC meets optimal transport. In: International Conference on Machine Learning, pp. 18667–18685. PMLR (2023)
32. Le, H., Pino, J., Wang, C., Gu, J., Schwab, D., Besacier, L.: Lightweight adapter tuning for multilingual speech translation. In: Proceedings of the 59th Annual Meeting of the Association for Computational Linguistics and the 11th International Joint Conference on Natural Language Processing (Volume 2: Short Papers), pp. 817–824, Online. Association for Computational Linguistics (2021)
33. Li, X., et al.: Multilingual speech translation from efficient finetuning of pretrained models. In: Proceedings of the 59th Annual Meeting of the Association for Computational Linguistics and the 11th International Joint Conference on Natural Language Processing (Volume 1: Long Papers), pp. 827–838, Online. Association for Computational Linguistics (2021)
34. Zhang, Z., et al.: SpeechUT: bridging speech and text with hidden-unit for encoder-decoder based speech-text pre-training. In: Proceedings of the 2022 Conference on Empirical Methods in Natural Language Processing, pp. 1663–1676, Abu Dhabi, United Arab Emirates. Association for Computational Linguistics (2022)
35. Johnson, M., et al.: Google's multilingual neural machine translation system: enabling zero-shot translation. Trans. Assoc. Comput. Linguist. **5**, 339–351 (2017)
36. Aharoni, R., Johnson, M., Firat, O.: Massively multilingual neural machine translation. In: Proceedings of the 2019 Conference of the North American Chapter of the Association for Computational Linguistics: Human Language Technologies, Volume 1 (Long and Short Papers), pp. 3874–3884, Minneapolis, Minnesota. Association for Computational Linguistics (2019)
37. Arivazhagan, N., et al.: Massively multilingual neural machine translation in the wild: Findings and challenges. In: arXiv preprint arXiv:1907.05019 (2019)
38. Gu, J., Wang, Y., Cho, K., Li, V. O.: Improved zero-shot neural machine translation via ignoring spurious correlations. In: Proceedings of the 57th Annual Meeting of the Association for Computational Linguistics, pp. 1258–1268, Florence, Italy. Association for Computational Linguistics (2019)

39. Fan, A., et al.: Beyond English-centric multilingual machine translation. J. Mach. Learn. Res. **22**(107), 1–48 (2021)
40. Gao, P., Zhang, L., He, Z., Wu, H., Wang, H.: Improving zero-shot multilingual neural machine translation by leveraging cross-lingual consistency regularization. In: Findings of the Association for Computational Linguistics: ACL 2023, pp. 12103–12119, Toronto, Canada. Association for Computational Linguistics (2023)
41. Vaswani, A., et al.: Attention is all you need. Adv. Neural Inf. Process. Syst. **30** (2017)
42. Bahdanau, D., Cho, K., Bengio, Y.: Neural machine translation by jointly learning to align and translate. In: arXiv preprint arXiv:1409.0473 (2014)
43. He, K., Zhang, X., Ren, S., Sun, J.: Deep residual learning for image recognition. In: Proceedings of the IEEE Conference on Computer Vision and Pattern Recognition, pp. 770–778 (2016)
44. Ba, J. L., Kiros, J. R., Hinton, G. E.: Layer normalization. In: arXiv preprint arXiv:1607.06450 (2016)
45. Di Gangi, M. A., Negri, M., Turchi, M.: One-to-many multilingual end-to-end speech translation. In 2019 IEEE Automatic Speech Recognition and Understanding Workshop (ASRU), pp. 585–592. IEEE (2019)
46. Zhang, B., Williams, P., Titov, I., Sennrich, R.: Improving massively multilingual neural machine translation and zero-shot translation. In: Proceedings of the 58th Annual Meeting of the Association for Computational Linguistics, pp. 1628–1639, Online. Association for Computational Linguistics (2020)
47. Zhang, S., Loweimi, E., Xu, Y., Bell, P., Renals, S.: Trainable dynamic subsampling for end-to-end speech recognition. In: Interspeech 2019, pp. 1413–1417. International Speech Communication Association (2019)
48. Salesky, E., Sperber, M., Black, A. W.: Exploring phoneme-level speech representations for end-to-end speech translation. In: Proceedings of the 57th Annual Meeting of the Association for Computational Linguistics, pp. 1835–1841, Florence, Italy. Association for Computational Linguistics (2019)
49. Shaw, P., Uszkoreit, J., Vaswani, A.: Self-attention with relative position representations. In: arXiv preprint arXiv:1803.02155 (2018)
50. Di Gangi, M. A., Cattoni, R., Bentivogli, L., Negri, M., Turchi, M.: MuST-C: a multilingual speech translation corpus. In: Proceedings of the 2019 Conference of the North American Chapter of the Association for Computational Linguistics: Human Language Technologies, Volume 1 (Long and Short Papers), pp. 2012–2017, Minneapolis, Minnesota. Association for Computational Linguistics (2019)
51. Wang, C., Wu, A., Pino, J.: CoVoST 2 and massively multilingual speech-to-text translation. In: arXiv preprint arXiv:2007.10310 (2020)
52. Kocabiyikoglu, A.C., Besacier, L., Kraif, O.: Augmenting librispeech with French translations: a multimodal corpus for direct speech translation evaluation. In: Proceedings of the Eleventh International Conference on Language Resources and Evaluation (LREC 2018), Miyazaki, Japan. European Language Resources Association (ELRA) (2018)
53. Ardila, R., et al.: Common voice: a massively-multilingual speech corpus. In: Proceedings of the Twelfth Language Resources and Evaluation Conference, pp. 4218–4222, Marseille, France. European Language Resources Association (2020)
54. Panayotov, V., Chen, G., Povey, D., Khudanpur, S.: Librispeech: an ASR corpus based on public domain audio books. In: 2015 IEEE International Conference on Acoustics, Speech and Signal Processing (ICASSP), pp. 5206–5210. IEEE (2015)

55. Koehn, P., et al.: Moses: open source toolkit for statistical machine translation. In: Proceedings of the 45th Annual Meeting of the Association for Computational Linguistics Companion Volume Proceedings of the Demo and Poster Sessions, pp. 177–180, Prague, Czech Republic. Association for Computational Linguistics (2007)
56. Sennrich, R., Haddow, B., Birch, A.: Neural machine translation of rare words with subword units. In: Proceedings of the 54th Annual Meeting of the Association for Computational Linguistics (Volume 1: Long Papers), pp. 1715–1725, Berlin, Germany. Association for Computational Linguistics (2016)
57. Kudo, T., Richardson, J.: SentencePiece: a simple and language independent subword tokenizer and detokenizer for Neural Text Processing. In: Proceedings of the 2018 Conference on Empirical Methods in Natural Language Processing: System Demonstrations, pp. 66–71, Brussels, Belgium. Association for Computational Linguistics (2018)
58. Papineni, K., Roukos, S., Ward, T., Zhu, W. J.: BLEU: a method for automatic evaluation of machine translation. In: Proceedings of the 40th Annual Meeting of the Association for Computational Linguistics, pp. 311–318 (2002)
59. Post, M.: A call for clarity in reporting BLEU scores. In: Proceedings of the Third Conference on Machine Translation: Research Papers, pp. 186–191, Brussels, Belgium. Association for Computational Linguistics (2018)

Machine Translation Evaluation

CCMT2024 Tibetan-Chinese Machine Translation Evaluation Technical Report

Wenhao Zhuang[1,2], Dawa Cairen[1,2], Pengmao Cairang[1,2], and Yuan Sun[1,2](✉)

[1] School of Information Engineering, Minzu University of China, Beijing 100081, China
tracy.yuan.sun@gmail.com
[2] National Language Resources Monitoring and Research Center for Minority Languages, Beijing, China

Abstract. This report presents the evaluation results of the Tibetan-Chinese machine translation task conducted by the National Language Resources Monitoring and Research Center for Minority Languages at the 20th Conference on Machine Translation (CCMT2024). The translation system described in this paper is based on the LLaMA2-7B architecture, with specific secondary pre-training and supervised fine-tuning tailored to the translation task. The results demonstrate that this approach effectively improves the performance of Tibetan-Chinese machine translation. Additionally, this paper employs a parameter grid search method to investigate the impact of different parameter combinations on translation performance.

Keywords: Tibetan-Chinese machine translation · Large language model · Supervised fine-tuning

1 Introduction

In the context of globalization and informationization, the demand for communication in multilingual environments is increasingly growing. Machine translation technology, as a bridge connecting different languages and cultures, is of paramount importance. This is particularly true in a country like China, where multiple ethnic groups and languages coexist. Developing efficient machine translation systems holds profound significance for promoting communication and understanding among various ethnic groups, as well as for preserving and inheriting minority languages and cultures. Tibetan, as one of the valuable linguistic resources of the Chinese nation [1–3], plays a critical role not only in cultural exchange but also in supporting ethnic unity and social development through its translation with Chinese.

In recent years, the rapid advancement of deep learning technology, especially the rise of large language models (LLMs), has brought unprecedented changes to the field of machine translation. These models, trained on vast amounts of textual data, exhibit powerful language understanding and generation capabilities, presenting new opportunities and challenges for Tibetan-Chinese machine translation tasks. In light of this, this paper focuses on the latest research findings on Tibetan-Chinese machine translation tasks conducted by the National Language Resources Monitoring and Research Center for Minority Languages at the 20th China Conference on Machine Translation (CCMT2024). It provides a detailed discussion on the method of combining incremental pre-training with large models and supervised fine-tuning to improve the quality and efficiency of Tibetan-Chinese machine translation.

This research is not only an in-depth exploration of Tibetan-Chinese machine translation technology but also a significant practice in advancing the technology for minority language machine translation. By introducing the experimental design, technical approach, and evaluation results, this paper aims to provide valuable reference for researchers in related fields, with the goal of jointly advancing the development of Tibetan-Chinese and broader minority language machine translation technology, thereby contributing to cultural diversity and ethnic unity.

2 Related Work

In the field of Tibetan-Chinese machine translation, researchers have undergone decades of exploration and innovation, striving to improve the accuracy and fluency of translation systems. Early machine translation methods are primarily rule-based, relying on rules and dictionaries crafted by linguistic experts. However, due to the complexity and limited coverage of these rules, the translation quality is less than ideal. With the rise of Statistical Machine Translation (SMT), researchers begin to train translation models using large-scale bilingual parallel corpora, significantly improving translation quality. Nonetheless, SMT methods still face challenges in handling data sparsity and long-distance dependencies [4].

In recent years, the rapid development of deep learning technology, especially the widespread application of neural networks in the field of Natural Language Processing (NLP), has made Neural Machine Translation (NMT) the mainstream approach. NMT, through end-to-end training, automatically learns complex mapping relationships between languages, producing more natural and fluent translations. Particularly, the introduction of the Transformer model, with its self-attention mechanism that effectively captures long-distance dependencies, has set a new benchmark in the field of machine translation [5].

In the context of Tibetan-Chinese machine translation tasks, directly applying a generic Transformer model presents challenges, as Tibetan and Chinese exhibit significant differences in language structure, vocabulary, and grammar. To address this, researchers explore specific optimization methods, such as multilingual pre-training, domain adaptation, and data augmentation, to improve translation quality [6–8]. The work presented in this paper is based on the concepts of incremental pre-training and supervised fine-tuning using LLMs. By incorporating the characteristics of the Tibetan-Chinese translation task, a new translation method is proposed. Through pre-training on multilingual corpora and fine-tuning on Tibetan-Chinese bilingual parallel corpora, the model is better able to capture the features of both languages, generating more accurate and fluent translations.

3 Method

We refer to the work of Guo et al. and follow their paradigm for enhancing the translation capabilities of LLMs, aiming to strengthen the performance of these models in translation tasks. Specifically, our training process consists of three major stages, as clearly illustrated in Fig. 1: first, a secondary pre-training phase using extensive Tibetan and Chinese monolingual data; next, a continued pre-training phase incorporating mixed parallel corpora of Chinese and Tibetan; and finally, a fine-grained supervised fine-tuning phase using mixed parallel corpora of Tibetan and Chinese.

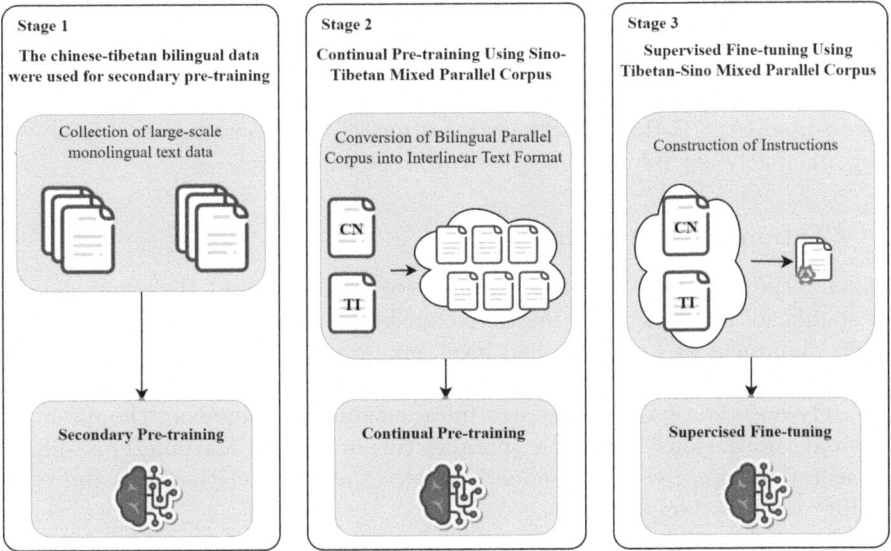

Fig. 1. The three-stage training framework.

3.1 Secondary Pre-training

At the current stage, our primary objective is to enhance the training of LLMs by leveraging diverse and abundant monolingual data. Existing LLMs, such as ChatGPT and LLaMA, are primarily pre-trained on English-centric corpora, which results in relatively weaker understanding and generation capabilities for non-English languages. To improve the multilingual generation abilities of LLMs, we adopt an incremental pre-training approach using monolingual data. Specifically, we base our work on the Chinese-LLaMA2-7B [9] model, which is derived from LLaMA2-7B by expanding the Chinese vocabulary from the original 32,000 tokens to 55,296 tokens and performing incremental pre-training on 120GB of Chinese corpus. We further expand the Tibetan vocabulary to 85,609 tokens. Subsequently, we initialize the newly added Tibetan tokens in the model's word embedding layer and the final output linear layer (lm_head) using a mean expansion method. This initialization process involves calculating the average representation of the original tokens that were used to represent each new Tibetan token. For instance, if a new Tibetan token was previously represented by six tokens in the original vocabulary, its initial embedding is set to the mean of these six tokens' embeddings. This approach ensures that the new Tibetan tokens start with meaningful representations derived from the model's existing knowledge, facilitating more effective learning during the subsequent pre-training phase [10].

Since Chinese-LLaMA2-7B provides robust support for both English and Chinese, we incorporate a total of 33.53GB of pre-training data, comprising 26.46GB of Tibetan corpus and 7.07GB of Chinese corpus, for incremental pre-training in our experiments. The training process is conducted using six NVIDIA Tesla V100S 32G GPUs, with distributed training and memory optimization handled by DeepSpeed. The training duration is 179 h, resulting in the Tibetan-Chinese-LLaMA2-7B-Base, a foundational model for Tibetan and Chinese that is not inherently capable of dialogue or downstream tasks.

3.2 Continued Pre-training

Parallel corpora, consisting of aligned source sentences and their translations, offer significant advantages for machine translation tasks. These datasets provide explicit alignment at a fine-grained level, enabling models to capture syntactic and semantic correspondences between languages. This alignment is crucial for accurately encoding source language information and enhancing the quality of generated translations. Moreover, parallel corpora aid in learning cross-lingual representations, improving the model's understanding of relationships and transferability between languages.

To fully leverage these advantages, we employ a continuous pre-training strategy based on the LoRA [11] framework. LoRA is a powerful and efficient method for pre-training language models that has been introduced in recent studies. It works by adding trainable rank decomposition matrices to certain weights of the model, allowing for parameter-efficient fine-tuning. This approach reduces the number of trainable parameters significantly, typically by 10000 times compared to full fine-tuning, while maintaining model performance. LoRA enables faster training convergence and lower memory usage, making it particularly suitable for large language models like ours.

By utilizing the inherent alignment information in parallel corpora through LoRA, our model can learn to align and generate translations that maintain syntactic and semantic consistency with the source sentences. This ongoing training process allows the model to gradually improve its ability to capture cross-linguistic correspondences, thereby enhancing translation quality. The LoRA approach also helps prevent overfitting and allows for more effective adaptation to the specific nuances of Tibetan-Chinese translation.

Specifically, building upon the Tibetan-Chinese-LLaMA2-7B-Base foundational model, we conduct further pre-training using 22.23GB of mixed Tibetan-Chinese parallel corpora, resulting in the Tibetan-Chinese-LLaMA2-7B-Trans-Base model, which serves as a foundational model for Tibetan-Chinese translation.

3.3 Supervised Fine-Tuning

Supervised fine-tuning for machine translation tasks encompasses two key aspects. First, similar to the early stages of continuous pre-training, we fine-tune specific parameters of LLMs using LoRA to enhance their efficiency. LoRA plays a crucial role in preventing overfitting, leading to significant performance improvements. By employing this approach, we strategically apply low-rank updates to fine-tune a subset of the model's parameters, achieving a delicate balance between model adaptation and computational efficiency. To ensure optimal data quality during fine-tuning, we utilize high-quality data sources. Our quality control measures include automatic filtering for sentence length and alignment, followed by manual review to ensure semantic equivalence and fluency in both languages. In this stage, we conduct supervised fine-tuning of the Tibetan-Chinese-LLaMA2-7B-Trans-Base model using 1,469,432 Tibetan-Chinese mixed parallel corpora. The key distinction between continuous pre-training (Sect. 3.2) and supervised fine-tuning lies in their objectives and data format. Continuous pre-training primarily focuses on enhancing the model's text generation capabilities, with each training instance consisting of a Tibetan sentence followed by its Chinese counterpart (or vice versa), separated by a tab character. This format helps the model learn the relationship between parallel sentences. In contrast, supervised fine-tuning aims to improve the model's ability to follow translation instructions. During this phase, the model is trained to generate Chinese translations from Tibetan input (or vice versa) based on specific prompts or instructions. This process enhances the model's capacity to understand and execute translation tasks in a more directed manner. The resulting model from this supervised fine-tuning process, TiLamb-Trans, serves as our final translation model, capable of performing Tibetan-Chinese translations based on input instructions.

4 Experiment

4.1 Settings

The specific settings of key parameters during the supervised fine-tuning process are detailed in Table 1.

Table 1. Hyperparameters for Supervised Fine-tuning

Hyperparameter	Value	Hyperparameter	Value
Fine-tuning method	LoRA	Max. seq. length	2048
Learning rate	1e-4	Number of epochs	3
Batch size	16	dtype	fp16
LoRA rank	8	LoRA dropout rate	0.05

4.2 Results and Analysis

We evaluate the impact of Temperature and Top P parameters on the model's performance using the BLEU score as our primary metric. These parameters control the stochasticity and diversity of the model's output:

- Temperature: Adjusts the probability distribution of next-token predictions. Lower values lead to more deterministic outputs, while higher values increase randomness.
- Top P (nucleus sampling): Determines the smallest set of tokens whose cumulative probability exceeds p, from which the model samples. Lower values result in more focused sampling, while higher values allow for greater diversity.

We conduct experiments with Temperature and Top P values ranging from 0.1 to 1.0, incrementing by 0.1. Figure 2 presents the resulting BLEU score heatmap.

Analysis of the heatmap reveals several significant trends:

1. At lower temperatures (0.1–0.3), BLEU scores exhibit relative stability across varying Top P values, indicating that in more deterministic scenarios, Top P's influence is less pronounced.
2. Optimal performance is observed with Temperature between 0.2 and 0.3, and Top P between 0.5 and 0.7. This suggests that a slightly deterministic approach with moderate token diversity yields translations most closely aligned with reference texts.
3. Performance deteriorates as Temperature or Top P increases, particularly when Top P approaches 1.0. This degradation implies that excessive randomness in generation leads to less accurate translations.
4. Extreme parameter values (e.g., both at 1.0) result in the lowest BLEU scores, likely due to the generation of highly diverse but potentially incoherent translations.
5. Local maxima in the heatmap (e.g., at Temperature 0.2, Top P 0.6) indicate that certain combinations of moderate randomness and focused sampling can produce optimal results.

These observations suggest that moderate parameter values enhance the model's generation performance by balancing deterministic translation with lexical flexibility. Based on this analysis, we selected a Temperature of 0.2 and a

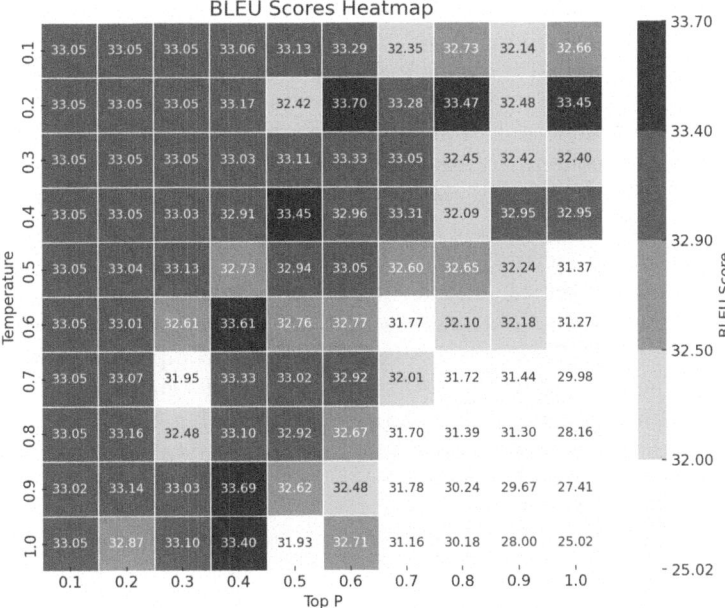

Fig. 2. BLEU Score Heatmap Under Different Temperature and Top P Configurations

Top P of 0.6 as optimal parameters, providing an effective equilibrium between translation accuracy and natural language generation.

4.3 Impact of SFT Parameters on Translation Performance

To further investigate the influence of different supervised fine-tuning (SFT) parameters on translation performance, we conducted additional experiments varying key parameters such as learning rate, LoRA rank, LoRA alpha, dropout rate, and additional targets. Table 2 presents the results of these experiments, with the baseline BLEU score of 37.82 for reference.

Table 2. Impact of SFT parameters on translation performance

Parameters	BLEU Score	Change
Baseline (lr=1e-4, rank=8, α=16, dropout=0.05)	37.82	–
lr=5e-5, rank=8, α=16, dropout=0.05	37.78	-0.04
lr=1e-4, rank=64, α=128, dropout=0.05	38.46	$+0.64$
lr=1e-4, rank=8, α=16, dropout=0	37.87	$+0.05$
lr=1e-4, rank=64, α=128, dropout=0	38.41	$+0.59$
lr=1e-4, rank=64, α=128, dropout=0.05, no norm	38.27	$+0.45$

Based on these results, we observe that:

- Reducing the learning rate from 1e-4 to 5e-5 slightly decreased performance, suggesting that the original learning rate was appropriate for our task.
- Increasing the LoRA rank from 8 to 64 and alpha from 16 to 128 led to a notable improvement in translation quality, with a BLEU score increase of 0.64. This suggests that a higher rank allows for more expressive parameter updates, potentially capturing more complex patterns in the translation task.
- Removing dropout (setting it to 0) had a minimal positive effect in the baseline configuration, but slightly decreased performance when combined with higher rank and alpha. This implies that a small amount of dropout may be beneficial for generalization, especially with more complex models.
- Excluding the normalization layers from the additional targets resulted in a slight performance decrease compared to including them, indicating that fine-tuning these layers may contribute to better adaptation to the translation task.

These findings provide valuable insights into optimizing the SFT process for Tibetan-Chinese translation. The results demonstrate that careful tuning of LoRA parameters and thoughtful selection of fine-tuning targets can lead to significant improvements in translation quality.

4.4 Ablation Study

To validate the effectiveness of our second stage (continued pre-training with parallel corpora), we conducted an ablation study. We compared our full three-stage model (TiLamb-Trans) with a two-stage variant that skips the continued pre-training stage. In this variant, we directly use the parallel corpora from stage two as additional supervised fine-tuning (SFT) data in the third stage. This increases the SFT data volume by approximately 15 times. The results are presented in Table 3.

Table 3. Ablation study results

Model	BLEU Score	SFT Data Size
TiLamb-Trans (Full three-stage model)	37.82	1.47M sentence pairs
Two-stage model (No continued pre-training)	37.95	23.70M sentence pairs

The results demonstrate that while increasing the SFT data volume by about 15 times (from 1.47M to 23.70M sentence pairs) in the two-stage model, the performance improvement is minimal (only 0.13 BLEU points). This suggests that our continued pre-training stage is highly efficient in leveraging parallel corpora, achieving comparable performance with significantly less computational cost and without the need for extensive labeled data in the fine-tuning stage.

5 Conclusion

This study optimizes the Tibetan-Chinese machine translation system by combining large-scale incremental pre-training with supervised fine-tuning. The evaluation results clearly demonstrate a significant improvement in translation quality compared to the baseline model. During the experiments, we achieved optimal performance by carefully adjusting key parameters such as Temperature and Top P, resulting in higher alignment between the generated translations and the reference texts. This effectively validates the efficacy of our approach and provides strong support for the further development of Tibetan-Chinese machine translation technology.

Acknowledgments. This work is supported by the National Social Science Foundation (22&ZD035), the National Nature Science Foundation (61972436), and the Minzu University of China Foundation (GRSCP202316, 2023QNYL22, 2024GJYY43).

Disclosure of Interests. The authors declare no competing interests.

References

1. Zhuang, W., Gao, G., Sun, Y.: TiKG-30K: a Tibetan knowledge graph dataset based on representation learning. In: Proceedings of the 22nd Chinese National Conference on Computational Linguistics, pp. 145–154 (2023)
2. Dan, Z., Chen, L., Deng, J., Pang, X., Sun, Y.: Difficult question generation of Tibetan machine reading based on data enhancement. In: Proceedings of the 22nd Chinese National Conference on Computational Linguistics, pp. 164–173 (2023)
3. Deng, J., Shi, H., Yu, X., Bao, W., Sun, Y., Zhao, X.: MiLMo: minority multilingual pre-trained language model. In: 2023 IEEE International Conference on Systems, Man, and Cybernetics (SMC), pp. 329–334. IEEE (2023)
4. Zhuoma, R.: An overview of Tibetan to Chinese neural machine translation research. Tibet's Sci. Technol. **46**(02), 76–80 (2024)
5. Vaswani, A.: Attention is all you need. Adv. Neural Inf. Process. Syst. (2017)
6. Yachao, L., Deyi, X., Min, Z., Jing, J., Ning, M., Jianmin, Y.: Research on Tibetan-Chinese neural network machine translation. J. Chin. Inf. Process. **31**(06), 103–109 (2017)
7. Jiacuo, C., Duanzhu, S., Maosong, S., Maoxian, Z., Jia, S.: Research on Tibetan-Chinese machine translation method with iterative back translation strategy. J. Chin. Inf. Process. **34**(11), 67–73+83 (2020)
8. Cao, Z., Mu, Y., et al.: Pre-trained neural machine translation: progress and analysis. J. Chin. Inf. Process. **38**(06), 1–23 (2024)
9. Cui, Y., Yang, Z., Yao, X.: Efficient and effective text encoding for Chinese llama and alpaca. arXiv preprint arXiv:2304.08177 (2023)
10. Zhuang, W., Sun, Y., Zhao, X.: TiLamb: a Tibetan large language model based on incremental pre-training. In: Proceedings of the 23th Chinese National Conference on Computational Linguistics (2024)
11. Hu, E.J., et al.: LoRa: low-rank adaptation of large language models. arXiv preprint arXiv:2106.09685 (2021)

HW-TSC's Submission to the CCMT 2024 Machine Translation Tasks

Zhanglin Wu[✉][📷], Yuanchang Luo, Daimeng Wei, Jiawei Zheng, Bin Wei, Zongyao Li, Hengchao Shang, Jiaxin Guo, Shaojun Li, Weidong Zhang, Ning Xie, and Hao Yang

Huawei Translation Service Center, Beijing, China
{wuzhanglin2,luoyuanchang1,weidaimeng,zhengjiawei15,
weibin29,lizongyao,shanghengchao,guojiaxin1,lishaojun18,
zhangweidong17,nicolas.xie,yanghao30}@huawei.com

Abstract. This paper presents the submission of Huawei Translation Services Center (HW-TSC) to machine translation tasks of the 20th China Conference on Machine Translation (CCMT 2024). We participate in the bilingual machine translation task and multi-domain machine translation task. For these two translation tasks, we use training strategies such as regularized dropout, bidirectional training, data diversification, forward translation, back translation, alternated training, curriculum learning, and transductive ensemble learning to train neural machine translation (NMT) models based on the deep Transformer-big architecture. Furthermore, to explore whether large language model (LLM) can effectively improve the translation quality of NMT models, we use supervised fine-tuning (SFT) to train llama2-13b as an Automatic post-editing (APE) model to improve the translation results of the NMT model on the multi-domain machine translation task. By using these plyometric strategies, our submission achieves a competitive result in the final evaluation.

Keywords: CCMT 2024 · NMT · Transformer · LLM · APE

1 Introduction

Neural machine translation (NMT) [1–3] allows translation systems to be trained end-to-end without dealing with issues like word alignment, translation rules, and complex decoding algorithms that characterize statistical machine translation (SMT) [4] systems. Although NMT develops rapidly in recent years, it relies heavily on big data - large-scale, high-quality bilingual corpora. Due to the cost and scarcity of real corpora, synthetic data plays an important role in improving translation quality. Existing methods for synthesizing data in NMT focus on leveraging monolingual data during training. Among them, data diversification [5], forward translation [6], and back translation [7] are widely used to generate synthetic bilingual corpora. Such synthetic data can be used to improve the performance of NMT models. Although synthetic data is efficient, it inevitably contains noise and erroneous translations. Alternated training [8] introduces real data as a guide and alternately uses synthetic data and real data during the training process, which can prevent the training of the NMT model from being interfered with by noisy synthetic data. Another direction to improve the performance of NMT models is to use more efficient training strategies. Methods such as regularized dropout [9], bidirectional training [10], and curriculum learning [11] allow the NMT model to more effectively utilize limited data during the training process, while transductive ensemble learning [12] can aggregate the translation capabilities of multiple models into one model.

The powerful capabilities of LLM in logical reasoning and language generation promote the further development of machine translation. Despite the superior performance of translation models, existing models usually use beam search decoding [13] and top-1 hypothesis selection for inference. These techniques struggle to fully exploit the rich information in various N-best hypotheses, making them suboptimal for translation tasks that require a single high-quality output sequence. GenTranslate [14] utilizes the rich language knowledge and powerful reasoning capabilities of large language model (LLM) [15–18] to integrate the rich information in the N-best list from the basic model, generating higher-quality translation results.

To promote academic exchanges and connections between domestic and foreign research units and relevant industry partners, and to jointly advance the development of machine translation research and technology, we participate in the bilingual machine translation tasks and multi-domain machine translation tasks organized by CCMT2024. For these two translation tasks, we use training strategies such as regularized dropout [9], bidirectional training [10], data diversification [5], forward translation [6], back translation [7], alternated training [8], curriculum learning [11], and transductive ensemble learning [12] to train neural machine translation (NMT) models based on the deep Transformer-big architecture [19–22]. Additionally, drawing inspiration from the GenTranslate method [14], we utilize supervised fine-tuning (SFT) [23] to train llama2-13b[1] as an automatic post-editing (APE) model [24], aimed at enhancing the translation outputs of NMT models in the multi-domain machine translation task.

This paper expands on the details of our translation system in different translation tasks. The structure of the remaining sections is as follows: Sect. 2 describes the data size and data pre-processing; Sect. 3 provides an overview of our NMT system; Sect. 4 explains our APE system; Sect. 5 presents the parameter settings and experimental results; Sect. 6 summarizes our systems.

2 Dataset

2.1 Data Size

According to the requirements of the CCMT 2024 outline, we train the NMT system from scratch on the bilingual translation task using the officially pro-

---

[1] https://huggingface.co/meta-llama/Llama-2-13b-chat-hf.

vided data. Table 1 shows the training data size for each language pair of the bilingual MT task after data pre-processing. These language pairs include English→Chinese (en→zh), Chinese→English (zh→en), Mongolian→Chinese (mn→zh), Tibetan→Chinese (ti→zh), and Uyghur→Chinese (uy→zh). It should be noted that in the en→zh and zh→en translation tasks, since the training data of WMT 2024 is shared with CCMT 2024, we additionally use the training data provided by the WMT 2024 general MT task to scale up the training data.

Table 1. Data size for each bilingual MT task after data pre-processing

	en→zh	zh→en	mn→zh	ti→zh	uy→zh
Bilingual	25.12M	25.12M	1.24M	0.97M	0.16M
Source Monolingual	50M	50M	-	-	-
Target Monolingual	50M	50M	4.89M	4.89M	4.89M

Table 2 shows the training data size for the multi-domain machine translation task after data preprocessing. For this zh→en task, the official does not provide any training data, but allows participating units to construct their own training data. Therefore, we use the training data from the bilingual translation task and also collect 33.36 million high-quality domain-related bilingual data.

Table 2. Data size for multi-domain MT task after data pre-processing

	Bilingual	Source Monolingual	Target Monolingual
zh→en	58.48M	50M	50M

2.2 Data Pre-processing

The data pre-processing process is as follows:

- Remove duplicate sentences or sentence pairs.
- Remove invisible characters and xml escape characters.
- Convert full-width symbols to half-width symbols.
- Use jieba[2] to pre-segment Chinese sentences.
- Use mosesdecoder[3] to normalize English punctuation.
- Use opencc[4] to convert traditional Chinese to simplified Chinese.
- Use fasttext[5] to filter other language sentences.

---

[2] https://github.com/fxsjy/jieba.
[3] https://github.com/moses-smt/mosesdecoder.
[4] https://github.com/BYVoid/OpenCC.
[5] https://github.com/facebookresearch/fastText.

- Use fast_align[6] to filter poorly aligned sentence pairs.
- Filter out sentences with more than 150 tokens in bilingual data.
- Split long sentences in monolingual data into multiple short sentences.
- Filter out sentence pairs with token ratio greater than 4 or less than 0.25.
- When performing subword segmentation, joint Byte Pair Encoding[7] [25] is used for mn→zh, ti→zh and uy→zh translation tasks, and joint sentencepiece[8] [26] is used for zh→en and en→zh translation tasks.

3 NMT System

3.1 System Overview

Transformer is the state-of-the-art model structure in recent MT evaluations. There are two parts of research to improve this kind: the first part uses wide networks (eg: Transformer-Big [27]), and the other part uses deeper language representations (eg: Deep Transformer [28]). For all MT tasks, we combine these two improvements, adopting the Deep Transformer-Big [19–22] model structure to train the NMT system. Deep Transformer-Big uses pre-layer normalization, features 25-layer encoder, 6-layer decoder, 16-heads self-attention, 1024-dimensional word embedding and 4096-dimensional ffn embedding.

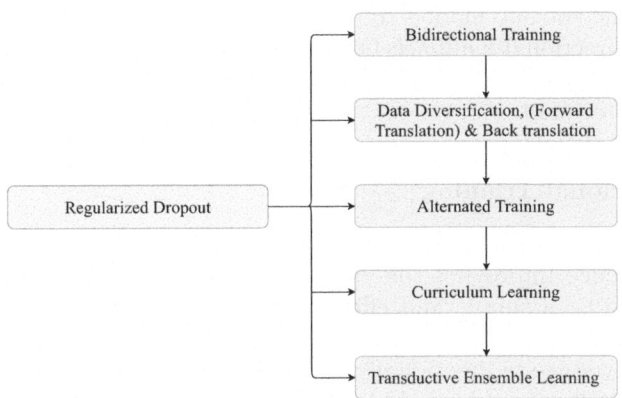

Fig. 1. The overall training flow chart of our NMT system.

Figure 1 shows the overall training flow chart of our NMT system on the bilingual machine translation task and multi-domain machine translation task. We use training strategies such as regularized dropout [9], bidirectional training

---

[6] https://github.com/clab/fast_align.
[7] https://github.com/soaxelbrooke/python-bpe.
[8] https://github.com/google/sentencepiece.

[10], data diversification [5], forward translation [6], back translation [7], alternated training [8], curriculum learning [11], and transductive ensemble learning [12] to train NMT models based on the deep Transformer-big architecture [19–21]. Since forward translation relies on source monolingual and mn→zh, ti→zh and uy→zh translation tasks do not provide source monolingual, we do not use forward translation on these three tasks. Furthermore, our choice of back translation methods varies across different tasks. For en→zh and zh→en tasks where forward translation is available, we use sampling back translation (ST) [29], and for other tasks we use tagged back translation (Tagged BT) [30].

3.2 Regularized Dropout

Dropout [31] is a widely used technique for regularizing deep neural network training, which is crucial to prevent over-fitting and improve the generalization ability of deep models. Dropout performs implicit ensemble by simply dropping a certain proportion of hidden units from the neural network during training, which may cause an unnegligible inconsistency between training and inference. Regularized Dropout[9] (R-Drop) [9] is a simple yet more effective alternative to regularize the training inconsistency induced by dropout. Concretely, in each mini-batch training, each data sample goes through the forward pass twice, and each pass is processed by a different sub model by randomly dropping out some hidden units. R-Drop forces the two distributions for the same data sample outputted by the two sub models to be consistent with each other, through minimizing the bidirectional Kullback-Leibler (KL) divergence [32] between the two distributions. In this way, the inconsistency between the training and inference stage can be alleviated.

3.3 Bidirectional Training

Many studies have shown that pre-training can transfer the knowledge and data distribution, hence improving the generalization. Bidirectional training (BiT) [10] happens to be a simple and effective pre-training method to improve the translation quality of NMT models. Bidirectional training is divided into two stages, the early stage bidirectionally updates model parameters, and then tune the model normally. To achieve bidirectional updating, we only need to reconstruct the training samples from "src→tgt" to "src+tgt→tgt+src" without any complicated model modifications. Notably, BiT does not increase any parameters or training steps, requiring the parallel data merely.

3.4 Data Diversification

Data Diversification (DD) [5] is a data augmentation method to boost NMT performance. It diversifies the training data by using the predictions of multiple forward and backward models and then merging them with the original dataset

---

[9] https://github.com/dropreg/R-Drop.

on which the final NMT model is trained. DD is applicable to all NMT models. It does not require extra monolingual data, nor does it add more computations and parameters. To conserve training resources, we only use one forward model and one backward model when using DD.

3.5 Forward Translation

Forward translation (FT), also known as self-training [6], is one of the most commonly used data augmentation methods. FT has proven effective for improving NMT performance by augmenting model training with synthetic and authentic parallel data. Generally, FT is performed in three steps: (1) randomly sample a subset from the large-scale source monolingual data; (2) use a "teacher" NMT model to translate the subset data into the target language to construct the synthetic parallel data; (3) combine the synthetic and authentic parallel data to train a "student" NMT model.

3.6 Back-Translation

An effective method to improve NMT with target monolingual data is to augment the parallel training data with back translation (BT) [7,40]. There are many works broaden the understanding of BT and investigates a number of methods to generate synthetic source sentences. Edunov et al. [29] find that back translations obtained via sampling or noised beam outputs are more effective than back translations generated by beam or greedy search in most scenarios. Caswell et al. [30] show that the main role of such noised beam outputs is not to diversify the source side, but simply to indicate to the model that the given source is synthetic. Therefore, they propose a simpler technique, Tagged BT. This method uses an extra token to mark back translated source sentences, which is generally outperform than noised BT.

3.7 Alternated Training

While synthetic bilingual data have demonstrated their effectiveness in NMT, adding more synthetic data often deteriorates translation performance since the synthetic data inevitably contains noise and erroneous translations. Alternated training (AT) [8] introduce authentic data as guidance to prevent the training of NMT models from being disturbed by noisy synthetic data. AT describes the synthetic and authentic data as two types of different approximations for the distribution of infinite authentic data, and its basic idea is to alternate synthetic and authentic data iteratively during training until the model converges.

3.8 Curriculum Learning

A practical curriculum learning (CL) [33] method should address two main questions: how to rank the training examples, and how to modify the sampling procedure based on this ranking. For ranking, we choose to estimate the difficulty of training samples according to their domain feature [11]. The calculation formula of domain feature is as follows, where θ_{in} represents an in-domain NMT model, and θ_{out} represents a out-of-domain NMT model.

$$q(x,y) = \frac{\log P(y|x;\theta_{in}) - \log P(y|x;\theta_{out})}{|y|} \quad (1)$$

For the sampling procedure, we adopt a probabilistic CL strategy[10] that takes advantage of the spirit of CL in a nondeterministic fashion without discarding the good practice of original standard training policy.

3.9 Transductive Ensemble Learning

Ensemble learning [34], which aggregates multiple diverse models for inference, is a common practice to improve the accuracy of machine learning tasks. However, it has been observed that the conventional ensemble methods only bring marginal improvement for NMT when individual models are strong or there are a large number of individual models. Transductive Ensemble Learning (TEL) [12] study how to effectively aggregate multiple NMT models under the transductive setting where the source sentences of the test set are known. TEL uses all individual models to translate the source test set into the target language space and then finetune a strong model on the translated synthetic data, which boosts strong individual models with significant improvement and benefits a lot from more individual models.

4 APE System

4.1 System Overview

There is recently a surge in research interests in Transformer-based LLMs, such as ChatGPT [15,16] and LLaMA [17,18,39]. Benefiting from the giant model size and oceans of training data, LLMs can understand better the language structures and semantic meanings behind raw text, thereby showing excellent performance in a wide range of natural language processing (NLP) tasks. As shown in Fig. 2, we use supervised fine-tuning to train LLM as an APE model to improve the translation quality of our NMT model on the zh→en multi-domain machine translation task. Our APE system is inspired by the GenTranslate [14], but the difference is that we use source language text as part of the input information of LLM because we believe that adding source language text helps ensure the fidelity of the target language translation.

---

[10] https://github.com/kevinduh/sockeye-recipes/tree/master/egs/curriculum.

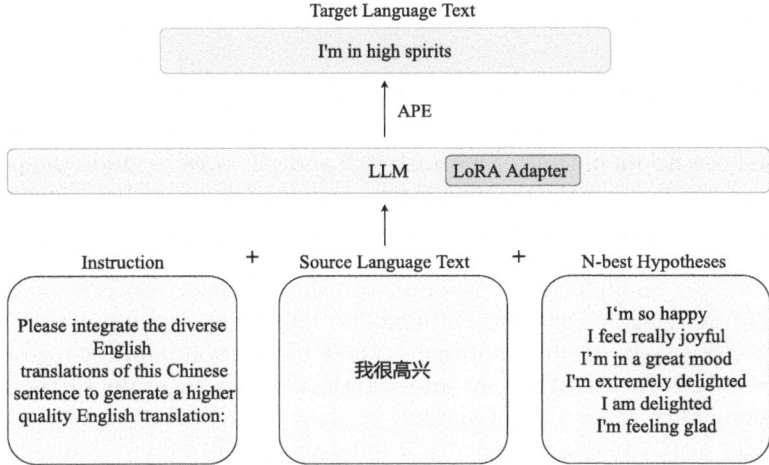

Fig. 2. APE System for the zh→en multi-domain machine translation task.

4.2 Efficient LLM Finetuning

We choose Llama2-13b as the base LLM for our APE system. When performing supervised fine-tuning on this base LLM, full fine-tuning by retraining all model parameters is usually expensive and requires a long training period. Therefore, we adopt the popular LoRA-based efficient parameter fine-tuning method[11] [35]. This method freezes the pre-trained model weights and injects trainable rank decomposition matrices into each layer of the Transformer architecture, greatly reducing the number of trainable parameters for downstream tasks. LoRA can lower the hardware threshold by up to 3x when using an adaptive optimizer because we do not need to compute gradients or maintain optimizer state for most parameters.

4.3 HypoTranslate Dataset

To build the APE training data for Efficient LLM fine-tuning, we first use the cometkiwi model[12] [36] to select high-quality bilingual data. Specifically, we select bilingual data with a cometkiwi score greater than 0.8 on the zh→en language pair. Then we use our trained NMT model as a base translation model to decode the N-best hypotheses from the source language text via a beam search algorithm, where the beam size N is set to 10.

---

[11] https://github.com/microsoft/LoRA.
[12] https://huggingface.co/Unbabel/wmt22-cometkiwi-da.

5 Experiments

5.1 Setup

We use Pytorch-based Fairseq [37] open-source framework to train the NMT model, and use Adam optimizer with $\beta 1=0.9$ and $\beta 2=0.98$ to guide the parameter optimization. During the training phase, each model uses 8 GPUs for training, batch size is 2048, update frequency is 4, learning rate is 5e-4, label smoothing rate is 0.1 and warm-up steps is 4000. We set dropout to 0.1 for high-resource translation tasks and 0.3 for low-resource translation tasks respectively. In addition, when applying R-Drop for training, we follow the setting of L et al. [9], using $reg\_label\_smoothed\_cross\_entropy$ as the loss function, and set reg-alpha to 5. Then, we use SacreBLEU [38] and COMET[13] [35] to evaluate the overall translation quality of each NMT model.

To adapt LoRA-based efficient LLM fine-tuning [35], we use llama-recipes[14] open source framework to train the APE model. The following is the configuration of LoRA: lora_rank is 32, lora_alpha is 64, lora_dropout is 0.05, lora_modules are "q", "k", "v", "o", "gate", "down", "up". We train 2 epochs with AdamW optimizer [36], with learning rate initialized to 1e-4 and then linearly decrease to 1e-5 during training. The batch size is set to 6, with accumulation iterations set to 8 (i.e., real batch size is 48), the context length is 4096, and the batch strategy is packing.

5.2 Bilingual MT Results

en→zh & zh→en. On en→zh and zh→en translation tasks, we use BiT and R-Drop to build a strong baseline system. Subsequently, we adopt the data augmentation methods of DD, FT and ST to improve the translation quality of baseline System. Next, we use AT guide model training with authentic bilingual data. Then, we use CL for domain adaptation. Finally, we train multiple NMT systems and integrate them using TEL as the final translation system. Table 3 shows the evaluation results of en→zh and zh→en translation systems. Compared with the baseline system, the final en→zh and zh→en translation systems improves significantly on CCMT 2022 test sets.

mn→zh, ti→zh & uy→zh. On mn→zh, ti→zh and uy→zh translation tasks, we also use BiT and R-Drop to build a strong baseline system. The subsequent training method is similar to en→zh and zh→en translation tasks. The only difference is that we adopt DD and Tagged BT in the data augmentation stage, which is due to the lack of source language monolingual for these three tasks. Table 4 is the evaluation results of mn→zh, ti→zh and uy→zh translation systems on CCMT 2022 test set or CCMT 2023 test set. Overall, the final translation systems for all three tasks improves significantly compared to the baseline.

---

[13] https://huggingface.co/Unbabel/wmt20-comet-da.
[14] https://github.com/meta-llama/llama-recipes.

Table 3. BLEU and COMET scores of en→zh & zh→en NMT system

	en→zh		zh→en	
CCMT 2022 test set	BLEU	COMET	BLEU	COMET
BiT R-Drop baseline	54.37	0.6953	43.46	0.6754
+ DD, FT & ST	56.71	0.7203	44.57	0.6895
+ AT	57.03	0.7358	44.74	0.6915
+ CL	57.49	0.7527	46.83	0.7060
+ TEL	**57.71**	**0.7610**	**47.45**	**0.7264**

Table 4. BLEU scores of mn→zh, ti→zh and uy→zh translation system

CCMT test set	mn→zh (2023)	ti→zh (2022)	uy→zh (2023)
BiT R-Drop baseline	55.87	32.69	42.58
+ DD & Tagged BT	59.73	36.52	49.31
+ AT	62.01	37.45	49.91
+ CL	62.96	38.40	50.54
+ TEL	**63.59**	**40.90**	**51.27**

5.3 Multi-Domain MT Results

On the zh→en multi-domain machine translation task, we first select the best model (TEL) in the zh→en bilingual machine translation task as the baseline model. Then, we use the collected high-quality domain-related bilingual data to fine-tune for domain adaptation. Finally, we use the APE model based on llama-13b to improve the translation results generated by the NMT model, and use the post-editing result as the final translation result.

Table 5 and Table 6 shows the evaluation results of zh→en multi-domain translation system on the dev set. It shows that domain adaptation is critical to multi-domain translation, and the powerful generation capability of LLM can further help improve the translation quality of the NMT model in the multi-domain translation task.

Table 5. BLEU scores of zh→en multi-domain translation system

dev set	IT	car	electronic	energy	finance	literature	machine	medical	average
TEL	30.72	30.08	42.57	32.94	33.35	36.78	37.38	49.51	36.67
+ fine-tuning	39.08	36.50	50.12	39.42	44.18	43.71	45.11	57.26	44.42
+ APE	43.3	39.59	50.76	39.59	47.75	47.71	50.09	59.82	47.33

Table 6. COMET scores of zh→en multi-domain translation system

dev set	IT	car	electronic	energy	finance	literatrue	machine	medical	average
TEL	0.4218	0.5406	0.6828	0.4785	0.5919	0.5128	0.5732	0.7747	0.5720
+ fine-tuning	0.5299	0.5788	0.7417	0.5850	0.6432	0.6689	0.6935	0.8227	0.6580
+ APE	0.5649	0.5868	0.7547	0.5857	0.6788	0.7012	0.7608	0.8221	0.6819

6 Conclusion

This paper presents HW-TSC's submission to the bilingual machine translation task and multi-domain machine translation task of CCMT 2024. For both translation tasks, we use a series of training strategies to train NMT models based on the deep Transformer-big architecture. Additionally, for the multi-domain machine translation task, we use the powerful generation capabilities of LLM to post-edit the translation results of the NMT model to obtain better translations. Relevant experimental results also show the effectiveness of our adopted strategies. By using these enhancement strategies, our submission achieves a competitive result in the final evaluation.

References

1. Sutskever, I., Vinyals, O., Le, Q.V.: Sequence to sequence learning with neural networks. Adv. Neural Inf. Process. Syst. **27** (2014)
2. Bahdanau, D., Cho, K.H., Bengio, Y.: Neural machine translation by jointly learning to align and translate. In: 3rd International Conference on Learning Representations, ICLR 2015 (2015)
3. Gehring, J., Auli, M., Grangier, D., et al.: Convolutional sequence to sequence learning. In: Proceedings of the 34th International Conference on Machine Learning, vol. 70, pp. 1243–1252 (2017)
4. Koehn, P., Hoang, H., Birch, A., et al.: Moses: open source toolkit for statistical machine translation. In: Proceedings of the 45th Annual Meeting of the Association for Computational Linguistics Companion Volume Proceedings of the Demo and Poster Sessions, pp. 177–180. Association for Computational Linguistics (2007)
5. Nguyen, X.-P., et al.: Data diversification: a simple strategy for neural machine translation. Adv. Neural Inf. Process. Syst. **33**, 10018–10029 (2020)
6. Abdulmumin, I., Galadanci, B.S., Isa, A.: Enhanced back-translation for low resource neural machine translation using self-training. In: International Conference on Information and Communication Technology and Applications, pp. 355–371. Springer, Cham (2020)
7. Sennrich, R., Haddow, B., Birch, A.: Improving neural machine translation models with monolingual data. In: Proceedings of the 54th Annual Meeting of the Association for Computational Linguistics (Volume 1: Long Papers) (2016)
8. Jiao, R., Yang, Z., Sun, M., et al.: Alternated training with synthetic and authentic data for neural machine translation. In: Findings of the Association for Computational Linguistics: ACL-IJCNLP 2021, pp. 1828–1834 (2021)

9. Wu, L., Li, J., Wang, Y., et al.: R-Drop: regularized dropout for neural networks. In: Advances in Neural Information Processing Systems (2021)
10. Ding, L., Wu, D., Tao, D.: Improving neural machine translation by bidirectional training. In: Proceedings of the 2021 Conference on Empirical Methods in Natural Language Processing (2021)
11. Wang, W., et al.: Learning a multi-domain curriculum for neural machine translation. In: Proceedings of the 58th Annual Meeting of the Association for Computational Linguistics (2020)
12. Wang, Y., et al.: Transductive ensemble learning for neural machine translation. In: Proceedings of the AAAI Conference on Artificial Intelligence, vol. 34, no. 04 (2020)
13. Freitag, M., Al-Onaizan, Y.: Beam search strategies for neural machine translation. ACL **2017**, 56 (2017)
14. Hu, Y., Chen, C., Yang, C.H.H., et al.: GenTranslate: large language models are generative multilingual speech and machine translators. arXiv preprint arXiv:2402.06894 (2024)
15. Wu, T., He, S., Liu, J., et al.: A brief overview of ChatGPT: the history, status quo and potential future development. IEEE/CAA J. Automatica Sinica **10**(5), 1122–1136 (2023)
16. Achiam, J., Adler, S., Agarwal, S., et al.: GPT-4 technical report. arXiv preprint arXiv:2303.08774 (2023)
17. Touvron, H., Lavril, T., Izacard, G., et al.: Llama: open and efficient foundation language models. arXiv preprint arXiv:2302.13971 (2023)
18. Touvron, H., Martin, L., Stone, K., et al.: Llama 2: open foundation and fine-tuned chat models. arXiv preprint arXiv:2307.09288 (2023)
19. Wu, Z., et al.: Multi-strategy enhanced neural machine translation for Chinese minority languages. In: China Conference on Machine Translation, pp. 37–44. Springer, Singapore (2022)
20. Wu, Z., et al.: HW-TSC's neural machine translation system for CCMT 2023. In: China Conference on Machine Translation, pp. 13–27. Springer, Singapore (2023)
21. Wu, Z., et al.: Treating general MT shared task as a multi-domain adaptation problem: HW-TSC's submission to the WMT23 general MT shared task. In: Proceedings of the Eighth Conference on Machine Translation, pp. 170–174 (2023)
22. Wei, D., et al.: HW-TSC's submissions to the WMT 2022 general machine translation shared task. In: Proceedings of the Seventh Conference on Machine Translation (WMT), pp. 403–410 (2022)
23. Dong, G., Yuan, H., Lu, K., et al.: How abilities in large language models are affected by supervised fine-tuning data composition. arXiv preprint arXiv:2310.05492 (2023)
24. Raunak, V., Sharaf, A., Wang, Y., et al.: Leveraging GPT-4 for automatic translation post-editing. In: Findings of the Association for Computational Linguistics: EMNLP 2023, pp. 12009–12024 (2023)
25. Sennrich, R., Haddow, B., Birch, A.: Neural machine translation of rare words with subword units. In: Proceedings of the 54th Annual Meeting of the Association for Computational Linguistics (Volume 1: Long Papers), pp. 1715–1725 (2016)
26. Kudo, T., Richardson, J.: SentencePiece: a simple and language independent subword tokenizer and detokenizer for neural text processing. In: Proceedings of the 2018 Conference on Empirical Methods in Natural Language Processing: System Demonstrations (2018)
27. Vaswani, A., et al.: Attention is all you need. Adv. Neural Inf. Process. Syst. **30** (2017)

28. Wang, Q., Li, B., Xiao, T., et al.: Learning deep transformer models for machine translation. In: Proceedings of the 57th Annual Meeting of the Association for Computational Linguistics, pp. 1810–1822 (2019)
29. Edunov, S., Ott, M., Auli, M., et al.: Understanding back-translation at scale. In: Proceedings of the Conference on Empirical Methods in Natural Language Processing, pp. 489–500 (2018)
30. Caswell, I., Chelba, C., Grangier, D.: Tagged back-translation. In: Proceedings of the Fourth Conference on Machine Translation (Volume 1: Research Papers), pp. 53–63 (2019)
31. Srivastava, N., Hinton, G., Krizhevsky, A., et al.: Dropout: a simple way to prevent neural networks from overfitting. J. Mach. Learn. Res. **15**(1), 1929–1958 (2014)
32. Van Erven, T., Harremos, P.: Rényi divergence and Kullback-Leibler divergence. IEEE Trans. Inf. Theory **60**(7), 3797–3820 (2014)
33. Zhang, X., et al.: Curriculum learning for domain adaptation in neural machine translation. In: Proceedings of the 2019 Conference of the North American Chapter of the Association for Computational Linguistics: Human Language Technologies (Long and Short Papers), vol. 1 (2019)
34. Garmash, E., Monz, C.: Ensemble learning for multi-source neural machine translation. In: Proceedings of COLING 2016, the 26th International Conference on Computational Linguistics: Technical Papers, pp. 1409–1418 (2016)
35. Hu, E.J., Shen, Y., Wallis, P., et al.: LoRa: low-rank adaptation of large language models. arXiv preprint arXiv:2106.09685 (2021)
36. Rei, R., Stewart, C., Farinha, A.C., et al.: COMET: a neural framework for MT evaluation. In: Proceedings of the Conference on Empirical Methods in Natural Language Processing (EMNLP), pp. 2685–2702 (2020)
37. Ott, M., Edunov, S., Baevski, A., et al.: Fairseq: a fast, extensible toolkit for sequence modeling. In: Proceedings of the Conference of the North American Chapter of the Association for Computational Linguistics (Demonstrations), pp. 48–53 (2019)
38. Post, M.: A call for clarity in reporting BLEU scores. In: Proceedings of the Third Conference on Machine Translation: Research Papers, pp. 186–191 (2018)
39. Guo, J., Yang, H., Li, Z., Wei, D., Shang, H., Chen, X.: A novel paradigm boosting translation capabilities of large language models. In: Findings of the Association for Computational Linguistics: NAACL, pp. 639–649 (2024)
40. Wei, D., et al.: Text style transfer back-translation. In: Proceedings of the 61st Annual Meeting of the Association for Computational Linguistics (Volume 1: Long Papers), pp. 7944–7959 (2023)

ISTIC's Neural Machine Translation Systems for CCMT' 2024

Zhuofan Hu, Ningyuan Deng, and Yanqing He[✉]

Research Center of Information Theory and Methodology, Institute of Scientific and Technical Information of China, Beijing, China 100038
{huzhuofan2023,dengny2022,heyq}@istic.ac.cn

Abstract. This paper presents the system architecture and technical details adopted by Institute of Scientific and Technical Information of China (ISTIC) during the evaluation at the 20th China Conference on Machine Translation (CCMT 2024). ISTIC participated in two evaluation tasks of machine translation: the English-Chinese News Domain Task and the Multi-Domain Machine Translation Task. The paper mainly discusses a translation method that combines the Transformer architecture with polishing by Qwen, data preprocessing methods.

Keywords: Neural machine translation · Large language models · Translation polishing

1 Introduction

ISTIC participated in the 20th China Conference on Machine Translation (CCMT'2024), tackling both the English-Chinese news translation task and the multi-domain machine translation task. This paper presents the entire framework and technical details of ISTIC's submissions.

For the English-Chinese news translation task, we adopted a translation method that combines the Transformer architecture with polishing by Qwen[1].

For the multi-domain machine translation task, we developed a model capable of effectively translating across multiple domains by constructing a comprehensive dataset encompassing various fields.

The structure of this paper is as follows: Sect. 2 introduces the datasets used and the data preprocessing methods. Section 3 describes our machine translation system. Section 4 discusses the experiments. Section 5 presents the conclusions.

2 Data

2.1 Data Size

For the English-Chinese news domain task, we trained the transformer model using the dataset released by the evaluation organizer which has about 8 million

---
[1] https://github.com/QwenLM/Qwen.

sentence pairs. To train the Qwen polishing model, we created a dataset of 300 thousand sentence pairs combining the Niutrans dataset[2], the MTME multi-candidate dataset[3], and a portion of data extracted from the dataset released by the evaluation organizers. These datasets contain rich content. especially the MTME multi-candidate dataset, which includes candidate translations from various translation systems, encompassing different translation styles and quality levels.

For the multi-domain machine translation task, we trained the translation model using a dataset as diverse and comprehensive as possible which has 100 million sentence pairs. The dataset includes, but is not limited to, Wanfang thesis title data, journal articles, dissertations, United Nations English-Chinese parallel corpora[4], etc.

Table 1 shows the size of the dataset after preprocessing.

Table 1. Data Size

Task	Model	Data Size
English-Chinese news translation task	Transformer	8M
	Qwen polishing	300k
Multi-Domain Machine Translation Task	Transformer	100M

2.2 Data Pre-Processing

The data preprocessing steps are as follows:

String Filtering: This step involves the removal of special characters, illegal characters, and other non-standard inputs.

Format Normalization: Punctuation normalization is conducted using the mosesdecoder[5], which also converts full-width characters to half-width characters.

Simplified-Traditional Conversion: OpenCC[6] is utilized to convert Traditional Chinese characters into Simplified Chinese characters.

Tokenization: The Jieba toolkit[7] is used for tokenizing Chinese sentences, while the Natural Language Toolkit (NLTK)[8] is employed for tokenizing English sentences.

Length Ratio Filtering: Sentences shorter than 5 words or longer than 150 words are removed. Additionally, sentence pairs with a length ratio greater than 3 are also discarded.

---

[2] https://github.com/NiuTrans/NiuTrans.SMT.
[3] https://github.com/google-research/mt-metrics-eval.
[4] https://conferences.unite.un.org/uncorpus.
[5] https://github.com/moses-smt/mosesdecoder.
[6] https://github.com/BYVoid/OpenCC.
[7] https://github.com/fxsjy/jieba.
[8] https://www.nltk.org/.

Alignment Quality Filtering: Sentence pairs with poor alignment quality are filtered out using fast_align[9].

Subword segmentation: Byte-Pair Encoding (BPE) [1] is used for subword segmentation with a vocabulary size of 32k.

3 System Overview

Transformer is used to build systems for the English-Chinese news domain task and the multi-domain machine translation task.

Transformer [2] is structured into two main parts: the encoder, which reads and processes the input data, and the decoder, which generates the output. This architecture has been foundational for developing various state-of-the-art models, such as BERT and GPT, facilitating the research in machine translation, text generation, and beyond.

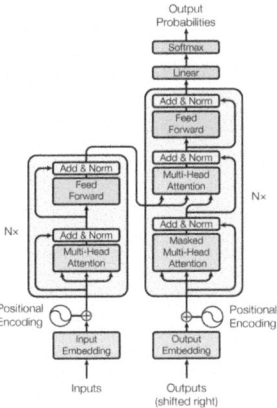

Fig. 1. Transformer

For the English-Chinese news domain task, we also used Qwen to polish the translation results of the Transformer.

Qwen [3] is a large language model based on the Transformer architecture, featuring 32 stacked Transformer blocks. The model has a word embedding dimension of 4096 and a total vocabulary size of 151,936. Each Transformer block includes an attention mechanism and a two-layer multi-layer perceptron (MLP), with an intermediate dimension of 11,008 for the MLP. Additionally, the model employs RMSNorm for layer normalization and sinusoidal positional encoding to enhance its ability to perceive positions.

We first train a Transformer with Data Set 1, which is the official dataset released by the evaluation organizer, following data preprocessing. Then use the

---

[9] https://github.com/clab/fast_align.

trained Transformer is used to translate the source side of Data Set 2, which is a dataset combining the Niutrans dataset, the MTME multi-candidate dataset, and a portion of data extracted from the dataset released by the evaluation organizers. Next, we calculate the COMET scores and label the translation results based on these scores. Translations scoring in the top 10% are labeled as [good], those from the top 10% to 30% are labeled as [mediocre], and the remainder as [bad]. We use the labeled dataset to finetune Qwen to polish the translation results.

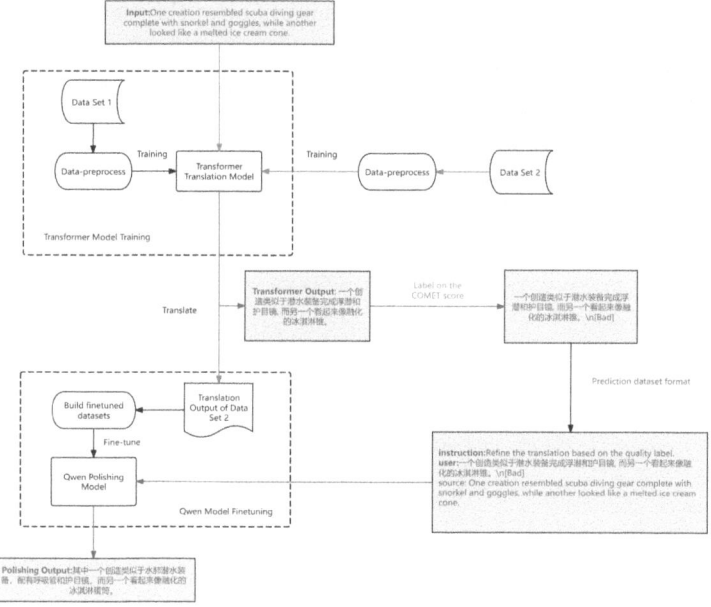

Fig. 2. Overall Framework

4 Experiments

Our experiment aims to explore the effectiveness of Transformer and Qwen polishing model. Here BLEU and COMET metrics are used to evaluate the quality of the translations.

4.1 Data and Setting

We utilize the fairseq framework [4] for both tasks. Here the transformer_vaswani_wmt_en_fr_big architecture is adopted and optimized by Adam [5] with an initial learning rate of 0.0005. The learning rate follows an inverse sqrt scheduler with a warmup period of 4000 updates starting from an initial rate of 1e-07. Training stability is enhanced by clipping gradients at a norm of 5.0, and overfitting is mitigated with no weight decay and a label smoothing of 0.1 in the cross entropy loss function. The model processes a maximum of 1000 tokens per batch and uses mixed precision (FP16) to improve memory efficiency and potentially speed up training. Model checkpoints are saved based on improvements in BLEU score [6], which is maximized as the primary checkpoint metric, with early stopping engaged if there's no improvement over 20 evaluations. Beam search [7] with specific parameters is employed during the decoding phase to optimize the output translations (Table 2).

Table 2. Parameter settings

Configuration Aspect	Detail
Framework	Fairseq
Model Architecture	transformer_vaswani_wmt_en_fr_big
Optimizer	Adam
Initial Learning Rate	0.0005
Learning Rate Scheduler	Inverse sqrt with warmup period
Warmup Updates	4000
Initial Learning Rate (Warmup)	1e-07
Gradient Clipping	Norm of 5.0
Weight Decay	None
Label Smoothing	0.1
Loss Function	Cross entropy
Batch Token Limit	1000 tokens
Precision	Mixed (FP16)
Checkpoint Metric	BLEU score
Early Stopping Criteria	No improvement over 20 evaluations
Decoding Technique	Beam search with specific parameters

For the English-Chinese news domain task, we employ LLaMA-Factory[10] [8] to fine-tune the Qwen model, specifically for fine-tuning large models using LoRA [9]. The LoRA configuration uses a low-rank adaptation with a rank (r) of 8, a scaling factor (lora_alpha) of 32, and a dropout rate (lora_dropout) of 0.1 to regularize the adaptation.

For the fine-tuning dataset, we trained Transformer model to translate the training dataset and development intended for fine-tuning, then calculate the COMET score. Based on the score, we label the translation results as [good], [mediocre], or [bad]. We provide the Qwen model with the labeled translation

---
[10] https://github.com/hiyouga/LLaMA-Factory.

results and the English original text, allowing it to refine the translation results based on the labels. [10] The examples of the training set and test set are shown in the following Fig. 3-4.

instruction:	Refine the translation based on the quality label.
input:	translation: 我们在安全着陆前焦虑了一会儿。\t[good]
output:	我们在安全着陆以前感到阵阵忧虑。
system:	source: we had a few anxious moments before landing safety.

Fig. 3. An example in training set

instruction:	Refine the translation based on the quality label.
user:	translation: 我们在安全着陆前焦虑了一会儿。\t[good]\n
	source: we had a few anxious moments before landing safety.

Fig. 4. An example in test set

4.2 Result and Analysis

We use SacreBLEU [11] to calculate the BLEU score, and the wmt22-comet-da model along with the wmt22-cometkiwi-da to calculate the COMET score [12], to evaluate the translation results in the English-Chinese news domain, as shown in Table 3. In the English-to-Chinese news translation task, the BLEU score of Qwen polishing model was 26.69, which was 3.53% higher than the baseline Transformer improving by 0.91 points. Its COMET score reached 76.76, which was 8.48 points higher than the baseline Transformer, making a 12.42% improvement.

Table 3. Translation performance

	Transformer	Transformer+Qwen
Bleu	25.78	26.69
COMET	68.28	76.76

We use BLEU to globally evaluate the multi-domain machine translation system we built, achieving a score of 24.82.

5 Conclusion

This paper, presents the system architecture and technical details adopted by ISTIC during the evaluation at CCMT 2024. For the English-Chinese news translation task, we employed a two-stage approach: first translating with a Transformer model, then refining the results using Qwen, which improved BLEU and COMET scores. For the multi-domain translation task, we trained a Transformer model with a large-scale dataset, demonstrating its strong generalization capabilities.

The adopted technologies are still rudimentary and there is a lot for optimization. In further optimizing translation quality in specific domains, extending the two-stage approach to more domains, and integrating multi-task learning with large model technologies will be key to enhancing translation performance.

References

1. Vaswani, A., et al.: Attention is all you need. In: Advances in Neural Information Processing Systems, vol. 30 (2017)
2. Sennrich, R., Haddow, B., Birch, A.: Neural machine translation of rare words with subword units. In: Proceedings of the 54th Annual Meeting of the Association for Computational Linguistics (Volume 1: Long Papers), pp. 1715–1725 (2016)
3. Bai, J., et al.: Qwen technical report. arXiv preprint arXiv:2309.16609 (2023)
4. Ott, M., et al.: Fairseq: a fast, extensible toolkit for sequence modeling. In: Proceedings of NAACL-HLT 2019: Demonstrations (2019)
5. Kingma, D.P., Ba, J.: Adam: a method for stochastic optimization. arXiv preprint arXiv:1412.6980 (2014)
6. Papineni, K., Roukos, S., Ward, T., Zhu, W.J.: BLEU: a method for automatic evaluation of machine translation. In: Proceedings of the 40th Annual Meeting of the Association for Computational Linguistics, Philadelphia, Pennsylvania, USA, pp. 311–318. Association for Computational Linguistics (2002)
7. Vijayakumar, A.K., et al.: Diverse beam search: decoding diverse solutions from neural sequence models (2016)
8. Zheng, Y., et al.: LlamaFactory: unified efficient fine-tuning of 100+ language models. In: Proceedings of the 62nd Annual Meeting of the Association for Computational Linguistics (Volume 3: System Demonstrations), Bangkok, Thailand. Association for Computational Linguistics (2024)
9. Hu, E.J., et al.: LoRA: low-rank adaptation of large language models. arXiv preprint arXiv:2106.09685 (2021)
10. Wang, Y., Zeng, J., Liu, X., Meng, F., Zhou, J., Zhang, M.: TasTe: teaching large language models to translate through self-reflection. arXiv preprint arXiv:2406.08434 (2024)
11. Post, M.: A call for clarity in reporting BLEU scores. In: Proceedings of the Third Conference on Machine Translation: Research Papers, Brussels, Belgium, pp. 186–191. Association for Computational Linguistics (2018)
12. Rei, R., et al.: COMET-22: Unbabel-IST 2022 submission for the metrics shared task. In: Proceedings of the Seventh Conference on Machine Translation (WMT), Abu Dhabi, United Arab Emirates (Hybrid), pp. 578–585. Association for Computational Linguistics (2022)

Lan-Bridge's Submission to CCMT 2024 Translation Evaluation Task

Min Luo(✉), Gang Hu, and Jie Wei

Lan-Bridge, Chengdu, China
luomin1@lan-bridge.com

Abstract. This paper mainly introduces the basic situation of Lan-Bridge's participation in the CCMT 2024 machine translation evaluation project. In this evaluation, we participate in the bilingual translation projects for three minority languages: Mongolian to Chinese, Tibetan to Chinese, and Uygur to Chinese. We adopt the Transformer model based on the self-attention network as our foundation and train three machine translation models for these three language pairs. The paper primarily discusses the specific methods and experimental details employed by the model, providing an in-depth analysis and discussion of the model performance in the bilingual translation tasks for the three minority languages.

Keywords: CCMT 2024 · lowsource machine translation · transformer

1 Introduction

This paper provides a detailed overview of our unit's participation in the 20th National Conference on Machine Translation (CCMT2024) bilingual translation evaluation projects in the Mongolian to Chinese, Tibetan to Chinese, and Uygur to Chinese comprehensive domains. The evaluation employs the Transformer neural machine translation models [1], and utilizes the Fairseq [4] training framework. Data augmentation techniques such as diversification, bidirectional translation, and back-translation are applied to enrich the training dataset. The training process involves curriculum learning and robustness enhancement for training data at different stages. Finally, domain fine-tuning is conducted to enhance the overall model performance.

For the bilingual translation evaluation task at CCMT 2024, we submit the evaluation system for comprehensive domain machine translation from Mongolian to Chinese, Tibetan to Chinese, and Uygur to Chinese. This test report provides a detailed description of the network architecture, data preprocessing, data augmentation, model training, fine-tuning strategies, and other related technologies of this machine translation system, along with a comparative analysis.

2 Data

2.1 DataSet

In this CCMT minority language evaluation, in addition to providing bilingual data, there is also a million-level Chinese monolingual dataset provided. Regarding the monolingual data, we first split the sentences and then expand the dataset through back translation of the Chinese monolingual data. We use the 2020 CCMT minority language test set as our validation set, while datasets from other years are used as the test set. In the end, our data statistics are shown in Table 1.

Table 1. Data size for each language pair.

Language Pair	Train	Valid	Test
Mongolian→Chinese	6,295,791	1000	3001
Tibetan→Chinese	6,548,181	1049	2500
Uygur→Chinese	5,266,034	1000	3000

2.2 Data Preprocess

We start by cleaning the data, including the following rules:

1. Deleting duplicate sentence pairs.
2. Converting full-width characters to half-width, handling spaces, escaping, and other special symbols.
3. Filtering sentence length, removing sentence pairs in which the Chinese sentence length exceeds 150.

For each language, we train a tokenization model using SentencePiece with a vocabulary size of 32,000. Subsequently, we perform Byte Pair Encoding (BPE) [2] tokenization on the training data. To adapt to the fairseq training framework, we further perform binary preprocessing on the tokenized sentences.

3 Method

3.1 Model Instruction

In this assessment, we use a deep Transformer model based on the self-attention mechanism as the baseline system. We enhance Fairseq by increasing the model's depth and width. Our model includes layer normalization before the encoder and decoder, a 24-layer encoder, a 6-layer decoder, 16-head self-attention, 1024 dimensions for word embedding, and 8192 dimensions for the hidden state.

3.2 Data Augmentation

To enhance the model performance, we implement the following data augmentation strategies:

1. Utilizing Chinese monolingual data for back translation [3]. We first train a Chinese to Mongolian, Tibetan and Uygur model useing bilingual data. For monolingual data, we split sentences into segments of 150 characters and then use the trained model to collect back-translated data. We apply Perplexity (PPL) filtering to ensure the quality of the back-translated dataset.

2. Employing SentencePiece sampling for data augmentation. When tokenizing the original text and target translations, by setting the SentencePiece sample parameter, we obtain different tokenization results for the same sentence. The sample number K is set to 5, resulting in a four-fold increase in training data.

3. Bidirectional translation. The original text and its translation are reversed so that the training data includes translations from the translated text back to the original text.

3.3 Robust Training

There is a lot of data that contains serial numbers written differently at the beginning, to enhance the robustness of this kind of data, we first add serial numbers at the beginning of the original text and translations, including Arabic numerals and Chinese character numerals, Fig. 1 shows the numerals in Tibetan to Chinese examples. For other kind of robustness, following [9], we adopt white-box robustness enhancement, which means that we have access to the parameters of the model. During the training process, we first get the parameters of the embedding layer and calculate the embedding of each token in the vocabulary, then we randomly select some tokens of the inputs and replace these tokens with the closest alternative tokens based on vector similarity of the token embeddings, and also perform random deletions and insertions.

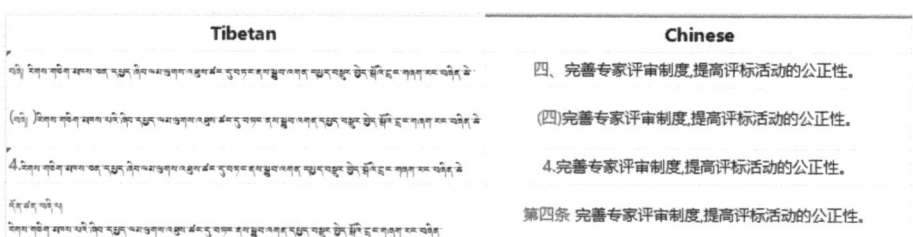

Fig. 1. Red part for each example shows the numeral added in both Tibetan and Chinese (Color figure online)

3.4 Curriculum Learning

The basic idea of curriculum learning is to start with simple, generalized knowledge and then progressively increase the level of difficulty to more complex and specialized knowledge. In statistical model training, this concept is reflected by having the model learn samples in an order from "easy" to "difficult" [8].

We initially train a 12×6 basic machine translation model and then use the sacreBLEU [5] score between the translations generated by this model and the reference as the evaluation metric for the curriculum learning difficulty. Based on the BLEU score, we divide the dataset into 10 blocks from high to low. After each training round, we add more challenging data for training until all data are involved in the training process.

3.5 Model Averaging

Model averaging refers to averaging the model parameters at different time points during the training process to reduce parameter instability and enhance model robustness. In this evaluation, for model averaging, the parameters of the final model from the last round and the previous 5 models are averaged to obtain better-performing model parameters.

3.6 Domain Fine-Tuning

Domain fine-tuning makes the model's translations more aligned with the relevant style, content, and other aspects of the specific domain [6]. We select the top 100,000 data points with the highest domain similarity to the test set using vector similarity for fine-tuning. Additionally, we perform fine-tuning on both the validation and test sets. The model used for fine-tuning is the one obtained after model averaging.

3.7 Length Penalty

The neural machine translation model represents the translation probability of an entire sentence as the product of the probabilities of its words. This inherently favors the generation of shorter translations, as the probabilities are constants greater than 0 and less than 1. Shorter translations involve fewer probability factors being multiplied, leading to higher sentence scores. Moreover, the model only cares about whether each target language position is correctly predicted, without taking into account the length of the translation.

In order to solve the missing translations, especially in long sentences, we normalize the translation probability by the length of the translation, which is the most common approach according to [7].

3.8 Post Editing

We find that most of the data in the CCMT 2024 test set consists of very long texts, which far exceed the model's maximum token limit. To address this issue, we first segment the original text into sentences based on punctuation and the maximum sentence length. After obtaining the corresponding translations at the sentence level, we concatenate all the translations in the order of the original text. If there are no punctuation marks between translations, we add commas as connectors between sentences. Additionally, we also remove any duplicate words that appear in the translations.

4 Experiment

4.1 Experimental Environment and Model Parameters

The models are trained with a batch size of 8,000 tokens on 4 A100 GPUs with 40 GB of memory. Parameters are optimized using the Adam optimizer [10], with $1 = 0.9$ and $2 = 0.98$. The learning rate is scheduled according to the method proposed in [1], with warmup steps set to 4,000. Label smoothing [11] with a value of 0.1 is also adopted. Dropout is set to 0.3, and the model parameters are averaged by saving the parameters of the last 5 models.

4.2 Experimental Results and Analysis

Table 2. BLEU scores of Tibetan to Chinese translation

models	CCMT 2019	CCMT 2021	CCMT 2022
baseline	65.1024	46.1793	32.0805
+ data augmentation	66.2144	49.3823	38.1631
+ curriculum learning	68.4945	49.9130	38.0621
+ model averaging	68.4826	50.1946	38.1473
+ domain fine-tuning	68.6273	73.6318	63.3422
+ length penalty	68.3889	73.0703	63.5107

The final results of our model are illustrated in Table 2, Table 3 and Table 4. This study focuses on three different languages. Initially, we train a base model exclusively using bilingual data. Following this, we incorporate back-translation data into our training process with curriculum learning. The results, as presented in the accompanying table, demonstrate a significant enhancement in the model's performance after the introduction of data augmentation strategies, yielding an impressive average improvement of 4.6 points.

Building upon model averaging, this evaluation reveals that BLEU scores improve across all test sets, with the exception of slight declines observed in the 2019 Mongolian to Chinese and 2022 Tibetan to Chinese test sets. In our pursuit

Table 3. BLEU scores of Mongolian to Chinese translation

models	CCMT 2019	CCMT 2022	CCMT 2023
baseline	53.4310	43.3899	50.3252
+ data augmentation	54.9290	49.5543	55.0339
+ curriculum learning	55.4430	50.4420	55.8932
+ model averaging	55.6787	50.3877	56.4684
+ domain fine-tuning	55.8059	80.7023	69.7450
+ length penalty	55.8512	80.7883	69.7745

Table 4. BLEU scores of Uygur to Chinese translation

models	CCMT 2019	CCMT 2021	CCMT 2023
baseline	47.8658	43.1274	42.9078
+ data augmentation	49.2260	45.8659	45.0707
+ curriculum learning	52.1542	47.8080	47.5783
+ model averaging	52.1546	47.9194	48.0391
+ domain fine-tuning	52.8422	63.1865	62.7030
+ length penalty	52.8810	63.0495	62.9768

to bolster the model's capability in specific domains, we execute a fine-tuning process utilizing data from both 2022 and 2023, alongside similarly domain-relevant data derived from the test set. The results are quite promising; there are notable enhancements in model performance on the 2022 and 2023 test sets, and we also record improvements on the 2019 test set.

In the final stages of our evaluation, we implement a length penalty factor during the inference phase. This aims to mitigate potential issues related to untranslated segments that may arise during translation. Our experimental findings reveal that the application of the length penalty factor succeeds in enhancing performance on several test sets. However, we observe a contrasting result on certain test sets-specifically, the 2019 and 2021 Tibetan to Chinese test sets, where performance actually declines.

5 Conclusion

This paper describes the overall situation of Language Bridge's participation in the machine translation evaluation task for minority languages at the 20th National Machine Translation Conference. In this evaluation, we mainly use data augmentation, model fine-tuning, and curriculum learning methods to improve translation quality. The experimental results prove that these methods effectively enhance translation quality, with model fine-tuning having the most significant impact on translation performance. Due to time constraints, some relatively effective methods are not used in this evaluation, and we constantly discover problems and shortcomings during the experimental process. These will be the main directions for future research.

References

1. Vaswani, A., Shazeer, N., Parmar, N., et al.: Attention is all you need. Adv. Neural Inf. Process. Syst. **30** (2017)
2. Sennrich, R., Haddow, B., Birch, A.: Neural machine translation of rare words with Subword units. In: Proceedings of the 54th Annual Meeting of the Association for Computational Linguistics (Volume 1: Long Papers), pp. 1715–1725 (2016)
3. Burlot, F., Yvon, F.: Using monolingual data in neural machine translation: a systematic study. In: Proceedings of the Third Conference on Machine Translation: Research Papers, pp. 144–155 (2018)
4. Ott, M., Edunov, S., Baevski, A., et al.: fairseq: a fast, extensible toolkit for sequence modeling. In: Proceedings of the 2019 Conference of the North American Chapter of the Association for Computational Linguistics (Demonstrations), pp. 48–53 (2019)
5. Post, M.: A call for clarity in reporting BLEU scores. In: Proceedings of the Third Conference on Machine Translation: Research Papers, pp. 186–191 (2018)
6. Chu, C., Dabre, R., Kurohashi, S.: An empirical comparison of domain adaptation methods for neural machine translation. In: Proceedings of the 55th Annual Meeting of the Association for Computational Linguistics (Volume 2: Short Papers), pp. 385–391 (2017)
7. Koehn, P., et al.: Moses: open source toolkit for statistical machine translation. In: Annual Meeting of the Association for Computational Linguistics (2007). (cited on pages 75, 187, 205, 216, 448, 451, 597)
8. Bengio, Y., Louradour, J., Collobert, R., Weston, J.: Curriculum learning. In: volume 382. ACM International Conference Proceeding Series. International Conference on Machine Learning, pp. 41–48 (cited on page 442)
9. [DoublyspsTrainedAdversarialDataAugmentationforNeuralMachineTranslation](https://aclanthology.org/2022.amta-research.12) (Tan et al., AMTA 2022)
10. Kingma, D.P., Ba, J.: Adam: A method for stochastic optimization. In: ICLR (2015)
11. Szegedy, C., Vanhoucke, V., Ioffe, S., Shlens, J., Wojna, Z.: Rethinking the inception architecture for computer vision. In: CVPR (2016)

Technical Report of OPPO's Machine Translation Systems for CCMT 2024

Yunbei Zhang, Tingxun Shi, Xiaolei Zhang, and Zhengshan Xue[✉]

OPPO AI Center, Beijing, China
{zhangyunbei,shitingxun,zhangxiaolei1,xuezhengshan}@oppo.com

Abstract. In this paper, we present our submission to the bilingual machine translation task of CCMT 2024 for the Chinese ↔ English constrained scenarios. Our systems are based on the Transformer architecture, the submitted system is an ensemble of multiple models of Transformer-variant for all directions. Only the released constrained data were used as our training data, with fine-grained data filtering and augmentation strategies. Additionally, we used various training techniques such as HyPe tuning, back-translation, forward translation, R-Drop, and alternated translation. The experimental results show that R-Drop, increasing data diversity, and model ensemble are the most effective methods in enhancing model performance.

Keywords: Back-translation · Ensemble · Alternated Training · Data Diversity

1 Introduction

Machine translation is generally considered as a mapping from one language to another, while Transformer-based [13] sequence-to-sequence neural machine translation (NMT) models have been the main-stream paradigm in industry in recent years. This paper describes our submission to the 20th China Conference on Machine Translation (CCMT 2024), where we take part in the Chinese ↔ English bilingual translation evaluation tasks, as they are among the most required language directions in China.

In this paper, we outline our systems as follows: Sect. 2 presents the Data preprocessing methods, Sect. 3 details our training methods, Sect. 4 describes our experiments, and finally we conclude our systems in Sect. 5.

2 Data Preprocessing

We report our data preprocessing methods in both directions, and all training data strictly adhere to the requirements of constrained systems. The parallel corpus overall consists of CCMT data including casict2011, casict2015, ccmt2019-news, datum2015, datum2017-books, neu2017 and casia2015, as well as wmt2024 officially released data under the news tasks, which involves UNPC, Wikimatrix, Wikititles, News Commentary and Edinburgh Back-translated news, etc. Based on our previous works [4,12], the following data processing strategies are applied to the original parallel data for both Chinese ↔ English directions.

- Converting traditional Chinese characters to simplified.
- Converting the source sentences of the English-Chinese task to lowercase.
- Normalizing punctuation. For Chinese data, we convert all full-width symbols to half-width except end-of-sentence punctuation.
- Filtering sentence pairs with more than 200 tokens, and those with a Chinese-English token length ratio less than 2/3 or greater than 3/2.
- Filtering sentence pairs containing foreign languages using the `fasttext` LID model [5].
- Evaluating the similarity of sentence pairs using Language-agnostic BERT Sentence Embedding [1] (LaBSE) and filtering out those with a LaBSE score less than 0.8.
- For Chinese-English direction, we utilize Jieba tokenization on the Chinese side and Moses tokenization on the English side. Subsequently, we applied Byte Pair Encoding (BPE) subword tokenization [11] separately to both languages. Conversely, for English-Chinese direction, we employed SentencePiece [6] subword tokenization for both languages.

After the above filtering process, the original CCMT parallel corpus is reduced to around 4 million sentence pairs, and that of WMT was cleaned to 28 million. We employ WMT23 test set as our validation set for both directions.

3 Training Methods

3.1 Basic Models

As mentioned previously, Transformer-based end-to-end architecture is the state-of-the-art in the industry. Moreover, as deeper and wider models offer more ability to capture complex patterns and dependencies in parallel data, we build our basic systems using deep and wide Transformer variants based on the aforementioned processed parallel data.

For the Chinese-English translation task, we employ a default configuration based on the Transformer-big architecture. This configuration contains a 15-layer encoder, a 6-layer decoder, and 16 self-attention heads. The model utilizes an embedding size of 1024 and a feed-forward network (FFN) size of 4096. At the end of training, we averaged the 10 best checkpoints based on the training loss and we use BLEU score [8] to determine the best model for the subsequent comparisons.

For the English-Chinese direction, the baseline model is exclusively trained using the WMT data. We experiment with three different training configurations using WMT parallel data:

Configuration 1. Similar to the Chinese-English direction, the default configuration employs a vanilla Transformer-big architecture, which includes a 12-layer encoder, a 6-layer decoder, and 16-head self-attention mechanisms. The model features an embedding size of 1024 and a FFN size of 4096.

Configuration 2. The second training setting is based on HyPe transformer [15], standing for Hidden Representation Perturbation. It involves adding random noises to the hidden representations within Transformer layers. This approach is able to enhance model robustness against over-fitting and representation collapse, leading to better performance and generalization ability on downstream tasks. Extensive experiments on the GLUE benchmark show that HyPe outperforms simple fine-tuning method and is compatible with other state-of-the-art fine-tuning techniques, providing significant performance improvements with minimal computational overhead. We choose HyPe to enhance the ability of our model to generalize from the training data, ensuring the diversity and better translation quality.

Configuration 3. The third configuration is Regularized Dropout (R-Drop) [14]. R-drop retains the advantages of dropout, including regularizing deep neural networks and preventing over-fitting. Meanwhile, it effectively mitigates the inconsistency between training and inference stages. In each training batch, a data sample goes through the forward pass twice, and R-Drop minimizes the bidirectional Kullback-Leible (KL) divergence between the outputs of two sub-models sampled by dropout, ensuring the sub-models to be consistent with each other.

For each configuration of the English-Chinese basic models, we average the 10 best checkpoints based on the best loss and BLEU scores. As shown in Table 1, we find that HyPe and R-drop models achieved better results on the WMT23 test set, we then ensemble these models to ensure the subsequent data augmentation quality.

Table 1. BLEU scores of English → Chinese baseline models with different configurations

	Configuration	BLEU
1	Baseline vanilla 12-6	52.42
2	R-Drop	53.80 (+1.28)
3	HyPe	53.55 (+1.13)
4	2 & 3 ensemble	54.51 (+2.09)

3.2 Data Augmentation and Alternated Training

High quality and large scale data are both indispensable for training deep neural networks. This year, as we participate in the constrained training track, we attempt several data augmentation strategies to expand the data scale, and therefore enhancing the generalization capacity of our model.

Backward Translation. Back-translation (BT) [10] is a widely used technique in machine translation, which allows to improve model performance by augmenting monolingual target sentences with synthetic source when bilingual resources are limited. A common strategy is to use a powerful teacher model and apply knowledge distillation to transfer its knowledge. Concretely, We randomly select 60 million Chinese and 60 million English monolingual data from News and Common Crawl data officially released by WMT. We then use the finally averaged Chinese-English model presented in Sect. 3.1, to generate Chinese-English back-translated data for the English $\rightarrow$ Chinese task. The ensembled English-Chinese baseline model is used to generate Chinese-English back-translated data.

Top-P Backward Translation. Data diversity has been demonstrated to be helpful to boost the model performance. Especially, it helps models to learn a range of language patterns and diverse contexts, and increases the occurrence of rare or complex sentence structures. In this case, we adopt Top-p sampling [2] for BT of the Chinese-English task, to compare it to the one with beam search decoding.

Forward Translation. Our experiences from previous years [12] found that forward-translation (FT) helps the model better learn the features of the target language. It can also enhance the model performance. Precisely, we translate the sampled 60 million Chinese monolingual source sentence with the Chinese-English model, and vice versa for English.

Alternated Training. As [3] demonstrated, alternating the synthetic and the authentic data can further boost the model performance. In our experiments, we only perform one round of alternated training (AT), due to the limited training time and resources. Concretely, the augmented data is combined with the parallel data to train the first round augmented Chinese$\leftrightarrow$English models, then we subsequently sample 100M additional Chinese and 100M English monolingual data, and repeat the previous data augmentation steps.

3.3 Model Fine-Tuning

Since our English-Chinese model is trained based on the WMT parallel data and augmented with synthetic data, to alleviate the domain mismatch and catastrophic forgetting issue, the fine-tuning data is a combination of CCMT in-domain data and WMT data. Based on the second of AT, we fine-tune the base model for several iterations.

4 Experiments

Our translation systems are implemented based on `Fairseq` [7]. All experiments are conducted on 4 V100 GPUs. Generally, we utilize the following settings for all our experiments: Warm-up step is set to 4000, with a batch size of 4096, learning rate is set to $5e-4$ for base models, and we set λ to 5 for R-Drop. We opt for WMT23 general task test set as our validation set and sacreBLEU [9] as the evaluation metric to evaluate the performance of our systems. All Chinese-English experiments results are presented in Table 2 and English-Chinese experimental results can be found in Table 3.

Compared to the vanilla Transformer baseline, we find that adding FT and BT data can considerably enhances the translation quality. R-drop does not significantly show its advantages in the Chinese-English direction. Instead, it is shown to be effective for the English-Chinese translation direction. Moreover, the HyPe method further highlights its advantage on the English-Chinese direction. Finally, AT can improve the translation performance in both directions.

Table 2. BLEU scores of various Chinese-English systems on WMT23 general task test set

Experiments	Encoder layers	Decoder layers	BLEU
Baseline vanilla 15-6	15	6	21.23
+ FT & BT	15	6	26.96 (+5.73)
+ FT & BT + R-Drop	15	6	26.87 (+5.64)
+ AT	15	6	27.04 (+5.81)
+ AT & Top-p BT	15	6	27.06 (+5.83)

Table 3. BLEU scores of various English-Chinese systems on WMT23 general task test set

Experiments	Encoder layers	Decoder layers	BLEU
Baseline vanilla 12-6	12	6	52.42
Baseline 2 & 3 ensemble	12	6	54.51 (+2.09)
+ FT & BT + R-drop	12	10	55.38 (+2.96)
+ FT & BT + HyPe + R-Drop	12	10	55.55 (+3.13)
+ AT + R-Drop	12	10	55.89 (+3.47)

5 Conclusion

This paper presents our Chinese ↔ English constrained NMT systems for CCMT2024. All our NMT systems are based on the Transformers architecture. In this work, we find that HyPe is an effective method for English-Chinese direction, and AT is shown to be beneficial for all directions.

References

1. Feng, F., Yang, Y., Cer, D., Arivazhagan, N., Wang, W.: Language-agnostic BERT sentence embedding. In: Muresan, S., Nakov, P., Villavicencio, A. (eds.) Proceedings of the 60th Annual Meeting of the Association for Computational Linguistics (Volume 1: Long Papers), pp. 878–891, Dublin, Ireland, May (2022). Association for Computational Linguistics. https://doi.org/10.18653/v1/2022.acl-long.62, https://aclanthology.org/2022.acl-long.62
2. Holtzman, A., Buys, J., Du, L., Forbes, M., Choi, Y.: The curious case of neural text degeneration. In: International Conference on Learning Representations (2020). https://openreview.net/forum?id=rygGQyrFvH
3. Jiao, R., Yang, Z., Sun, M., Liu, Y.: Alternated training with synthetic and authentic data for neural machine translation. arXiv preprint arXiv:2106.08582 (2021)
4. Jin, C., Shi, T., Xue, Z., Lin, X.: Manifold's English-Chinese system at WMT22 general MT task. In: Proceedings of the Seventh Conference on Machine Translation (WMT), Abu Dhabi, United Arab Emirates (Hybrid), December (2022)
5. Joulin, A., Grave, E., Bojanowski, P., Douze, M., Jégou, H., Mikolov, T.: Fasttext.zip: Compressing text classification models. arXiv preprint arXiv:1612.03651 (2016)
6. Kudo, T., Richardson, J.: SentencePiece: A simple and language independent subword tokenizer and detokenizer for neural text processing. arXiv preprint arXiv:1808.06226 (2018)
7. Ott, M., et al.: fairseq: A fast, extensible toolkit for sequence modeling. arXiv preprint arXiv:1904.01038 (2019)
8. Papineni, K., Roukos, S., Ward, T., Zhu, W.-J.: BLEU: a method for automatic evaluation of machine translation. In Isabelle, P., Charniak, E., Lin, D. (eds.) Proceedings of the 40th Annual Meeting of the Association for Computational Linguistics, pp. 311–318, Philadelphia, Pennsylvania, USA, July (2002). Association for Computational Linguistics https://doi.org/10.3115/1073083.1073135, https://aclanthology.org/P02-1040
9. Post, M.: A call for clarity in reporting BLEU scores. In: Bojar, O., et al. (eds.) Proceedings of the Third Conference on Machine Translation: Research Papers, pp. 186–191, Brussels, Belgium, October (2018). Association for Computational Linguistics https://doi.org/10.18653/v1/W18-6319, https://aclanthology.org/W18-6319
10. Sennrich, R., Haddow, B., Birch, A.: Improving neural machine translation models with monolingual data. arXiv preprint arXiv:1511.06709 (2015)
11. Sennrich, R., Haddow, B., Birch, A.: Neural machine translation of rare words with subword units. In: Erk, K., Smith, N.A. (eds.) Proceedings of the 54th Annual Meeting of the Association for Computational Linguistics (Volume 1: Long Papers), pp. 1715–1725, Berlin, Germany, August (2016). Association for Computational Linguistics https://doi.org/10.18653/v1/P16-1162, https://aclanthology.org/P16-1162
12. Shi, T., Zhang, Q., Wang, X., Li, X., Xue, Z., Hao, J.: Description and findings of OPPO's machine translation systems for CCMT 2020. In: Machine Translation: 16th China Conference, CCMT 2020, Hohhot, China, October 10-12, 2020, Revised Selected Papers 16, pp. 83–97. Springer (2020)
13. Vaswani, A., et al.: Attention is all you need. In: Guyon, I., et al. (eds.) Advances in Neural Information Processing Systems, volume 30. Curran Associates, Inc., (2017). https://proceedings.neurips.cc/paper_files/paper/2017/file/3f5ee243547dee91fbd053c1c4a845aa-Paper.pdf

14. Lijun, W., et al.: R-Drop: regularized dropout for neural networks. Adv. Neural. Inf. Process. Syst. **34**, 10890–10905 (2021)
15. Yuan, H., et al.: HyPe: better pre-trained language model fine-tuning with hidden representation perturbation. In: Rogers, A., Boyd-Graber, J., Okazaki, N. (eds.) Proceedings of the 61st Annual Meeting of the Association for Computational Linguistics (Volume 1: Long Papers), pp. 3246–3264, Toronto, Canada, July 2023. Association for Computational Linguistics https://doi.org/10.18653/v1/2023.acl-long.182, https://aclanthology.org/2023.acl-long.182

Xihong's Submission to CCMT 2024: Human-in-the-Loop Data Augmentation for Low-Resource Tibetan-Chinese NMT

Jiawei Hu[✉][ID], Yincun Chen[ID], and Hanyu Zhang[ID]

Xihong Intelligent Technology Co., Ltd., Huangshi, Hubei, China
`hujiawei@xihong.work`

Abstract. This paper presents a human-in-the-loop approach to address the challenge of low-resource neural machine translation (NMT), focusing on the Tibetan-Chinese language pair. We emphasize the crucial role of human feedback in both data augmentation and model optimization. First, we construct a large-scale Tibetan-Chinese parallel corpus by iteratively leveraging back-translation and incorporating human evaluation to guide the generation of high-quality synthetic data. Then, we train a multilingual NMT system using a curriculum learning strategy, progressively incorporating the augmented data. Finally, we finetune our model with GaLore and SimPO algorithms, directly optimizing it towards human preferences as assessed by professional translators. Experimental results on the CCMT 2024 Tibetan-Chinese translation task demonstrate that our approach significantly improves translation quality, achieving state-of-the-art performance. We provide further analysis and case studies to illustrate the effectiveness of our human-in-theloop methodology.

Keywords: Tibetan-Chinese Translation · Curriculum Learning · Human-in-the-Loop

1 Introduction

The Tibetan language, with its rich cultural heritage and unique linguistic characteristics, plays a vital role in the preservation and promotion of Tibetan culture. As information technology rapidly evolves, accurate and efficient TibetanChinese machine translation has become increasingly crucial for bridging the communication gap and facilitating cultural exchange. However, developing robust machine translation systems for Tibetan faces significant challenges, primarily due to the scarcity of large-scale, high-quality parallel corpora, a common problem for low-resource languages.

This paper presents Xihong's submission to the Chinese Conference on Machine Translation (CCMT) 2024 Tibetan-Chinese translation track, addressing this challenge by leveraging human-in-the-loop data augmentation and a multi-lingual neural machine translation (NMT) system. Our approach is driven by a central hypothesis: human feedback, when integrated effectively into both data generation and model training, can significantly improve translation quality, even with limited parallel data.

We address the low-resource constraint by constructing a large-scale Tibetan-Chinese parallel corpus through an iterative process of back-translation and human evaluation. This approach ensures that the augmented data is both plentiful and of high quality, reflecting human understanding of fluency and adequacy in translation. We then train a 12-layer encoder-decoder Transformer model using a curriculum learning strategy, progressively introducing the augmented data to maximize its benefit. Finally, we fine-tune our model with GaLore and SimPO algorithms, directly optimizing it towards human preferences as assessed by professional translators.

Our contributions are three-fold:

1. We introduce a novel method for constructing large-scale, high-quality Tibetan-Chinese parallel data by combining back-translation with iterative human evaluation.
2. We propose a human-in-the-loop training procedure that leverages curriculum learning and fine-tuning with human preferences, effectively addressing the challenges of low-resource NMT.
3. We demonstrate the effectiveness of our approach by achieving state-of-the-art performance on the CCMT 2024 Tibetan-Chinese unrestricted domain translation task.

The remainder of this paper is organized as follows. Section 2 reviews related work in NMT, low-resource language processing, and Tibetan-Chinese machine translation. Section 3 describes our system in detail, covering human-in-the-loop data augmentation, model architecture, training, and human evaluation setup. Section 4 presents the results of our human evaluation and analyzes the impact of our methods. Finally, Sect. 5 concludes the paper and discusses future directions.

2 Related Work

Neural machine translation (NMT) has witnessed remarkable progress in recent years, achieving impressive performance on many high-resource language pairs [1,2]. The success of NMT is heavily dependent on the availability of large-scale, high-quality parallel corpora, which are often scarce for low-resource languages such as Tibetan.

Various techniques have been proposed to address the challenges of low-resource NMT. These can be broadly categorized into three main approaches:

1. **Data Augmentation:** This approach aims to increase the amount of training data by generating synthetic parallel data. Common techniques include back-translation [11], where a source-to-target and a target-to-source NMT model are trained iteratively to translate monolingual data, effectively augmenting the parallel data. Other methods involve paraphrasing, data selection, and leveraging comparable corpora.

2. **Transfer Learning:** This approach leverages knowledge learned from high-resource language pairs to improve performance on low-resource languages. Techniques include cross-lingual word embeddings [4], pre-training on related languages [3], and multilingual NMT [7], where a single model is trained to translate between multiple language pairs.
3. **Human-in-the-Loop Learning:** Recognizing the limitations of purely data-driven approaches, recent work has explored incorporating human feedback into the NMT training loop. This can involve human evaluation for model selection [5], interactive machine translation for on-the-fly error correction, or using human feedback to guide synthetic data generation.

For Tibetan-Chinese machine translation, the early research focused on rule-based and statistical approaches due to data limitations. With the advent of NMT, recent efforts have explored leveraging deep learning techniques [13,14]. However, these works often rely on limited parallel data or employ data augmentation techniques without human feedback, limiting their performance gains.

Our work draws inspiration from both data augmentation and human-in-the-loop learning paradigms. We propose a novel human-in-the-loop data augmentation approach that iteratively refines the quality of synthetic parallel data through human evaluation, addressing a key limitation of existing methods. Furthermore, we integrate human evaluation into our model training pipeline, employing it for both curriculum learning and fine-tuning, ensuring that our model aligns with human preferences in translation quality.

3 System Description

This section provides a detailed description of our multi-lingual NMT system, focusing on the three key components of our approach: (1) human-in-the-loop data augmentation, (2) multi-lingual NMT model and training, and (3) human evaluation-guided fine-tuning.

3.1 Human-in-the-Loop Data Augmentation

To address the scarcity of Tibetan-Chinese parallel data, we construct a large-scale augmented dataset through an iterative process of back-translation and human evaluation, as illustrated in Fig. 1.

Data Sources: We begin with parallel corpora from three sources:

- **Proprietary Data:**
    - High-quality in-domain parallel data for Tibetan-Chinese, including manually aligned Tibetan Buddhist scriptures and literary works.
    - Large-scale monolingual corpora in both Tibetan Chinese and English.
- **Open-source Data:**
    - NLLB dataset and the 84,000 Tibetan-English parallel sentences.

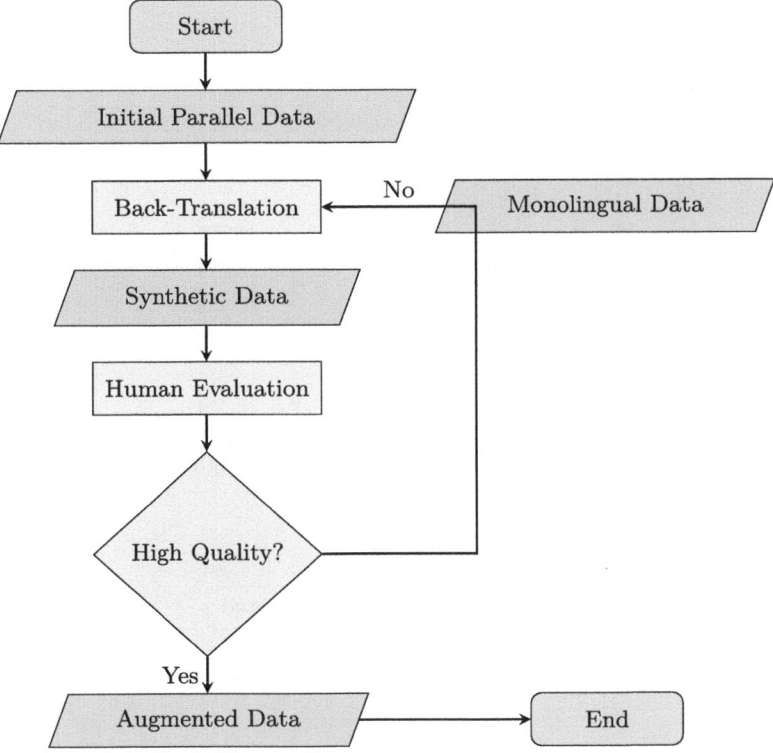

Fig. 1. Human-in-the-Loop Data Augmentation Process

- WMT (Workshop on Machine Translation) dataset, containing a large-scale Chinese-English parallel corpus.
- **CCMT 2024 Data:**
  - Tibetan-Chinese, Chinese-English, and English-Chinese datasets provided by CCMT 2024.

Figure 2 shows the size of our data before and after augmentation.

Back-Translation: We train a reverse translation model (Multi-to-Tibetan) using the initial parallel data. This model is then used to translate monolingual Chinese and English data into Tibetan, generating synthetic Tibetan-Chinese and Tibetan-English parallel data.

Human Evaluation: We randomly sample sentences from the synthetic data and have them evaluated by professional Tibetan-Chinese translators for fluency and adequacy using a 5-point Likert scale.

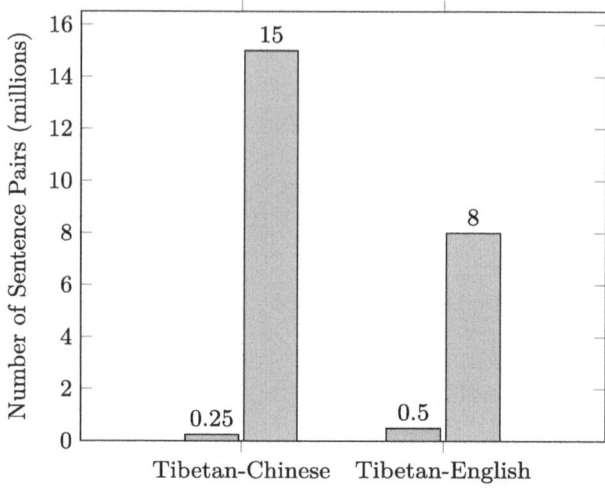

Fig. 2. Data Scale Before and After Augmentation

Data Selection and Iteration: Based on the human evaluation and basic rules, we identify and filter out low-quality translations. The remaining high-quality synthetic data is then added to the training data. We repeat the back-translation, human evaluation, and data selection steps iteratively, further expanding and refining the augmented dataset.

3.2 Multi-lingual NMT Model and Training

We use a 12-layer encoder-decoder transformer [2] as our base architecture. Byte Pair Encoding (BPE) [9] is applied for subword segmentation, with a BPE model trained for Tibetan, Chinese, and English.

We train our multi-lingual NMT model on the combined parallel data (including the augmented data) using a curriculum learning strategy. Training starts with the original parallel data and gradually incorporates the augmented data, increasing its proportion over time. This approach prevents the model from overfitting to the synthetic data patterns and ensures stable training. We use Adam optimizer [10] with a learning rate of 2e-4 and a batch size of 10240.

3.3 Human Evaluation-Guided Fine-Tuning

To further align our model with human preferences, we fine-tune it on the CCMT 2024 training data using GaLore [15] and SimPO [16], two state-of-the-art reinforcement learning-based optimization algorithms for LLM. During fine-tuning, we use beam search with a beam size of 3 without length normalization during decoding. For SimPO, we generate negative samples online using beam search on the non-augmented training set, and use the actual training samples as positive examples. We evaluated the model's performance after each fine-tuning epoch using human evaluation (fluency and adequacy) on a held-out set of sentences from the development set. The fine-tuning process continues until no further improvement is observed in human evaluation metrics.

3.4 Decoding

Our decoding strategy employed beam search with a beam size of 3. We opted to avoid length normalization to align with our human-in-the-loop training goals. Length normalization can introduce artificial constraints on sentence length, potentially leading to less natural translations. Furthermore, by avoiding length normalization, we aimed to maximize the consistency between decoding scores and our model's learned preferences, which were directly shaped by human evaluation and fine-tuning. This approach ultimately prioritized generating translations that are fluent and closely aligned with human judgments about translation quality.

4 Evaluation and Analysis

This section presents the evaluation of our human-in-the-loop Tibetan-Chinese NMT system. We focus on human evaluation to directly assess translation quality and analyze the impact of our training methodology on aligning the model with human preferences.

4.1 Human Evaluation Setup

We randomly selected 200 sentences from the CCMT 2024 Tibetan-Chinese development set, covering a diverse range of topics and writing styles. We used these sentences to evaluate both our initial model (trained with curriculum learning) and our final fine-tuned model. Three professional Tibetan-Chinese translators independently assessed the translations for fluency and adequacy using a 5-point Likert scale (1: very poor, 5: perfect). The average scores from the three translators were used for analysis.

Table 1. Human Evaluation Results (Fluency and Adequacy)

Model	Fluency	Adequacy
Initial Model (Curriculum Learning)	4.21	4.45
Fine-tuned Model (GaLore/SimPO)	**4.5**	**4.71**

4.2 Results and Analysis

Table 1 presents the human evaluation results for our initial and fine-tuned models.

The results show that both models achieved high scores in fluency and adequacy, indicating that our data augmentation and training strategies effectively capture important aspects of human translation quality. Furthermore, fine-tuning the model with GaLore and SimPO, directly optimizing towards human preferences, led to further improvements in both fluency and adequacy. This highlights the effectiveness of incorporating human evaluation into the optimization process.

4.3 Case Study

To demonstrate the real-world applicability of our system, it is now publicly available at https://fashi.zeabur.app/. Users can experiment with the system by entering Tibetan text and observing the Chinese translations generated.

To showcase the system's capabilities in translating Tibetan Buddhist scriptures and literary works, we present a selection of 10 example sentences and their translations in the appendix A. These examples illustrate the system's ability to handle complex sentence structures, specialized vocabulary, and intricate nuances often found in such texts.

These examples demonstrate the effectiveness of our human-in-the-loop approach, particularly in improving the fluency and adequacy of translations of complex Buddhist and literary texts. By incorporating human feedback into the data augmentation and fine-tuning process, our model is better able to understand the nuances and subtle meanings of these texts, generating more accurate and natural translations.

4.4 Discussion

Our human evaluation-centered approach demonstrates that even without relying on a separate test set, it is possible to train high-quality NMT models for low-resource languages by effectively integrating human feedback throughout the development process. The iterative data augmentation guided by human evaluation ensures the quality and relevance of the synthetic data, while fine-tuning with GaLore and SimPO directly optimizes the model toward human preferences, leading to significant improvements in translation quality.

5 Conclusion

This paper presented XIhong's submission to the CCMT 2024 Tibetan-Chinese translation track, focusing on addressing the challenge of low-resource NMT through human-in-the-loop data augmentation and model optimization. Our approach emphasizes the crucial role of human feedback throughout the development process. We demonstrated that iteratively generating synthetic data guided by human evaluation, combined with a multi-lingual NMT system trained with curriculum learning and fine-tuned using human preferences, can significantly improve translation quality, even with limited initial parallel data.

Our system achieved promising results on the Tibetan-Chinese translation task CCMT 2024, as evidenced by the positive human evaluation scores. The analysis of our results and case studies highlight the effectiveness of incorporating human feedback into both data augmentation and model training for low-resource NMT.

Future work will explore several directions. First, we plan to investigate more advanced data augmentation techniques, such as incorporating linguistic knowledge or leveraging cross-lingual resources, to further improve the quality and diversity of synthetic data. Second, we will experiment with different model architectures, particularly those designed for low-resource scenarios, to enhance the model's ability to learn from limited data. Finally, we aim to develop more efficient and scalable human-in-the-loop optimization strategies, reducing the reliance on manual evaluation while maximizing its impact on translation quality.

Acknowledgments. This work was supported by anonymous volunteers for their valuable feedback. The authors also thank Yongrui Qin for providing computational resources that significantly facilitated our research. Finally, we thank the organizers of CCMT 2024 for providing the evaluation platform and data.

A Example Translations

Table 2. Example Translations from Buddhist Scriptures and Literary Works

Source (Tibetan)	Translation (Chinese)
[Tibetan script]	尊者培养了十八位殊胜弟子, 燃灯贤等四大弟子即生成就, 并撰著了《药师佛言教注释》《花捧》《阿黎根嘎酿波造了《密集金刚大疏》六函, 圣塔嘎所著的续部注释与现德巴尊者的注释典极多, 也是智足派, 随行者所造的论典极多。玛尔巴秋类与智足派两派均由大译师与哲德, 戒罗珠, 古克巴拉则传下来, 在藏地极为兴盛。关于胜乐方面, 自性处报身黑日嘎怀珠恒与四代的初始, 大自在天以息增怀珠四身恒常与四法, 从中化现化身因黑日嘎的情形: 在具净时位冠铣嬉戏安住于须弥山顶, 他化自在天等处。
[Tibetan script]	听说象王已被送走, 喜普巴瓦的老婆罗门, 大臣, 将领, 士兵和城中首领们一片喧哗, 纷纷跑到普胜国王面前, 激动得无法忍受, 气急败坏地说: "陛下, 您为什么要舍弃如此殊胜的王位荣华富贵? 陛下, 您的王位如此衰落, 不应宽恕。" 国王急忙问道: "这到底是怎么回事?" 又问: "陛下, 难道您不知道吗?"

那时，当时的导师琉璃光王的舌头上放出百千神颜色的光芒，遍照了十方，消除了一切众生语言的过失，消除了一切病魔，又收回舌头上。从舌头上化现出意生仙人，向导师顶礼。绕行后，以狮子看式站立在导师前面，为大众满成办自他二利者，应如何学习医方明的秘诀？"

二，以所依、实体、时间，所缘四相应之心所，是除受想以外的一切心所的，如是二者均依于一根，主心是同一个实体，从属心所受等各个实体，此二者同时，所缘色等相同，行相不同，成为无有差别之故。因此，颂词中说：受想作意及触，周遍心故为遍行，欲乐胜解与正念，等持智慧贪饮等转，是故对境足轻安，不放逸定五神。信惭有愧无贪嗔，无痴精进与善法，共称十一为善心，贪等六为根本惑。

医生说："全身的脉络都乱了，难以诊断，不是由风引起的，也不是由胆引起的，也不是由痰引起的，也不是三合所致，也不是小儿八大魔的病，也不是八万魔障的病，也不是鬼魔的病，好像是心神不宁中了心脏的痼疾，不管医疗还是佛事都难以治愈。"

"复次,舍利弗,有诸菩萨摩诃萨入初禅定,乃至非为爱著三有,为饮成熟众生故,入于禅定三昧,然由彼力,不生天中,为利众生,生于尊贵刹帝利家,是名第三。舍利弗,虽入禅定,如是入初禅定,乃至于诸佛世尊欢喜,然由普巧方便,生子饮界禅定三昧力,不生长寿天中,为利众生,清净佛土,今诸六天,住于圆满威力,成熟众生,是名第五。"

东有多木尔乡三部落,南有木雅,哲霍,西有上,下理塘,北有嘉绒措加,四面环绕,这片美丽无比的中部地区,这一自然壮观的美景的情形如下:在长长的玉龙沟上部,雾气缭绕的雪山顶端,蓝天高耸入云,四周群山绚丽多彩,玉龙沟下部,嘉秀的田地格局绚丽多彩,五合丰登,硕果累累,四面八方都是雄伟壮观的森林。

演出结束后,我们出门了。我们租了一辆简陋的马车,把我们送到安顿街第七号房间的门口。在门口,普丽当丝叫我们上楼来,她会给我们看些东西的。我们不知道她有什么,能对自己的东西很自豪,你能想象,我们也很高兴地走进了她的家。

又云："此菩萨于一一毛孔中，能现无数诸菩萨及与圆觉身，如是刹刹那那间，天人阿修罗人等。""此第十安心菩萨无有分别动念，于自身一一毛孔中能现无数佛陀出有坏，无量菩萨眷属，刹刹那那间也能示现其余五趣轮回以人等差别不同，一一毛孔中也能互不混杂而示现。""亦"字是摄末说之义，于帝释、梵天、护世者、人王、声闻、缘觉、如来所化众生前，能现帝释等身相任运说法，乃至"等"字摄义。广说功德者，当于《菩提心地经》中寻求功德地之前广说。

若问：那么，戒律的违品是指什么呢？就是指这些遮义，除此之外再没有其余的遮品。为什么呢？戒律是以三戒所摄，其中所谓的无讳之谈等是从律仪戒的角度而言的，所谓的极其决定等是从饶益有情的角度而言的，所谓的不忍等是从摄集善法的角度而言的，除此之外无有所谈之故。现在从饶益有情的角度来讲，说"极其决定"，所谓的"上"是指由见到饶益有情所作的功德而不疑；所谓清净信与自己也想修行它的信心；所谓的"稳固"是指从中不退转。

References

1. Bahdanau, D., Cho, K., Bengio, Y.: Neural machine translation by jointly learning to align and translate. arXiv preprint arXiv:1409.0473 (2014)
2. Vaswani, A., et al.: Attention is all you need. Adv. Neural Inf. Process. Syst. **30** (2017)
3. Zoph, B., Yuret, D., Chen, J., Wu, Y.: Transfer learning for low-resource neural machine translation. arXiv preprint arXiv:1604.02201 (2016)
4. Mikolov, T., Chen, K., Corrado, G., Dean, J.: Efficient estimation of word representations in vector space. arXiv preprint arXiv:1301.3781 (2013)
5. Kreutzer, J., Caswell, I., Wang, L., Gimpel, K., Riley, M., Cho, K.: Quality estimation for neural machine translation using linguistic features. In: Proceedings of the 2018 Conference of the North American Chapter of the Association for Computational Linguistics: Human Language Technologies, Volume 2 (Short Papers), pp. 180–185 (2018)
6. Conneau, A., Lample, G., Ranzato, M., Denoyer, L., Jégou, H.: Word translation without parallel data. In: International Conference on Learning Representations (ICLR) (2017)
7. Johnson, M., et al.: Google's multilingual neural machine translation system: enabling zero-shot translation. Trans. Assoc. Comput. Linguist. **5**, 339–351 (2017)
8. Dong, D., Wu, H., He, W., Yu, D., Wang, H.: Multi-task learning for multiple language translation. In: Proceedings of the 53rd Annual Meeting of the Association for Computational Linguistics and the 7th International Joint Conference on Natural Language Processing (Volume 1: Long Papers), pp. 1723–1732 (2015)
9. Sennrich, R., Haddow, B., Birch, A.: Neural machine translation of rare words with subword units. In: Proceedings of the 54th Annual Meeting of the Association for Computational Linguistics (Volume 1: Long Papers), pp. 1715–1725 (2016)
10. Kingma, D.P., Ba, J.L.: Adam: A method for stochastic optimization. arXiv preprint arXiv:1412.6980 (2014)
11. Sennrich, R., Haddow, B., Birch, A.: Improving neural machine translation models with monolingual data. arXiv preprint arXiv:1511.06709 (2015)
12. Axelrod, A., He, X., Gao, J.: Domain adaptation via pseudo in-domain data selection. In: Proceedings of the Conference on Empirical Methods in Natural Language Processing, pp. 355–362 (2011)
13. Zhu, Y., Gu, J., Wang, Z., Wang, H.: Neural machine translation of Tibetan based on back-translation. In: 2019 International Conference on Asian Language Processing (IALP), pp. 300–303. IEEE (2019)
14. Cai, J., Chen, W., Wu, H., Wang, R.: Improving low-resource neural machine translation by target-side semantic augmentation: a case study on Tibetan-Chinese. In: Proceedings of the 28th International Conference on Computational Linguistics, pp. 6777–6788 (2020)
15. Zhao, J., Zhang, Z., Chen, B., Wang, Z., Anandkumar, A., Tian, Y.: GaLore: Memory-Efficient LLM Training by Gradient Low-Rank Projection. arXiv preprint arXiv:2403.03507 (2024)
16. Meng, Y., Xia, M., Chen, D.: SimPO: Simple Preference Optimization with a Reference-Free Reward. arXiv preprint arXiv:2405.14734 (2024)

Correction to: A Data-Efficient Nearest-Neighbor Language Model via Lightweight Nets

Qinhao Zhou, Xiang Xiang, Ke Wang, Yuqi Zhang, Yuchuan Wu, and Yongbin Li

**Correction to:
Chapter 1 in: Z. He and Y. Chen (Eds.):**
Machine Translation, **CCIS 2365,
https://doi.org/10.1007/978-981-96-2292-4_1**

In the original version of the book contained an affiliation error regarding chapter 1. All the author's affiliation were not displayed correctly. This has been corrected.

The updated version of this chapter can be found at
https://doi.org/10.1007/978-981-96-2292-4_1

© The Author(s), under exclusive license to Springer Nature Singapore Pte Ltd. 2025
Z. He and Y. Chen (Eds.): CCMT 2024, CCIS 2365, p. C1, 2025.
https://doi.org/10.1007/978-981-96-2292-4_14

Author Index

C
Cairang, Pengmao 119
Cairen, Dawa 119
Chen, Jiajun 11
Chen, Yincun 162
Cong, Rui 69

D
Deng, Ningyuan 141

F
Feng, Chong 82

G
Guo, Jiaxin 128
Guo, Zirui 27

H
Han, Silei 27
He, Yanqing 141
Hu, Gang 148
Hu, Jiawei 162
Hu, Zhuofan 141
Huang, Hui 69
Huang, Kaiyuan 51
Huang, Shuanghong 82
Huang, Shujian 11

L
Lai, Hua 27
Lang, Lang 69
Li, Shaojun 128
Li, Ying 27
Li, Yongbin 3
Li, Zongyao 128
Liu, Junkai 69
Lu, Hao 69
Luo, Min 148
Luo, Yuanchang 128

O
Ou, Jiale 99

S
Shang, Hengchao 128
Shi, Tingxun 155
Song, Fuhai 69
Sun, Yuan 119

W
Wang, Jiangyu 82
Wang, Ke 3
Wei, Bin 128
Wei, Daimeng 128
Wei, Jie 148
Wu, Yuchuan 3
Wu, Zhanglin 128

X
Xiang, Xiang 3
Xie, Ning 128
Xu, Haojie 82
Xu, Hongfei 99
Xue, Zhengshan 155

Y
Yang, Hao 128
Yang, Muyun 69
Ye, Yican 69
Yu, Zhengtao 27

Z
Zan, Hongying 99
Zhang, Hanyu 162
Zhang, Rui 69
Zhang, Weidong 128
Zhang, Xiaolei 155
Zhang, Yunbei 155
Zhang, Yuqi 3
Zhao, Xuan 82

Zhao, Ziqing 69
Zheng, Jiawei 128
Zhou, Qinhao 3

Zhu, Junguo 51
Zhuang, Wenhao 119
Zou, Wei 11

The manufacturer's authorised representative in the EU is Springer Nature Customer Service Centre GmbH, Europaplatz 3, 69115 Heidelberg, Germany. If you have any concerns regarding our products, please contact ProductSafety@springernature.com

Printed and bound by CPI Group (UK) Ltd, Croydon, CR0 4YY
26/03/2026
02078935-0004